To my mom, Georganne, my wife, Marihya,
and my children, Brittney, Tripp, Autumn and Sam.
I love you each so very much.

THE UNIVERSITY LA[N]
RESOURCES AND HIGHE[R] EDUCATION IN TEXAS
1838-1996

BY TODD HOUCK, PH.[D]

Todd Houck
2023

COPYRIGHT 2011 WINDY FOX PUBLISH
MIDLAND, TEXAS

ACKNOWLEDGEMENTS

I wish to thank the numerous people who provided me with direction and support while I completed this project. I also want to thank a few people who have given me support and friendship in general. While I cannot thank everyone, I am also grateful to those I fail to mention.

First and foremost I owe everything to my Lord, Jesus Christ. None of this would have been possible without his saving grace.

Dr. Paul H. Carlson at Texas Tech University deserves my infinite gratitude for his invaluable encouragement and thoughtful criticism throughout the research and writing of this project. He taught me how to write ... period. Dr. Carlson is one of the finest writers in the state. Dr. Briggs L. Twyman deserves special thanks for his guidance and friendship, I miss his sense of humor and laugh. The other members of my committee at Texas Tech, including Dr. Alwyn Barr, Dr. John M. Howe, Dr. Donald R. Walker and Dr. Jeff Johnson, each provided some measure of assistance for which I am equally thankful.

The executive director of University Lands West Texas Operations (WTO), Steve Hartmann, was particularly helpful in providing personal insight into the last three decades of operations and in allowing me unfettered access to documents and records used in the course of the study. Other current employees of University Lands WTO who aided me with the collection of scattered information include Jim Benson, Sharon Burkes, Dave Campbell, Rick Doehne, Jim Evans, Tim Hunt, Melba McKandles, and Michael "Doc" Weathers. Former employees of University Lands Mineral Interests who graciously talked with me about their experiences include Wallie P. Gravitt, Laddie F. Long, and Lynward Shivers. Susan Dorsey of the Texas General Land Office went beyond the call of duty in helping with my research in the archives of the General Land Office at Austin, but also in promptly responding to my long distance pleas for information that I neglected to obtain while I was there. Lisa Struthers at the San Jacinto Museum of History also deserves a special thanks for expediting my photo request.

I would like to give a special thanks to Kathy Shannon and Leslie Meyer at the Permian Basin Petroleum Museum were also important in my obtaining most of the photos contained herein.

Former State Senator W. E. "Pete" Snelson supplied important details about legislative developments regarding university lands and the permanent university fund. His sincerity and commitment towards education in Texas is worthy of numerous plaudits.

I would like to extend my appreciation to my many colleagues, peers and friends, who include Will Morris, Lee Almaguer, Michael Dixon, Damon Kennedy, Frank DeLaO, Paula Marshall-Gray, Donna Thompson, Mike Schneider, David Edens, Russell Goodyear, Monica Sosa, David Daniel, Richard Jolly, Stan Jacobs, Rex Peebles, Steve Thomas, Chris Hieb [for the cover design and maps], Norma Duran, Billy Feeler, Lula Lee, Chloice Shofner, Larry Hagler, Martin Garcia, Jane Phares, Betty Orbeck, Edward Garza, Doug Avery, Mike Makowsky, Martin Rangel, Carl Strain, Father Tom Finney, Father Eric Vowels, Father Jonathon Hartzer, Father Jim Liggit, Deacon Tom Burns, Judge John Hyde, Paul Best, Roger Traxel, Stephen J. Frank, Gary Clayman, Rosanna Catalasan, Warren Taylor, Herb Blankenship, Diana Olien, Mike Leach, and Ron Power. Edna McGinnis, Autumn

Hunt, Mason Hunt, and Samuel Jobe also deserve a special thanks. Each provided useful suggestions, but, more importantly, they gave me their friendship and support for many years.

Finally, I want to thank my father Mike. My Dad is my friend and I always knew his love. To my beautiful wife Marihya I can never thank her enough for her love and support. My grandmother, Deana, deserves credit for my appreciation of history. I wish to thank my daughter Brittney for inspiring me every day and filling my life with joy. My son Tripp for making me laugh and giving me hope for the future. Last but not least, I want to thank my mother, Georganne, for giving me life, unconditional love, and an education. To paraphrase Henry Ward Beecher: my mother gave me roots, but she also gave me wings.

TABLE OF CONTENTS

ACKNOWLEDGEMENTS.. i

LIST OF ILLUSTRATIONS... v

INTRODUCTION.. 1

CHAPTER

I. LAND FOR HIGHER EDUCATION..5

II. WEST TEXAS LANDS, 1874-1895 37

III. SURFACE LEASING, 1896-1996 79

IV. MANAGING SUB-SURFACE RESOURCES, 1896-1996........131

V. THE PERMANENT AND AVAILABLE UNIVERSITY FUNDS, 1896-1996.. 181

VI. CONCLUSION 223

BIBLIOGRAPHY..236

INDEX 250

List of Illustrations & Photos

Figure 1: Mirabeau B. Lamar, 4

Figure 2: Map of the Original 50 Leagues, 11

Figure 3: Map of constitutional and Legislative millions, 47

Figure 4: Oran M. Roberts, 58

Figure 5: R. E. L. Saner, 88

Figure 6: Frank Friend Survey Crew, 107

Figure 7: Texon Oil & Land Company Office, 142

Figure 8: Dr. Hal P. Bybee, 153

Figure 9: UT dignitaries & oilmen at Santa Rita #1, 161

Figure 10: Berte R. Haigh, 164

Introduction

The 2.1 million-acre land reserve of the University of Texas and Texas A&M University, called "university lands," played a significant role in the financial history of both institutions. The university lands are also an important part of the history of Texas, and in particular, West Texas.

The impetus for this project, which was my doctoral dissertation, was a suggestion from Betty Orbeck one morning in 2000. She had known Berte Haigh and felt that his book was not the last word on the subject. I wrote a straightforward version of the work that satisfied the requirement for my Doctorate at Texas Tech University in 2004. I let it sit and simmer for 7 years before I so much as revisited a single page. As I started to read I felt the old creative juices flowing and began to give the entire manuscript the old once over. I am quite proud of the original manuscript and any variations are not overly significant. I was particularly happy with the exposition and left it pretty much as originally written. I am publishing not for vanity, or glory, or for money, but so that anyone who delves into the story of the university lands must reckon with my work. My contribution may be faint in the chorus of the history of Texas, but people will know I was here.

As I searched for the truth, as historians profess to do, I found the truth as I saw it and it is shaped by my own interpretations, preconceptions, and prejudices. This is a sincere effort to write a serious history of the University Lands and I am satisfied that I gave it my best. Using documents and other sources I felt that I had witnessed this story from afar ... like watching through binoculars... backwards. I left the footnotes in so the reader can go right to any of my sources. Any mistakes are mine and mine alone.

The narrative of the book traces the history of the university lands from 1838 to 1996. President Mirabeau B. Lamar in 1838 announced plans to set aside a fifty-league land reserve for the establishment and maintenance of a university. In 1876, the Constitution called for the establishment of a University of Texas, the Permanent University Fund (PUF), the Available University Fund (AUF), and a grant of one million acres of land, known as the "constitutional million." An additional land grant in 1883 represented the so-called "legislative million" and completed the present-day university lands. The study examines the development, use, and management of the university lands.

Following the establishment of the University of Texas in 1881, the University of Texas Board of Regents began lobbying for exclusive control over the sale and lease of university lands. Following two decades of such efforts, lawmakers granted the regents' request in 1895.

The year 1896 marked a watershed in the history of university lands. The regents hired an agent to lease and sell university lands on their behalf. Income increased almost immediately and surface use diversified in the following years, but, more importantly, oil was discovered on university lands in 1923.

The year 1929 was also important in the history of university lands. That year the legislature established the University Lands Surface Office and University Lands Geology Office. Lawmakers also set up the Board for Lease of University Lands to handle mineral lease sales and the University Lands Survey Office to re-survey the entire 2.1 million-acre university lands.

Surface leasing provided considerable income for the AUF throughout the twentieth century, but oil revenues proved to be the real windfall. Through sound policies, university lands management organization helped make the PUF the largest endowment of a public institution of higher learning in the United States.

By the 1990s, oil revenues began to decline and the regents looked to investment management to continue sustained growth of the PUF. In 1996 the regents established the University of Texas Investment Management Company (UTIMCO) to manage PUF investments. They also placed the three management organizations, University Lands Surface, Mineral Interests, and Accounting, under a single director and designated the combined organizations as University Lands West Texas Operations (WTO).

Figure 1: Mirabeau B. Lamar, Second President Republic of Texas, 1838-41. On December 20, 1838 he called on the 3rd Congress to set aside, among other things, land for higher education. Photo courtesy of the San Jacinto History Museum.

CHAPTER I

LAND FOR HIGHER EDUCATION

    The history of the university lands began during the first years of the Republic of Texas. The period from President Mirabeau B. Lamar's call for an appropriation of land for higher education in 1838 to the opening of Texas A&M College in 1874 was a time of constant and drastic political change for the state and the nation. Texas had four constitutions during the period, each one dealing with the issue of a land endowment for a university differently from the preceding one. Ideas regarding democracy, education, and manifest destiny had a profound impact on the developing society of early Texas. Successive legislatures made attempts to establish a state university and to select, survey, and sell the land that had been set aside, but destructive political currents and the Civil War interrupted their efforts.

    When he arrived in Texas in 1832, Georgia native Mirabeau B. Lamar carried with him the ideas of education, territorial expansion, and the spread of American democracy. A classically educated, former teacher whose reputation as an academic was widely known, Lamar, during the Sam Houston administration, served as the first Vice President of the Republic of Texas.[1] Houston was such a forceful presence in Texas politics during the period that the political leadership was divided into pro-Houston

---

[1] Jack C. Ramsay, Thunder Beyond the Brazos: Mirabeau B. Lamar, a Biography (Austin: Eakin Press, 1985), 9-10.

and anti-Houston groups. Acquaintances since the Battle of San Jacinto, Lamar and Houston at first enjoyed a good relationship, but the friendship soured following independence. Later animosity and open criticism marked the relationship.[2] While President Houston made it immediately clear he sought statehood for the young Republic, Lamar believed Texas should remain independent. He saw the future of Texas in terms of expansionist policies that prevailed among many of the adventuresome Texas revolutionary generation. Such fundamental differences of philosophy, and what seems to be a personal dislike of one another, perhaps caused Houston and Lamar to oppose the policies of one another.

Because the Constitution of 1836 specifically forbade the first president from serving more than two years, Houston's supporters had to find a candidate who would continue the general's policies. Peter W. Grayson and James Collinsworth briefly divided the support of the pro-Houston group although neither lived to see the election. Houston supporters then gave the endorsement to a promoter of the town of Houston, Robert Wilson of Harris County. Nonetheless, Lamar won the November 16, 1838, election with a sound majority to become the second President of the Republic of Texas.[3]

It did not take long for the new president to make clear his intention to depart from the frugal policies of the previous administration. As Vice President, Lamar knew

---

[2] James L. Haley, Sam Houston (Norman: University of Oklahoma Press, 2001), 213.

[3] Rupert N. Richardson, Adrian Anderson, Cary D. Wintz, and Ernest Wallace, eds., Texas: The Lone Star State, 8th ed. (Upper Saddle River, New Jersey: Prentice Hall, 2001), 137.

Texas had over 216 million acres at its disposal.[4] He also knew that land was the most abundant resource available to the government and a possible source of revenue for a system of free education. At his December 20, 1838, address to the Third Congress of the Republic, Lamar introduced a bold plan of activist government focused on education. In his speech he called on legislators to set aside land for " . . . the establishment of a free public education system, a state asylum, and two colleges or universities."[5] The legislature responded by appointing a committee to devise a system of general education. It included Ashbel Smith, W. Y. Allen, Robert Irion, Andrew J. Yates, Anson Jones, and Lorenzo de Zavala. John Wharton, who died before the committee finished its work, chaired the committee.

Ezekial W. Cullen, who replaced Wharton as chairman of the committee, submitted a report to the Third Congress on January 4, 1839. The report began by reminding lawmakers that Mexico had failed to set up a system of general education, which was one of the grievances set out in the Texas Declaration of Independence. The committee pointed to the need for trained teachers and noted precedents for land grants for education. The report stated that Texas "has boundless sources of national wealth still dormant in its soil, its forest,

---

[4] Thomas Lloyd Miller, The Public Lands of Texas: 1519-1970 (Norman: University of Oklahoma Press, 1971), xi.

[5] Act of January 26, 1839, Acts of the Third Congress, Regular Session (1839), H. P. N. Gammel, ed., The Laws of Texas, I (Austin: H. P. N. Gammel, 1900), 135-136.

and its minerals."[6] The committee's recommendations echoed the sentiments of Lamar's inauguration speech, urging Congress to endow a school system while the public domain was still available.

On January 9, 1839, Cullen submitted a bill to the congress. The bill went through three readings and some debate over amendments, mostly focused on whether there should be one university or two. In the meantime, on January 14, a bill passed that designated Austin as the seat of government, a move that caused further animosity between Lamar and his predecessor.[7] Finally, on January 26, 1839, the Congress passed a law setting aside three acres of land in each county for establishing a primary school or academy in that county and fifty leagues of land for two institutions of higher learning. The law stipulated that the president appoint a competent surveyor, although it is unclear exactly when the appointment took place.[8] Lamar immediately signed the measure into law, thus, earning the title "father of education in Texas."[9]

That Lamar saw a connection between land, education, and democracy is evident in his first speech before the Third Congress. From the outset, Lamar spoke eloquently about his ideas on education, and he did so with

---

[6] Harry Y. Benedict, ed., "A Source Book Relating to the History of the University of Texas: Legislative, Legal, Bibliographical and Statistical," University of Texas Bulletin, no. 1757 (Austin: University of Texas, 1917): 8.

[7] Ramsay, Thunder Beyond the Brazos, 69; Haley, Sam Houston, 213-214.

[8] An Act to Appropriate Fifty-Leagues for the Establishment of a State University, Acts of the Fourth Congress, Regular Session (1840), Gammel, Laws of Texas, II, 131-132.

[9] Ramsay, Thunder Beyond the Brazos, 207.

the rustic language of the agrarian republican. Lamar stated that "It is admitted by all, that [a] cultivated mind is the guardian genius of democracy."[10] The yeoman allusion to educating oneself as necessary to governance was evident in his appropriation of the original fifty leagues. Lamar's position regarding land abundance and education was part of a broader trend tied to American expansion. Edith Helene Parker, an historian who wrote on the history of land grants for education, argues there was a prevailing attitude regarding the issue of land abundance and education. Parker contends that "the rights of the people to equal opportunities for education and equal participation in the public domain were in the foreground of the national consciousness."[11]

Most of Lamar's contemporaries recognized that a system of education for children was imperative, but an institution of higher learning was a different matter. Some people felt that establishing a university was putting the proverbial cart before the horse. Others believed that the state had no business supporting such an institution at all.

Lamar's desire to get something done with expedience proved to be impossible. Indian problems existed on the frontier. Furthermore, opposition to his administration came from the highest levels. Sam Houston, for example, did nothing to help advance Lamar's cause, favoring a policy of "caretakerism": that is, simply taking care of Texas until it became a part of the United States. Lamar, however, envisioned an independent Texas that extended to the Pacific coast and rivaled the United States for hegemony in North America. Although it failed, the 1841

---

[10] Benedict, "Source Book," 8.

[11] Edith Helen Parker, "History of Land Grants for Education in Texas" (Ph.D. diss., University of Texas, 1952), iii, 1-15.

expedition to Santa Fe to assert Texas' civil authority in New Mexico is evidence of Lamar's plans for Texas.[12]

Jack C. Ramsay argues that Sam Houston did his best to make Lamar's job more difficult. Ramsay notes that Anson Jones, an ardent pro-Houston man and enemy of Lamar, said that "The fact that Houston's only intent was that of making Lamar's administration as odious as possible . . . He [Houston] is willing the government be a failure in order that he might say there is no one but 'Old Sam' that people can depend upon."[13]

Still while the Fourth Congress was in regular session, lawmakers, on January 5, 1840, passed a bill that appropriated money for the survey of land adjoining the Austin town site. They designated forty acres north of the capital grounds for the state university.[14] After the bill passed, there is no more mention of a state university in the legislative record of the Republic.[15] As the issues of establishing civil control in Santa Fe, frontier defense, and a foreign loan consumed most of the President Lamar's attention, the Austin site remained undeveloped during the remaining year of his administration,

Nonetheless, the issue of the university lands to endow education was not absent from the minds of Lamar and officials of his administration. In a report dated October 20, 1840, acting Secretary of State Joseph Waple

---

[12] Ramsay, Thunder Beyond the Brazos, 123, 131-132.

[13] Ibid., 150-151; H. P. Gambrell, Anson Jones: The Last President of Texas (Austin: University of Texas Press, 1964), 203.

[14] Joint Resolution for the Survey and Sale of the Austin town tract, Acts of the Fourth Congress, Regular Session (1840), Gammel, Laws of Texas, II, 377-378.

[15] Parker, "Land Grants," 1-15.

Figure 2: The Original Fifty Leagues, map drawn by Chris Hieb.

wrote President Lamar that none of the surveys had been completed. In another letter to Lamar, Land Commissioner Thomas William Ward attached a list of counties surveyed to that date. He reported that fifty leagues had been selected and surveyed in Fannin, Robertson, and Nacogdoches counties, although many of the surveys were not actually completed. Ward also included the names of the surveyors Lamar appointed: William H. Hunt and B. A. Vansiclele.[16]

There is no extant account of the survey expeditions, but at some point in 1839 or 1840, President Lamar, or agents of Lamar, decided where the fifty leagues should be located. The surveyor likely chose the general locations based on the availability of water and timber and the quality of the soil as farmland. Then came the appointment of Hunt and Vansieclele to carry out the surveys. Finally, the surveyors hired crews and traveled to remote areas in northeast Texas to carry out their work. Except for their maps in the General Land Office, there is no mention of Hunt or Vansieclele in available sources. Still, records show that they were among many active surveyors in the region.

The 1830s and 1840s were a boom period for surveyors in Texas. As the state disposed of its public lands at ever increasing rates, surveyors found themselves in greater demand. Because they were required to demarcate virgin lands well beyond the line of settlement, the biggest problem facing them was Indian activity.[17] There are endless accounts of Indian attacks on survey parties during the period. The most infamous being the Battle Creek Massacre of October 8, 1838, in which Indian warriors killed eighteen members of a twenty-five man

---

[16] Letter from Thomas William Ward to Mirabeau B. Lamar, Mirabeau B. Lamar Papers, Texas State Archives, 1909/1-22.2096.

[17] Forrest Daniel, "Texas Pioneer Surveyors and Indians," in One League to Each Wind, ed. Sue Watkins (Austin: Texas Surveyors Association, 1964), 57-58.

survey crew.[18] Indian problems slowed the efforts of surveyors, and it is plausible that such attacks account for delays in the university land surveys.

The surveys continued during the 1840s. Because district surveyors contracted deputies to do the actual fieldwork, a lack of uniformity in survey results occurred. Moreover, a sizable percentage of the surveys were of questionable accuracy. Backlogs in the General Land Office and remote locations of surveys also contributed to the problems. The need to hurry caused many surveyors to cut corners and increased the likelihood of mistakes. To avoid hostile Indians, some surveyors would only locate a corner or two of a tract and compute the other sides, quite a common practice for the period.[19] Many of the surveys conducted during the 1840s were unreliable and led to problems that later required legislative remedy.

Another problem with the surveys was the lack of communication between government agencies involved in disposing of the public domain. For example, private parties surveyed land in Nacogdoches County that later ended up in parts of Rusk and Smith counties and conflicted with university land surveys in the same counties. Part of the problem was the failure of university surveyors to file their notes in the General Land Office. The land commissioner, knowing nothing about the university surveys, sold university land to the parties who

---

[18] R. Ernest Lee, "Pioneer Surveyors," in One League to Each Wind, ed. Sue Watkins (Austin: Texas Surveyors Association, 1964), 5.

[19] Edwin P. Arnesen, "The Early Art of Terrestrial Measurement and Its Practice in Texas," in One League to Each Wind, ed. Sue Watkins (Austin: Texas Surveyors Association, 1964), 16.

properly filed paper work and purchased the land in good faith.[20]

Another reason for the delay in the surveys and the establishment of a state university is that officials lost interest. During the 1840s private colleges and academies diverted attention of officials. When they appropriated the original fifty leagues for a university, lawmakers also gave four leagues of land to establish a private school called De Kalb College in Red River County. A group of Methodists established the first Protestant denominational school, Rutersville College, near La Grange in 1840. Five years later, the Baptists established Baylor University in Independence.[21] Advocates of a public university argued that the problem with private schools was that they were expensive and not everyone had access to them. The cost of private school education explains the continuing issue of a state university. However, Indian troubles along the western edge of settlement and developments regarding annexation continued to dominate the efforts of politicians in the early 1840s. Nonetheless, at the end of the Lamar administration the initial steps towards progress on the survey and disposition of the university lands was underway.

At the commencement of his second administration, Sam Houston stated publicly his belief that the time was not right to waste government efforts on education.[22] He criticized the previous administration for the size of the debt, as well as every other policy that differed from his own. Houston and his supporters made every effort to cast

---

[20] Berte R. Haigh, Land, Oil, and Education (El Paso: Texas Western Press, 1986), 6.

[21] Parker, "Land Grants," 186.

[22] Haley, Sam Houston, 189, 196.

blame on Lamar, but they never offered any solutions of their own. Houston's anger towards Lamar is due, in part, to the removal of the capital from the President's namesake town of Houston to Austin early in the previous administration.

In March 1842, President Houston again brought up the question of annexation to the United States. At the same time, concerns over the British influence in Texas prompted United States President John Tyler to reopen the question of annexation, and in October 1843 he began negotiations with envoys from the Texas Republic. Houston agreed to negotiate under two conditions: the United States must defend Texas in the event of a Mexican invasion and the talks had to be kept secret. Efforts continued through the 1844 election, and James K. Polk campaigned on a promise of annexation. Tyler's Secretary of State John C. Calhoun and Texas' Special envoys Isaac Van Zandt and James Pinckney Henderson signed a treaty on April 12, 1844, but the United States Congress did not ratify it. In December 1844, President Tyler said Polk's election was a mandate to annex Texas and on March 4, 1845, signed a joint resolution to annex the troubled country.[23] Sam Houston's dream of the United States' annexation of Texas came to fruition.

With statehood came a new constitution: the Constitution of 1845. The tenth article of the new constitution reflected Houston's view that common schools should be a prerequisite to the establishment of a state university. The constitution instructed the legislature to establish a system of common schools but said nothing about a college or university. The most important aspect of annexation is that Texas retained its public lands, perhaps its most abundant resource. Land, or the sale of the land,

---

[23] Richardson, Anderson, Wintz, and Wallace, Texas, 152-154.

could be used for internal improvements and the endowment of educational institutions.[24]

During the late 1840s, Anglo settlers continued to arrive in Texas. Some settlement promoters advertised the possibility that Texas might contain valuable mineral deposits, something the Spanish had long believed true of the area. In an 1841 report, William Kennedy, a British diplomatic secretary, traversed the state and for prospective American settlers wrote of the geological diversity of Texas. Kennedy's report, writes Walter Keene Ferguson, was responsible for "the myth that Texas contained extensive and valuable surface mineral deposits."[25] Kennedy's description of extensive coal reserves from the Trinity River to the Rio Grande, and stories of Spanish gold and silver mines in the vicinity of the San Saba, came to the attention of Prince Carl of Solms-Braunfels. Prince Carl headed a German immigration association called the *Adelsverein*, which settled in the Texas Hill Country. Carl began to seek professional aid in determining mineral potential to attract settlers. When it came time to hire someone to conduct a mineral survey, Carl went to Europe and procured the services of a Berlin trained geologist named Ferdinand von Roemer.[26]

Roemer arrived in Texas in 1845. He then conducted a survey on behalf of the *Adelsverein*. He traveled throughout the state during 1846 and 1847 and published his findings in the American Journal of Science. Roemer's survey failed to uncover any significant mineral deposits.

---

[24] Constitution of Texas (1845), Gammel, Laws of Texas, II, 1297; Benedict, "Source Book," 17-18.

[25] Walter Keene Ferguson, Geology and Politics in Frontier Texas, 1845-1909 (Austin: University of Texas Press, 1969), 10.

[26] Ibid., 12.

Of more significance, however, Roemer's survey, writes Ferguson, set the "precedent for the use of geological survey to promote the exploitation of minerals and the development of virgin lands."[27]

Continued conflicts with surveys during the 1840s prompted the Third Legislature to pass, in 1849, a joint resolution entitled "Chapter 92." The law canceled the university surveys and reaffirmed all good faith purchases. This time the legislature instructed the land commissioner, not the chief executive, to employ a surveyor to demarcate three leagues from any appropriated lands in exchange for those already sold in Rusk and Smith counties. The legislature also passed a resolution calling on the committee on education to consider the "expediency of establishing a college or university."[28]

International and national events connected to American expansion in the 1840s also impeded progress on selection and survey of university lands. Increased focus on the issue of statehood caused suspicions of how Mexico would respond. Since 1836, the Mexican government had threatened that it would view the annexation of Texas as an act of war. Following annexation in 1845, President James K. Polk sent General Zachary Taylor into the disputed area of the Trans-Nueces. The resulting Mexican War, 1846-48, was partially due to the United States' annexation of Texas, but also it was due to Polk's desire to take California. Two years later, the Treaty of Guadalupe Hidalgo ended the war. The United States got California, the New Mexico and Utah territories, and paid Mexico $15 million, plus other

---

[27] Ibid., 12-13.

[28] Chapter 92, Acts of the Third Legislature, Regular Session (1849), Gammel, Laws of Texas, II, 534-53; Benedict, "Source Book," 19-20.

benefits. Mexico recognized Texas as part of the United States.

Almost immediately after the Mexican War, the State of Texas came into conflict with the United States government over the state's western boundary. Texas claimed land west to the Rio Grande, land the federal government considered part of New Mexico. Several prominent officials submitted proposals for setting the western boundary of Texas and debated what was fair compensation for the land Texas would ultimately forfeit. As part of the Compromise of 1850, Governor Peter H. Bell signed a settlement on November 25, 1850, in which the United States agreed to pay Texas $10,000,000. In turn, the State of Texas forfeited to New Mexico sixty-seven million acres east of the Rio Grande. The state legislature deposited $100,000 of the money in the treasury to the credit of the "university fund."[29] Not long afterward, as a result, attention returned to the idea of establishing a state university with a sizeable, but not permanent land endowment, for the proceeds from the sale of land would support the school.

Despite the political upheaval and sectional tension of the 1850s, there were continued efforts to complete the selection and survey of the university lands and to establish the actual institution. In a message to the Fourth Legislature on November 10, 1851, Governor Bell renewed the discourse over the establishment of two universities and the still incomplete fifty-league land endowment.[30] There is no evidence, however, that anything was done at that time. In 1853, Bell told the Fifth Legislature that the

---

[29] W. J. Spillman, "Adjustment of the Texas Boundary in 1850," Southwestern Historical Quarterly 7, no. 3 (January 1904): 180-181.

[30] Benedict, "Source Book," 21-22.

selection and survey of the university lands must be completed because private interests were acquiring the most valuable lands in the unappropriated public domain. Bell strongly urged appropriations for the cost of survey operations and the establishment of two colleges or universities.[31] Despite the urgency of his pleas, the legislature did nothing.

The first Texas governor to make serious progress toward founding a state university was Elisha M. Pease. Governor Pease took office in December 1853 and in his address to the Fifth Legislature spoke of his thoughts on a state university. In the first of many such appeals to legislators, he called on them for legislation to pay for the completion of the surveys and urged the establishment of a single university. Pease argued that one institution securely endowed was preferable to two with nominal endowments. Following several days of Senate debate over one institution, or two, or none at all, legislators could reach no agreement. Despite Pease' urging and best efforts, they again took no action.

On January 6, 1854, the Fifth Legislature's committee on education reported on the progress of the selection and survey of the university lands. It stated that 199,102 acres had been surveyed with 22,250 acres still left to be located.[32] The committee report notes each of the counties where university lands were located and surveyed, as well as the total acreage in each county. The report lists the committee's findings as follows: Grayson 73,645 acres; Cooke 22,215 acres; Fannin 39,515 acres; Hunt 7,544 acres; Collin 1,677 acres; McClellan 41, 212 acres; and Lamar 13,285. Some of the land was previously located in

---

[31] Haigh, Land, Oil, and Education, 6-7.

[32] Chapter 15, Acts of the Fifth Legislature, Special Session (1854), Gammel, Laws of Texas, III, 1455-1459.

part of the much larger counties of Fannin, Robertson, and Nacogdoches, which had been carved into smaller counties as the population began to increase.

Besides the renewed efforts to complete the university surveys in the 1850s, the decade was also the beginning of a period of railroad construction. Cost of construction was expensive and the state used land as an initiative to build new lines. In 1854, legislators passed "Chapter 15," also called the "Railroad Grant Act." The law gave railroad companies sixteen sections of land for every mile of track built. The railroads got alternate sections of land in exchange for the cost of the surveys, while the state retained possession of the sections opposite the railroad lands. The terms were quite generous to the railroads and the act sparked intense debate over the state government subsidizing internal improvements. Before the law's repeal in 1882, the railroads got over 32,400,000 acres of land from the state.[33]

On November 6, 1855, Governor Pease addressed the Sixth Legislature and again stressed the importance of establishing a state university. With urgency, he reported that the survey and selection of the fifty leagues was still incomplete and that none of the land had been sold. He solicited $300,000 in United States bonds from the state treasury and a second appropriation from general revenue to finish the surveys of the university lands. The legislators, especially in the Senate, spent considerable time and effort debating the merits of Pease's request, but they did nothing at the time.

Finally, in August 1856, the legislature passed "Chapter 144" and a companion bill, "Chapter 156." Governor Pease immediately signed both into law. Chapter

---

[33] Aldon S. Lang, "A Financial History of the Public Lands in Texas," The Baylor Bulletin 35, no. 3 (July, 1932), 107.

144 gave control of the survey and selection of the remaining balance of the original fifty leagues to the governor. It stated that the governor should appoint experts to locate and survey 22,250 acres. The law also instructed surveyors to mark plainly the lines of each tract, with intersection points and corners clearly marked, "with good and substantial material."[34] The surveyors divided 640-acre sections into 160-acre tracts and prepared maps and notes with descriptions of resources for the General Land Office. The classification and descriptions included water, timber, and the character of the soil. The law gave the governor the power to execute sales within a clearly defined set of standards. Advertisement for such sales was to be made well in advance of the sale, with date, time, and location of the auction provided in the announcement. The minimum price for land was $3.00 per acre, and the 160-acre tracts were to be sold with a twenty-year contract at eight percent interest.[35] The first sale of university lands took place in December 1856 at the county courthouse in Sherman, Grayson County, Texas. The sale price for land was $3.50 per acre.[36] After seventeen years of effort, the value of the university fund would begin to grow and benefit from income from the sale of university lands.

In November 1857, Governor Pease once again addressed the legislature and implored lawmakers to act while they had the means to establish a state university. He proclaimed:

> On former occasions, I have called the attention of the Legislature to the importance of establishing a

---

[34] Chapter 156, Acts of the Sixth Legislature, Adjourned Session (1856), Gammel, Laws of Texas, II, 502-503.

[35] Ibid.

[36] Haigh, Land, Oil, and Education, 10.

State University, where all the facilities can be furnished for obtaining a thorough education that are to be found in other states; and I feel that I should be wanting in duty, did I fail to urge this measure upon your consideration. No Country was ever better situated to commence such an undertaking. We have ample means in the treasury, not needed for other objects, with which to erect the necessary buildings; and we have two hundred twenty one thousand and four hundred acres of land already set apart by your predecessors for a University, the proceeds of which, if properly managed, will be a liberal endowment, and will enable us to command the services of the ablest professors in every department of learning.[37]

In the address, Pease also reported that the balance of the fifty leagues was surveyed and divided in accordance with Chapter 144. He noted, however, that the work of one surveyor had to be sent back and corrected, and he advised against selling any more land until the surveys were compliant with the law. Nevertheless, Pease' emphasis on the university lands and their value demonstrates common attitudes regarding land abundance and the establishment of the university.

Prompted by Pease' speech, Representative Pleasant Williams Kittrell of Huntsville offered a resolution calling for the Committee on Education to look at the possibility of establishing two universities. Debates again revealed that there was a group that favored two institutions: one east of the Trinity River and one to the west of it; another group favored the establishment of one institution; and a final group was against any state supported university

---

[37] Governor Elisha M. Pease, Message to Seventh Legislature (November 2, 1857), in Benedict, "Source Book," 65.

whatsoever.[38] Political maneuvering and debates continued well into the next year.

On January 21, 1858, the Senate sent to the governor a bill entitled "An Act to establish the University of Texas." Two days later Representative Kittrell reported on behalf of the education committee and urged the establishment of a single institution to avoid sectional rivalry within the state. He argued that, "over two hundred youths of Texas [are] being educated in Northern schools . . . where their young and plastic minds imperceptibly imbibe sentiments and feelings hostile to our Southern institutions and principles."[39] Kittrell's rhetoric was sure to incite emotion at the thought of young Texans being indoctrinated in Yankee culture. On February 8, 1858, a bill relating to the establishment went to a vote. The refusal of many to vote and the subsequent threat to announce publicly the names of those that refused to vote are evidence of significant disagreement over the contents of the bill. Nonetheless, "Chapter 116" passed with a final count of 48 in favor and 13 opposed. Governor Pease signed Chapter 116 into law on February 11, 1858.[40]

Chapter 116 is significant. It set out the plan under which the University of Texas would be established. Section three of the law gave control of the management and supervision of the university to a ten-member Board of Administrators. The board consisted of the Governor, Chief Justice of the Supreme Court, and eight persons appointed by the Governor with Senate approval. Section

---

[38] Haigh, Land, Oil, and Education, 11-13.

[39] Benedict, "Source Book," 95.

[40] Chapter 116, Acts of the Seventh Legislature, Regular Session (1858), Gammel, Laws of Texas, IV, 148-151.

four mandated the subjects to be taught.[41] Had national affairs not taken a downturn and secession not taken place, Chapter 116 would have been the vehicle to establish the University of Texas in the 1860s.

Another important feature of Chapter 116 is that it also appropriated a significant amount of additional land for the university endowment. Often called the "One-In-Ten Railroad Act," Chapter 116 stipulated that out of the alternate sections of railroad land reserved for the state under the Railroad Grant Act (1854), every tenth section was reserved for the university fund. Some of this land proved to be quite valuable, and by 1886 the one-tenth reserved for the university totaled over 1,600,000 acres. But national events precluded efforts to survey and sell the land.[42] The intensely divisive issues of slavery and secession became the focus of lawmakers, who made no efforts to begin the necessary surveys.

In 1859, Sam Houston was reelected to the governor's office on a campaign promise of loyalty to the Union. With sectional turmoil tearing at the fiber of the Union, Houston also became concerned that Indians might make trouble along the northern and western line of settlement. In a speech to the Eighth Legislature on January 13, 1860, Governor Houston questioned the feasibility of the state supporting a university at the time and asked for a loan from the university fund for "frontier defense."[43] On January 31, 1860, the legislature passed "Chapter 32," which allowed for the appropriation of $100,000 in United States bonds from the university fund over the next two

---

[41] Ibid., 149.

[42] Miller, Public Lands, 124.

[43] Benedict, "Source Book," 173-174.

years. The law stated explicitly that the money was to be paid back without interest. The amount borrowed for the purpose under Chapter 32 totaled $109,472.26.[44]

In December 1860, Texas was moving towards secession. A group of radicals, including future Governor Oran M. Roberts, met in Austin and drew up an appeal to the voters of Texas to send delegates to a convention in Austin on January 28, 1861, to consider secession. Governor Houston's request that the legislature convene on January 21, 1861, in a special session was all but ignored. On the second day of the convention delegates passed a resolution that called for the voters to settle the secession question at an election on February 23. The popular vote of roughly 46,000 to 14,000 indicates a clear majority of folks favored leaving the Union. The Secession Convention reconvened on March 2, and on March 5 the delegates voted to apply for admission to the Confederate States of America.[45] On March 16, 1861, the Legislature declared the governor's office vacant, and Lieutenant Governor Edward Clark replaced Sam Houston.

During the same session the legislature again diverted money from the university fund. On January 29, 1861, lawmakers passed "Chapter 5," which instructed the treasury to hand over $9,768.62 from the sale of university lands to pay mileage and expenses of members of the Eighth Legislature. Chapter 5 also called for repayment of the loan when the money was available, but it said nothing about interest.[46] A week later the legislature passed

---

[44] Chapter 32, Acts of the Eighth Legislature, Regular Session (1860), Gammel, Laws of Texas, V, 1391-1392.

[45] Richardson, Anderson, Wintz, and Wallace, Texas, 213-214.

[46] Chapter 5, Acts of the Eighth Legislature, Extra Session (1861), Gammel, Laws of Texas, V, 342-343.

"Chapter 23," calling on the comptroller and treasury officials to accept State Treasury bonds as payment for land purchases and credit the amounts to the appropriate fund.[47] At the same time state officials were moving toward secession.

There were a number of other measures passed during the war regarding repayment of the money to the university and school funds. In January 1862, the Ninth Legislature passed "Chapter 86," which allocated the remaining university funds to pay their own contingent expenses. The fund showed a balance of $1,520.97, of which lawmakers diverted $1,520.40, leaving the university fund with fifty-seven cents.[48] Clearly, during the Civil War, the university was not a priority for the state government, but lawmakers were concerned that money from the university and school funds be paid back.

The Ninth Legislature, in January 1862, enacted other measures concerning repayment of loans from various agency funds. "Chapter 47," for example, stipulated the aforementioned loans from the university fund could be paid with Texas non-interest-bearing notes and Confederate States of America promissory notes.[49] "Chapter 50" allowed purchasers to stop making payments on state lands until January 1864, or six months after the war ended. Again, lawmakers wanted to insure that the money was paid back.

Two additional pieces of legislation dealt with the payment for lands purchased on installments before the war. The Tenth Legislature passed "Chapter 52," which

---

[47] Ibid., 355.

[48] Chapter 86, Acts of the Ninth Legislature, Regular Session (1862), Gammel, Laws of Texas, V, 500-501.

[49] Ibid., 481.

repealed Chapter 50, and called for a period of twelve months after peace for individuals to pay all installments and interest due to the university and public school funds.[50] The Tenth Legislature passed "Chapter 6" on November 12, 1864, which approved the exchange of Confederate Treasury notes for a later issue of the same.[51] Lawmakers were clearly focused on preserving the university fund and its money.

The decision to join the Confederate States of America, however, had significant consequences relating to the loans taken from the university fund. When Texas reentered the Union in 1865, Democrats and Republicans debated the repudiation of the state's wartime debts, which included money borrowed from the university fund. Repudiation of the debt would leave the university fund without the $100,000 from the Compromise of 1850 and the almost $10,000 from the sale of lands. It was also necessary to write a new state constitution and ratify the Thirteenth and Fourteenth Amendments to the United States Constitution.

With the Civil War over, officials convened in Austin in early 1866 to begin work on a new state constitution. Delegates elected James W. Throckmorton president of convention. In a message to the delegates on February 10, 1866, Governor A. J. Hamilton discussed the state war debt and pointed out that some purchasers of university lands had paid with worthless Confederate notes. He asked the General Land Commissioner to give an accounting of all land sales prior to February 1, 1861. In response to the report, the convention on March 15, 1866, passed two ordinances: one which validated all sales before secession

---

[50] Chapter 52, Acts of the Tenth Legislature, Regular Session (1863), Gammel, Laws of Texas, V, 689.

[51] Ibid., 839.

and the other nullified the state war debt. The former measure stipulated that all purchasers who paid with Confederate notes would be credited the market value of the notes at the time the payments were made. The state comptroller would determine the market value.[52] To insure that taxpayers were not liable for the debts of the wartime government, lawmakers supported the measures. They did not intend, however, to penalize purchasers of university lands for payments made in Confederate notes either.

Delegates to the convention came up with a series of amendments to the Constitution of 1845, and the resulting Constitution of 1866 reflected the views of conservative Democrats. It provided for an elaborate system of internal improvements for education. Article Ten, Section Three of the Constitution of 1866 reaffirmed prewar legislation that set aside alternate sections of railroad land for the public school and university funds. Section Eight stipulated that proceeds from the sale of public school and university lands must be placed in a fund and invested, but that the legislature shall have no power to use the money except for the intended purpose. The final part of Section Eight urged the legislature to organize and establish a university at the earliest possible date. Each of these constitutional provisions is essentially a reiteration of aspects of the Constitution of 1845.[53] The reestablishment of civil government, however, had to be achieved before any action could be taken towards establishing a state university.

Voters took up the proposed Constitution of 1866 and a slate of candidates for state office at a special election held June 25, 1866. They narrowly passed the new constitution, and Democratic candidate James W.

---

[52] Benedict, "Source Book," 188-191, 193.

[53] Ibid., 192-193.

Throckmorton easily defeated Union stalwart Elisha M. Pease for the governor's office. Democrats also held a majority in the state legislature.[54] The Democratic legislature elected former Confederate and president of the Secessionist Convention O. M. Roberts and former Unionist David G. Burnet to the United States Senate.[55]

The newly elected Eleventh Legislature convened in August and passed numerous measures regarding the university lands. "Chapter 43," for example, gave purchasers of university lands until January 1, 1869, to make payment of interest due on their purchases. "Chapter 95" facilitated the sale of the university lands at a price of not less than $3.00 per acre. "Chapter 148" amended the Act of 1858 to establish the university and set forth a procedure to make contracts for construction. "Chapter 152" made provision for the survey of the remainder of the fifty leagues. Finally, "Chapter 167" appropriated $134,472.26 in five per cent state bonds to pay for the wartime loans from the university fund.[56] The Democratic controlled Eleventh Legislature obviously wanted to set Texas' hopes for education on the course begun before secession, and it ignored Republican assertions that the wartime debt should be repudiated altogether.

Conflict between President Andrew Johnson and "radicals" in the United States Congress became increasingly hostile, and in Texas the conflict undermined

---

[54] William Whatley Pierson, Jr. "Texas *Versus* White," Southwestern Historical Quarterly 18, no. 4 (January 1915): 351-352.

[55] Charles W. Ramsdell, Reconstruction in Texas, 2nd ed., (Austin: University of Texas Press, 1970), 115-116; Richardson, Anderson, Wintz, and Wallace, Texas, 239-240.

[56] Benedict, "Source Book," 198-204; Ramsdell, Reconstruction in Texas, 114-119, 126.

Throckmorton's attempts to reestablish civil government. Like most other southern states in the immediate post-*bellum* period, the Radical Republicans, who controlled the United States Congress, deemed the Texas Constitution of 1866 unacceptable, for it lacked safeguards for the rights of newly freed slaves. The radical leadership in the United States Congress refused to seat the Texas congressional delegation because its members could not take the ironclad oath, meaning they had never been disloyal to the Union. The refusal left the fate of Texas' statehood in limbo.[57] Congressional Republicans did not want to see southern state governments returned to prominent Confederate leaders and immediately initiated measures for Congressional Reconstruction.

Following passage of the Reconstruction Acts of 1867, federal law mandated that the Texas Constitution of 1866 had to be revised. The measure placed the former Confederacy under five military districts. General Philip Sheridan commanded the Military Division of the Southwest, headquartered at New Orleans. Texas and Louisiana made up the Fifth District, with Texas under the direct command of General Charles Griffin. Military Authorities removed Governor Throckmorton and replaced him with former Governor Elisha M. Pease.[58]

To craft a new state document, a Constitution Convention convened in Austin on June 1, 1868. Of the ninety-four delegates, only twelve were conservatives. The proceedings, however, were disrupted by a major division in Republican ranks over the issue of *ab intio*, or the affirmation of all laws passed during the war not in conflict with the United States Constitution. Due to infighting the

---

[57] Richardson, Anderson, Wintz, and Wallace, Texas, 240-241; Constitution of Texas (1866), Gammel, Laws of Texas, V, 884.

[58] Pierson, "Texas *Versus* White," 353.

delegates never finished their work. Military officials gathered the convention's materials and published them as the Constitution of 1869. The Constitution of 1869 reflected the Republicans' desire to limit the influence of former Confederates. Although it provided for a common school system, the 1869 Constitution contained no provision for a state university. The lack of such a provision signifies the first break since 1839 in legislative and constitutional continuity regarding the state university.

On November 30, 1869, the voters ratified the Constitution of 1869 and elected E. J. Davis to the governor's office. Some conservatives stayed away from the polls, while about sixty-three percent of eligible freedmen voted. The legislature ratified the Thirteenth and Fourteenth Amendments to the Unites States Constitution in February and elected Morgan Hamilton and J. W. Flanagan, both Republicans, to the United States Senate. President Ulysses S. Grant, on March 30, 1870, signed the congressional order admitting the Texas Congressional delegation, and on April 16, General J. J. Reynolds ended military rule in Texas.[59] The Republican dominated state government and the Constitution of 1869 were both controversial, and after military rule ended, many Texans believed that yet another constitutional convention was in order.

In a message to the Twelfth Legislature on April 29, 1870, Governor Davis discussed the common school and university funds, which he characterized as one and the same. He explained that railroad loans taken from the two funds in 1856 were in arrears, no payment had been made since 1860. He also suggested that the legislature extend relief to the railroad companies because the war had hampered their ability to repay the loans. If the legislature did not act, he argued, the law compelled him to proceed in

---

[59] Richardson, Anderson, Wintz, and Wallace, Texas, 249.

accordance with the Act of 1856 with a sale of those railroads that were in default. When the legislature instead took up a bill to confirm the title to university lands and called for their immediate sale, Davis protested. In a letter to Speaker of the House Ira H. Evans in August 1870, Davis argued:

> This act is objectionable, particularly in the respect that it compels the Governor to proceed to sell out the remaining university lands at once. Whether these lands belong to the University or the general school fund, it is obvious that a large fund may be realized for the benefit of education by due care in the sale of them - they being some of the best lands in the State. There is no necessity existing which would require their immediate sale. Within a year or two such lands will probably bring two or three times what they will sell for now. In the meantime the university, even if organized, will not require other funds than are already on hand.[60]

Davis's argument clearly made an impression on lawmakers. They defeated the measure soundly by a vote of 59-2.

Although dissatisfaction with Republican rule in Texas hampered progress in a lot of ways, Davis kept attention focused on the issue of higher education. In a speech before the Twelfth Legislature on January 10, 1871, he urged lawmakers to cancel the bonds issued in 1866. They were bonds that had replaced United States bonds in the public school and university funds the state had borrowed and spent during the Civil War. He argued that the bonds should be canceled because it was not fair for

---

[60] Benedict, "Source Book," 207-208.

taxpayers to pay the interest on those loans.[61] The legislature seems to have ignored Davis' request because there is no record of the bonds being canceled at that time.

More importantly, however, during the same speech Davis announced that he had studied the provisions of an 1862 piece of federal legislation entitled the Morrill Land-Grant College Act. Senator Justin Morrill of Vermont first introduced a resolution in 1856 that called for the development of "National agricultural schools."[62] Morrill presented slightly different versions of his plan in subsequent years, but it was not until 1862 that the Republican-dominated Congress passed a revised version of the bill. Originally, the law was designated to expire in 1867, but in 1866, the United States Congress extended the law for another five years. Davis explained to lawmakers that the United States Congress had made an appropriation of script equal to 180,000 acres for the establishment of a college, which provided instruction in the agricultural and mechanical arts. He reported that he had applied for the grant, which Texas was awarded, and urged lawmakers to pass "an act applicable to that case."[63]

The legislature answered the Governor's request with the passage of "Chapter 44." The law called for the governor to appoint a commission of three to select a site for the institution, "on not less than 1,280 acres of land."[64]

---

[61] Ibid., 209.

[62] Henry C. Dethloff, A Centennial History of Texas A&M University, 1876-1976, vol. 1 (College Station: Texas A&M University Press, 1975), 10.

[63] John J. Lane, "History of Education in Texas," United States Bureau of Education Circular of Information, no. 2 (Washington, 1903), 260-261.

[64] Dethloff, History of Texas A&M, 14.

It also allocated 1,280 acres of land for that purpose and $75,000 for the cost of construction. The final section of the act took the unique step of specifying that the institution be placed under the state university, which, of course, had not yet been established.[65] The sale of the federal land script gave the institution an endowment of $176,000, with an annual income of $14,280.[66] The amount was hardly enough to sustain the institution and caused years of financial uncertainty for the school.

More importantly, however, the Republican establishment of the Agricultural and Mechanical College of Texas under Chapter 44 was a clear circumvention of Chapter 116, the 1858 law that set forth the means to establish a state university. In a move characteristic of reconstruction politics in Texas, Republicans ignored the *ante-bellum* legislation and instead used federal money and passed their own law to establish an institution of higher learning. The action is obviously the reason subsequent Democratic controlled legislatures appropriated very little for the operation of the school.

Reconstruction politics also played a role in the selection of the site for the new institution. Davis' selection committee appointees included John G. Bell, F. E. Grothaus, and John B. Slaughter. Each of the individuals was a Republican holding a seat in the state legislature. The commissioners visited sites in Grimes, Brazos, and Austin counties, with each community lobbying heavily for consideration as the site of the school. The community of Bryan, in Brazos County, became the front-runner, but Bell

---

[65] Chapter 44, Acts of the Twelfth Legislature, First Session (1863), Gammel, Laws of Texas, VI, 938-940; Benedict, "Source Book," 211.

[66] Haigh, Land, Oil, and Education, 29.

insisted that the school be located in his home district at Bellville, Austin County. To avoid prolonging the selection, Davis replaced Bell with Charles W. Gardiner, an advocate of the Bryan site. Following a meeting at Houston in June 1871, the committee elected Bryan as the site.[67] Many years of controversy surrounded the decision that was largely considered a partisan move by the unpopular Republican administration.

Republican leadership in Texas was waning as reconstruction slowly ended throughout the South. In 1871, the Democrats regained the four seats in the national Texas Congressional delegation. The following year the Democrats got a majority in the state legislature.[68] Among the various actions of the Democratic-controlled Thirteenth Legislature was the appointment of a group of eight administrators for the not yet established University of Texas. They also passed a bill to give the Agricultural and Mechanical College twenty of the original fifty leagues of university lands, a portion of the five percent bonds paid to the university fund in 1866, and $40,000 to complete construction. Governor Davis vetoed the bill on June 3, 1873, arguing that it was fiscally irresponsible.[69]

During the 1873 gubernatorial election, the Democratic candidate Richard Coke of Waco defeated incumbent Davis for the governor's seat. In a desperate attempt to retain control of the governor's office, Davis supporters protested that the election was invalid due to a technicality. President Grant, however, refused to intervene on Davis' behalf. Republicans locked Democrats

---

[67] Dethloff, History of Texas A&M, 15-19.

[68] Benedict, "Source Book," 213.

[69] Dethloff, History of Texas A&M, 24-25.

out of the capital and placed state troops on the ground floor. But Democrats, using ladders, gained access to the second floor of the capital, convened the legislature, and Governor Coke took office in January 1874.[70] Reconstruction had ended, but many Texans attempted to wipe out the vestiges of Radical Republican rule, especially the Constitution of 1869. Almost immediately there were calls for a constitutional convention.

During the period 1838-1874, Texans saw an almost continuous stream of legislation and constitutional amendments that provided state land for the establishment and maintenance of a state university. But no university appeared. Several factors account for delays in achieving the objectives of Mirabeau B. Lamar's original fifty-league grant. First, Sam Houston's opposition to Lamar and his policies proved to be a powerful force working against progress on the matter. Second, problems related to Indian raiders on the frontier and remote locations of selected tracts accounted for much of the delay in completing the university surveys. Also, political developments from the period of the Republic to the end of reconstruction diverted attention of officials from such issues as the establishment of a state university.

As reconstruction ended in Texas, people began to look to the vast lands in the western part of the state and the opportunities that the land opened to settlers. Land was still viewed as an abundant resource, but Indian removal and the continuance of railroad construction were necessary to open the western part of the state for settlement. Also in West Texas, lawmakers set aside two million acres of land for the endowment of a state university.

---

[70] Alwyn Barr, Reconstruction to Reform: Texas Politics, 1876-1906 (Austin: University of Texas Press, 1971), 8.

CHAPTER II

WEST TEXAS LANDS, 1874-1895

The period from 1874 to 1895 is important for the history of the university lands. It is not only the period when lawmakers finally established the University of Texas, but also when they completed the appropriation of the present-day university lands. In accordance with the Constitution of 1876, the legislature, and later the University of Texas Board of Regents, made provisions for the selection, survey, and classification of the university lands. Also during this period control over the lands used for an endowment passed from the governor, to the ill-fated State Land Board, to the commissioner of the General Land Office, and finally in 1895 to the regents.

After gaining control of the legislature in the 1872 elections, Redeemer Democrats, former Confederates and states rights supporters, wanted to remove all vestiges of Radical Republican rule, especially the Constitution of 1869.[1] When it was written in 1868, the document had some conservative support, and Republicans were divided over the *ab initio* issue, that is, repealing all laws passed between 1861 and 1865. Although it had provisions for a common school system, the Constitution of 1869 said nothing about higher education. The lack of a provision for higher education was an obvious point of contention for university advocates.

---

[1] Seth Shepard McKay, Seven Decades of the Texas Constitution of 1876 (Lubbock: Texas Technological College Press, 1944), 47.

When the Fourteenth Legislature convened in a regular session in January 1874, lawmakers discussed various bills dealing with the sale and leasing of the university lands. One of them became "Chapter 32." It gave relief to purchasers of university lands under the Acts of August 13, 1856, and November 12, 1866. Chapter 32 gave buyers until March 1, 1875, to make the first payment on the notes.[2] The law is clear evidence that many people who purchased university lands on credit had difficulty making their payments because of the depressed economy of the 1870s, and state officials wanted to insure that they did not default on their purchase agreements.

More significantly, the Fourteenth Legislature passed "Chapter 43," which amended an earlier act to sell university lands, and designated the governor to dispose of the remainder of the fifty leagues for the benefit of the university fund. The law instructed the land commissioner to appoint a surveyor within sixty days to divide the land into quarter sections, for which he was to be paid $3.00 per linear mile surveyed. The law further directed that the surveyor deposit all maps and field notes with the General Land Office and send copies to respective counties in which university lands were located. Section five of the law designated the governor to appoint three commissioners in each county to set minimum values on the surveyed land at not less than $1.50 per acre. The commissioners were also supposed to be compensated at a rate of $3.00 per day until they finished the valuation.[3] The passage of Chapter 43 indicates that state and university

---

[2] Harry Y. Benedict, ed., "A Source Book Relating to the History of the University of Texas: Legislative, Legal, Bibliographical and Statistical," University of Texas Bulletin, no. 1757 (Austin: University of Texas, 1917), 215-216.

[3] Ibid., 216-220.

officials were well aware that disposal of university lands must be given careful consideration to insure sale at a maximum price. In fact, officials sought to maximize profits on all public and governmental agency lands.

During the same period, Governor Coke threw his support behind Texas A&M College. Originally conceived by Republican Governor E. J. Davis, the institution, contends Henry C. Dethloff, did not long remain associated with its Republican origins. Dethloff argues that the A&M College had become a "Redeemer" rather than a "Radical" institution before it ever opened, pointing to numerous instances of Democratic support for the college. Governor Coke first visited the institution in 1873 during the gubernatorial campaign, and following his election spoke of the need to support the institution, which prompted the Fourteenth Legislature to appropriate $40,000 to finish construction of the main building. Upon completion of construction, the governor personally inspected the building and in January 1874 he reported to the legislature, "it furnishes the means of supplying immediately in Texas the great want of an institution of learning of the highest grade."[4] His official endorsement went a long way in persuading the public that A&M College was a vital aspect of higher education in Texas, a sentiment echoed by many of Coke's predecessors.

In response to Redeemer Democratic calls in 1874 for constitutional revision, Governor Coke and the conservative elements in the legislature created a joint legislative committee to carry out the necessary revisions, because they believed a constitutional convention would entail enormous and unnecessary expense. When the joint

---

[4] Henry C. Dethloff, A Centennial History of Texas A&M University, 1876-1976, vol. 1 (College Station: Texas A&M University Press, 1975), 25-27.

committee, chaired by state Senator J. L. Camp and Representative W. B. Sayers, turned out an entirely new constitution in April 1874, the Senate approved its work, but the House rejected it. Seth S. McKay contends that the work of the Camp-Sayers committee was superior to the Texas Constitution of 1869, as well as the one adopted in 1876.[5] John Walker Mauer argues, "A majority of the House of Representatives, however, argued that anything but a convention was anti-Democratic."[6] The rejection of the new constitution led to more pronounced public displeasure and Governor Coke called the legislature into special session in January 1875 to address calls for a constitutional convention. Advocates of the not yet established state university were among the most vocal of the proponents for constitutional convention.

At the outset of the called session of the Fourteenth Legislature in January 1875, Governor Coke addressed the body about the things he desired from lawmakers, including his ideas on education and the state of the university lands. He boasted of the success of Chapter 43, the law that spelled out the procedure to sell the university lands. He reported that the land commissioner had appointed surveyors to subdivide the university lands and indicated that a number of sales had been completed. He added that more lands had been surveyed and were ready for sale. Of particular importance, he called for the establishment of one or more universities to educate teachers for the common schools. The governor's speech struck a nerve with lawmakers. On February 15, the

---

[5] McKay, Constitution of 1876, 56-58.

[6] John Walker Mauer, "Constitution Proposed in 1874," The Handbook of Texas Online. <http://www.tsha.utexas.edu/handbook/online/articles/view/CC/mhc12.html> [Accessed Sun Jan 18 21:14:52 US/Central 2004].

legislature passed a resolution asking Land Commissioner J. J. Groos to report on university land sales under Chapter 43. Two days later, Commissioner Groos disclosed that there were sixteen sales completed at an average of $4.00 per acre.[7] Chapter 43 was an obvious success and the continued sale of university lands was assured for a number of years to follow. Supporters of the university were pleased with such progress.

During the same session, the Fourteenth Legislature passed "Chapter 48," once again extending relief to purchasers of university lands. The law required that a new contract be negotiated with a university agent by May 15, 1875. If buyers did not renegotiate, the original sale would be nullified and the land would be resold. The law further instructed the governor to appoint agents in all counties with university lands to execute the new sales contracts in accordance with the law.[8] Officials wanted to end problems associated with delinquent payments for university lands.

In response to a land dispute in McClennan and Hill Counties, lawmakers on March 6, 1875, passed "Chapter 51." The law suspended payments for purchasers of disputed land until pending litigation resolved the matter.[9] University supporters wanted to keep good relations with purchasers to insure against default on their payments.

In a move that prompted considerable dismay among university advocates, the legislature created a board of directors for A&M College, a group independent of the board of regents established in 1872 for the state university.

---

[7] Benedict, "Source Book," 223-4.

[8] Ibid., 224-6.

[9] Ibid., 226.

The A&M board, which first convened at Bryan on June 1, 1875, became a source of agitation for the university regents and seemed to contradict the 1871 legislation which established the college as a branch of the university. The creation of a separate administrative structure for A&M College was intended to expedite the opening of the school, and because the state university did not exist, made perfect sense at the time.[10]

One of the final acts of the Fourteenth Legislature was the passage of a joint resolution to convene in Austin the first Monday in September 1875 to address the calls for a new constitution. When delegates finally convened in September, the issue of constitutional revision was the most prominent public issue in Texas. Of the ninety delegates, seventy-five were Democrats, fifteen, including six African Americans, were Republicans. Due to the growth in the Patrons of Husbandry (also called the Grange) in the early 1870s, there was strong agrarian influence among delegates. About half of the delegates were members of the Grange.[11] Most of the delegates were Redeemer Democrats. Members contemplated and debated numerous issues, including the issue of land grants for internal improvements. State officials had long used land grants to finance a wide variety of projects, including railroad construction and education.

Delegates engaged in heated debate over the policy of granting land to railroads to subsidize construction. The Grangers generally argued that they did not trust the railroad officials who failed to increase mileage in spite of generous land donations. Interestingly, the debate over railroads divided some delegates not only along party lines

---

[10] Dethloff, History of Texas A&M., 27.

[11] Alwyn Barr, Reconstruction to Reform: Texas Politics, 1876-1906 (Austin: University of Texas Press, 1971), 9.

but also sectional lines. Some Republican leaders were affiliated with railroad companies, while some Democrats opposed the use of land for railroad construction. Likewise, East Texans believed the policy should be discontinued, while West Texans felt their region should benefit from state subsidized railroad construction, as had their East Texas counterparts.[12] Similar divisions appeared among delegates regarding the issue of land grants for education.

On the issue of land grants for education, conservative Democratic delegates argued for a continuation of the *ante bellum* policy of allocating half of the public domain for the public school fund. After considerable debate, Redeemer Democrats laid out a general plan for public education and the establishment of a state university. The actions of some delegates reflected a desire to undo policies begun by Governor Davis and the Radical Republicans. When he had initiated the establishment of the A&M College under federal legislation in 1871, Davis had done so in lieu of establishing the state university as called for by the 1858 "Act to Establish the University of Texas."[13] Even though some Redeemers embraced A&M College, many conservative delegates may have viewed it as the creation of Republicans with federal funds and subordinate to the Democratic sponsored state university. The attitude is evident in the new constitution's reaffirmation of the status of A&M College as a branch of the state university. Understandably, the reaffirmation added a political dimension to the rivalry between the two, one that lasted for many years. In a related matter, Texas A&M College

---

[12] McKay, Constitution of 1876, 109.

[13] Dethloff, History of Texas A&M, 10.

matriculated its first students in October 1876, even though the state university still did not exist.

When the convention adjourned on November 24, 1875, delegates by a vote of 53-11 adopted the new constitution. Convention members anticipated criticism, especially the length of the section dealing with education, which the press vehemently attacked. Ratification of the new constitution faced considerable opposition: the state Democratic Convention failed to endorse it, and the Republicans denounced it by a unanimous vote. The proposed constitution was submitted to the voters for ratification on February 15, 1876, and in what has been commonly described as a quiet election, the Constitution of 1876 passed by a vote of 136,606 to 56,652.[14] Contents of the new state document reflected the era of agrarian unrest and the retrenchment policies of conservative Democrats.

Members of both parties and the press attacked various aspects of the new constitution, but none more than the section pertaining to education. Disapproval was primarily focused on why lawmakers dismantled what many considered a good education system set up by Republicans under the Constitution of 1869. Democrats argued that the school system of the 1869 constitution was extravagant, drained state coffers, and placed an undue burden on taxpayers. They pointed to the generously endowed school and university funds, which removed much of the educational burden from taxpayers.[15]

Article Seven of the Constitution of 1876 dealt with education and it is long, containing fifteen sections. The

---

[14] Rubin Richardson, Adrian Anderson, Cary D. Wintz, and Ernest Wallace, Texas: The Lone Star State (Upper Saddle River, New Jersey: Prentice Hall, 2001), 262.

[15]Ibid.

first eight sections deal with public schools, and the ninth deals with state asylums. Sections ten through fifteen deal specifically with the establishment and maintenance of the University of Texas. Section ten lays out a detailed plan for the establishment of the university. Here the framers followed Chapter 116, entitled "An Act to establish the University of Texas," as passed by the legislature in 1858.[16]

In Section Eleven, the framer's created the Permanent University Fund, or PUF. Part of the important section reads:

> In order to enable the Legislature to perform the duties set forth in the foregoing section, it is hereby declared that all lands and other property heretofore set apart and appropriated for the establishment and maintenance of 'The University of Texas,' together with the proceeds of sales of the same, heretofore made or hereafter to be made, and all grants, donations and appropriations that may hereafter be made by the State of Texas, or from any others source, shall constitute and become a permanent university fund...[17] Section eleven also stated that money generated from the sales of the university lands was to be invested by university officials, with the interest placed in the Available University Fund, or AUF. The aspect of section eleven that caused much dismay among university supporters was that the framers canceled the One-In-Ten Railroad Act of 1858, stating that such lands, "shall not be included in

---

[16] Article 7, Section 10, Constitution of Texas (1876), H. P. N. Gammel, ed., Laws of Texas, VII, (Austin: Gammel, 1900), 811; Benedict, "Source Book," 233.

[17] Article 7, Section 11, Constitution of Texas (1876), Gammel, Laws of Texas, VII, 812.

or constitute a part of the permanent university fund."[18]

To counter the loss of such money, framers provided for other monies in section fifteen. The section reads:

> In addition to the lands heretofore granted to the University of Texas, there is hereby set apart, and appropriated, for the endowment, maintenance and support of said university and its branches, one million acres of the unappropriated public domain of the State, to be designated and surveyed as may be provided by law; and said lands shall be sold under the same regulations, and the proceeds invested in the same manner as is provided for the sale and investment of the permanent university fund; and the Legislature shall not have the power to grant any relief to the purchasers of said lands.[19]

Critics of section fifteen estimated that the railroads received 17,500,000 acres under the original 1854 legislation, meaning the institution missed out on 1,750,000 acres of prime agricultural land in central Texas. As it was carried out with little regard for the rightful claims of the university, the land substitution remained a point of contention between university supporters and lawmakers for many years. A plausible explanation for why framers favored the land substitution is that at the time of the constitutional convention the state was still in possession of a considerable amount of unappropriated public domain. Convention members probably saw little reason to grant the

---

[18] Benedict, "Source Book," 233.

[19] Ibid., 234.

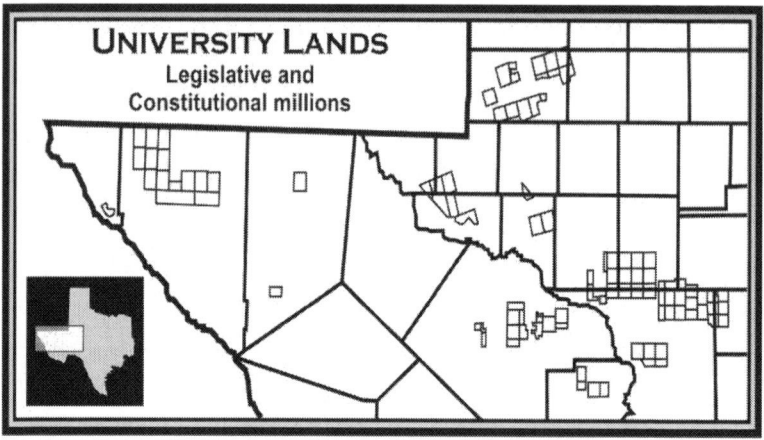

Figure 3: "Constitutional and Legislative millions," map by Chris Hieb.

more valuable railway land for an institution that did not yet exist. Delegates also knew that public lands would eventually run out, which explains why they took the fortuitous step of appropriating one million acres of land for the state university in Crockett and Tom Green counties, commonly called the "constitutional million." Supporters of the university argued that because of a lack of surface water and vegetation, the land was marginal. Clearly the land was less valuable than the railroad land, which lay in the northeastern part of the state and was generally good agricultural land with some surface water and timber.[20]

There were other sections of article seven that had direct implications for the university lands. Section twelve stipulated that university lands be sold in accordance

---

[20] Thomas Lloyd Miller, The Public Lands of Texas, 1519-1970 (Norman: University of Oklahoma Press, 1971), 121.

47

with laws of the legislature, but that the legislature should have no right to grant relief to purchasers.[21] The section is due to repeated legislative efforts after the Civil War to grant relief to purchasers of university lands. Framers of the constitution, it seems, felt compelled to protect the PUF by ensuring the collection of money for it.

When the Fifteenth Legislature convened on April 18, 1876, lawmakers passed several measures dealing with university lands. "Chapter 69" validated the sale of eighty-acre parcels. The measure was a move to increase sales of university lands. By making smaller parcels available, legislators hoped to attract a greater number of buyers. On August 12, 1876, legislators passed "Chapter 89," which instructed the land commissioner to appoint a surveyor to undertake the selection and survey of the "constitutional million." Because of the remote location of the newly appropriated land, the survey expeditions took some time to organize. Finally, "Chapter 128" called for the investment of the PUF in six per cent state bonds.[22] Lawmakers considered investment in state bonds a safe course of action and insured that the state government would benefit from the use of PUF funds. Each of the measures is evidence that state officials hoped that higher education might capitalize on income derived from the university lands.

As noted, the survey of the constitutional million took some time to work out. Although the land commissioner was to appoint a surveyor to demarcate the constitutional million, several issues had to be considered before making the appointment. Foremost among them was the problem of Indian depredation. Many Indian people refused to go to

---

[21] Article 7, Section 12, Constitution of Texas (1876), Gammel, Laws of Texas, VII, 812-813.

[22] Benedict, "Source Book," 236-238.

reservations, instead they attacked settlers, taking hostages and destroying property. After an 1871 Kiowa attack on a wagon train in Salt Creek valley that left several teamsters dead, the federal government focused efforts of its troops in Texas on missions along the western edge of settlement. They also built a line of forts from the Red River to the Rio Grande. When southern plains tribes under Quanah, a Comanche leader, launched attacks in spring 1874, President Grant canceled the Quaker Peace Policy, a policy advocated by Quakers to make treaties with Indians rather than using military force against them. In August, Colonel Ranald S. Mackenzie and others led troops into the Panhandle and within a year quelled major Indian threats in West Texas.[23] Nonetheless, survey parties needed to be vigilant, for Indian warriors and hunting parties still rode over West Texas in the late 1870s. At the same time, a resurgence in railroad construction occurred. It was due to radical Republican patronage and the desire to push settlement to the arid lands between San Antonio and El Paso.

    The role of the railroad in the settlement of West Texas cannot be overstated. The Texas & Pacific Railroad, which initiated the push of railroads into far West Texas, began construction in Longview in 1872 and reached Fort Worth in 1876. Construction did not begin anew until 1880, when the Texas & Pacific continued westward toward El Paso, joining up with the Southern Pacific line at Sierra Blanca in 1882.[24] The grant of land for railroad

---

[23] Paul H. Carlson, The Plains Indians (College Station: Texas A&M Press, 1998), 159.

[24] William Curry Holden, Alkali Trails, or Social and Economic Movements on the Texas Frontier, 1846-1900, 2nd ed., Double Mountain Books – Classic reissues of the American West (Lubbock: Texas Tech University Press, 1998), 190-194.

construction and the reservation of alternate sections within the grant for the state meant that taxpayers would not bear the cost of surveying state lands. University supporters favored the extension of rail transportation into West Texas. They saw railroad extension as having a positive impact on the sale of university lands.

At about the same time, the state university came to fruition. No Texas politician did more during the late 1870s and early 1880s to establish the University of Texas and to protect and increase the university lands than Oran M. Roberts. Roberts had served as president of the secession convention in 1861, and he was one of two senators refused his seat in the United States Congress in 1866. More importantly, he was a long-time advocate of a state university. Roberts emerged as the leading Democratic candidate for governor in 1878 and he soundly defeated his opponent in the general election.

In an address to the Sixteenth legislature on January 14, 1879, Roberts spoke explicitly about the university lands. He expressed displeasure over the cancellation of the One-In-Ten Railroad Grant as part of the permanent university fund and argued that the railroad land had an average value of $3.50 per acre. Roberts contended that under current laws, which stipulated sales to settlers only and in smaller parcels, years would pass before the land sales would effectively benefit the available university fund. He also discussed the land dispute between state officials and individuals in McLennan County. Citizens in the county claimed land the state considered part of the original fifty leagues. Robert's argued that the state should assert the university's title and reimburse the purchasers for both principle and interest paid to that point.[25] The speech, it turns out, foreshadowed Roberts' land policy, one

---

[25] Benedict, "Source Book," 238-239.

designed to dispose of all public lands quickly, even at prices as low as $0.50 per acre.

In his inaugural address on January 21, 1879, Roberts again spoke of disposing of public lands for the benefit of education, including the public school, the asylum, and the university. He reiterated his position that current policies were restrictive, that sales would merely continue at a snail's pace, and that the respective funds would not grow as quickly as the student population. By implication, Roberts' suggested that taxpayers would have to make up any deficiencies not covered by interest on the respective funds. He added that the restrictive policies would "postpone indefinitely the building of a university, which should be erected at the capital of the State for the education of Texas youths, instead of sending them out of the State to be educated, and to return home strangers to Texas."[26] Roberts' attitude reveals the existence of continued sectional distrust among the Democratic Party ranks.

In early February, Roberts once again addressed the legislature and spoke directly to the issue of land sales to fund all levels of education. He began with a discussion of university land and reported that of the original fifty leagues appropriated in 1839 some 219,800 acres remained unsold. The requirement that only settlers could purchase the tracts, he argued, had given rise to fraud. Because many of the lands were in league size tracts, a survey to divide them into smaller parcels was required. Such a survey would entail added expense and make land sales more costly. He stated explicitly that if it were continued, the same policy could take as long as forty years before the university would be established. Instead, Roberts advocated the immediate sale of the remaining fifty

---

[26] Ibid., 239.

leagues, as well as the constitutional million, without restrictions on size of parcels and who may purchase them. Only in this manner, he maintained, would the means to establish a university be achieved in the quickest way possible.[27] Roberts' policy towards university lands was actually a part of a broader policy regarding all public lands that developed during his first administration.

Roberts also stated that the A&M College was no substitute for the long awaited state university, and he expressed satisfaction that it was a constitutionally prescribed branch of the main institution. Roberts argued that the original intent of the Morrill Act (1862) was not "to promote the cause of scientific and literary education ... but rather to educate skilled laborers ... to secure skilled labor at home, instead of importing it from abroad."[28] The statement reflects the fact that for some years the A&M College placed less emphasis on its constitutionally mandated purpose to focus on instruction in the agricultural and mechanical arts instead following a curriculum that Roberts felt was more appropriate for a university.

Despite the considerable prodding by the newly elected governor, the Sixteenth Legislature passed no measures addressing Roberts' suggestions regarding the university lands. In a joint resolution passed February 19, however, the legislature called for the attorney general to begin legal proceedings to assert the state's title to disputed university lands in McLennan and Hill counties. On March 20, lawmakers followed with "Chapter 39," which instructed the land commissioner to issue patents to all

---

[27] William Elton Green, "Land Settlement in West Texas: Tom Green County, a case study," (Ph.D. diss.: Texas Tech University, 1981), 139-141.

[28] Dethloff, History of Texas A&M, 39.

purchasers of university lands under the law of August 30, 1856. In a politically expedient move, the legislature passed "Chapter 159," which provided for the establishment and support of a Normal School at Prairie View for the education of African American teachers.[29] The failure of the legislature to respond to the governor's desires suggests that some opposition to his policies existed.

The reluctance of lawmakers to address Roberts' concerns prompted the governor to call the Sixteenth Legislature into a special session. It met from June 10 to July 9, 1879. After Roberts delivered an impassioned speech at the outset of the session, lawmakers passed two measures that had some relevance on the subject. "Chapter 18" prescribed that coupon bonds in each of the respective education funds at the treasury be changed to manuscript-registered bonds. The law was intended to insure that proper credit be given purchasers for the sale of public lands. The other measure, "Chapter 49," was an appropriations bill for the next two years. It gave $7,500 per year to A&M College and a one time $1,600 grant for the Prairie View School for African Americans in Waller County.[30] The funds were to be drawn from the PUF, much to the dismay of university supporters, including Governor Roberts.

The Sixteenth Legislature, in July 1879, passed at the prompting of Governor Roberts another important measure that affected the university lands. The so-called "fifty-cent law" prescribed the sale of public lands in fifty-four West Texas counties for $0.50 per acre. Under the shortsighted law a huge amount of the public domain was sold below

---

[29] Benedict, "Source Book," 246.
[30] Ibid., 247.

market value.[31] Roberts reasoned that selling the public land cheaply, for cash or interest-bearing bonds, enabled the government to function without deficit spending. He favored selling lands of public institutions, such as the university lands, at low prices because they were producing no tax revenues. Roberts once opined that deferring land sales for future benefit was essentially "damned nonsense."[32] The policy, however, had the unexpected effect of driving down land prices and the abundance of cheap land caused the market value of university lands to drop.

In 1880, Democratic newspapers and lawmakers criticized Roberts' efforts to sell huge tracts of the public domain. The most surprising source of opposition to Roberts' land policy came from his Lieutenant Governor Joseph D. Sayers, who challenged Roberts for the Democratic gubernatorial nomination. Sayers called for higher school appropriations and land sales to settlers only.[33]

Despite the efforts of his opponents, Roberts garnered the Democratic nomination and won the general election. In office for another term, he reduced taxes on landowners and continued to raise revenue through the sale of the public lands. The sale of land was popular because it meant a reduced tax burden. Roberts was a man of action. The surveys of university lands in West Texas began in earnest under his administration.

---

[31] Miller, Public Lands, 62; Barr, Reconstruction to Reform, 78; Aldon S. Lang, "A Financial History of the Public Lands of Texas," The Baylor Bulletin 35, no. 3 (July, 1932), 57-58.

[32] Kenneth E. Hendrickson, Jr., The Chief Executives of Texas: from Stephen F. Austin to John B. Connally, Jr. (College Station: Texas A&M University Press, 1995), 108.

[33] Barr, Reconstruction to Reform, 58-59.

Land Commissioner W. C. Walsh was responsible for setting up the surveys. He used a system of competitive bids to save the state money, for surveys at the going rate would have cost the state as much as $20,000. He accepted ten bids to survey the lands. They ranged from $10 to $4.25 per section surveyed. C. W. Holt and A. W. Thompson submitted the lowest bid and Walsh awarded them the contract. The pair put up a bond of $10,000 and took on the responsibility of paying a land agent, appointed by Walsh, whose responsibility was to accept or reject land Holt and Thompson chose on behalf of the university. Walsh appointed M. B. Moore as land agent and instructed him to classify the land as agricultural, grazing, or timbered, and to report on the availability of water. Moore filed his reports in the General Land Office, and by all accounts completed his job in a most satisfactory way.[34]

Holt and Thompson put together two crews of five men each. In the fall of 1880, they set out for Crockett, Tom Green, and Pecos counties, which at the time were much larger than their present boundaries. The group arrived at Fort Concho in late fall, and upon reaching the designated region of Tom Green County, ascertained that the land appeared to be poor enough that it was hardly worth surveying. Thompson sent a telegraph to Land Commissioner Walsh and reported on the poor condition of the land. He further expressed the opinion that the land was not even suitable for grazing. Walsh instructed the surveyor that there was no choice in the matter because the law stipulated that a certain amount of the land had to be selected in Tom Green County. Thompson's crew

---

[34] W.C. Walsh, Report of the Commissioner of the General and Office of the State of Texas for the Fiscal Year Ending August 31, 1880 (Galveston: Book and Job Office of the Galveston News, 1880), 5-6.

continued its work throughout the winter and into the late spring of 1881.[35]

The survey crew faced hardships out beyond the settled areas. R. M. Thompson, a member of the crew and the younger brother of A. M. Thompson, described the difficulties. He reported that there were no water sources available for their camps, and they had to haul water in by wagon. Although by the mid-1870s, the U.S. Army supposedly had removed most Indian groups from West Texas, survey crews still had to be vigilant. Thompson recounted:

> Our survey of the million acres of University lands . . . was made at the very close of the era of the Indian and buffalo in West Texas. If we had undertaken the work a year before, it is not unlikely that we could have met with exciting experiences with hostile bands of Indians . . . A few months before Indians had killed the driver of the stage . . . The last onslaught on the buffalo was just being concluded when we were there . . . While we did not see any live buffaloes, we saw their carcasses and hides . . . their skeletons by the hundreds.[36]

Although the surveys took place after the removal of the Indian threat, the crew had no way of knowing that the danger had been mitigated.

Meanwhile, back in Austin, in a speech at the opening of the Seventeenth Legislature in January 1881, Governor Roberts once again made an impassioned plea to establish a state university as prescribed by the Constitution of 1876.

---

[35] Edith Helene Parker, "History of Land Grants for Education in Texas" (Ph.D. diss., University of Texas, 1952), 254-255.

[36] Ibid., 256.

He argued that enough land had been sold to establish the school. Subsequently, Lieutenant Governor L. G. Story addressed the legislature and pressed for the establishment of a university, arguing that Texans were building up universities in other states when they sent their children out of state to be educated. On January 29, Roberts noted that the State Teachers Association gave its endorsement for the proposed institution.[37] The governor and other officials led a determined effort to establish the school by appealing to Texans' pragmatism as well as sectionalism.

On January 31, 1881, both houses began debate on a bill to establish a state university. A minority opinion of the House Committee on Education signed by George W. L. Fly, J. P. Ayers, and John A. Peacock, dated February 8, 1881, stated that the fledgling public schools and the A&M College should be set on secure footing before considering the establishment of a university.[38] Lawmakers considered the university lands an important aspect of the proposed state university. They passed "Chapter 73" on March 30, 1881. It was intended to insure state title to university lands in McLennan and Hill Counties. That same day, a major milestone in the history of Texas higher education took place when the Seventeenth Legislature passed "Chapter 75," the legislation that finally launched the University of Texas.[39] The measure spelled out precisely how the institution would be organized, administered, financed, and operated.

---

[37] John J. Lane, History of the University of Texas (Austin: Henry Hutchings, 1891), 197-198; Benedict, "Source Book," 247-250.

[38] Benedict, "Source Book," 257.

[39] Joe B. Franz, The Forty Acre Follies: An Opinionated History of the University of Texas (Austin: Texas Monthly Press, Inc., 1983), 11-13.

Figure 4: Oran M. Roberts presided over the Texas secession convention in 1861, as governor he established the University of Texas in 1881, and served as Chief Justice of the Texas Supreme Court, and later on the Faculty of the UT Law School. Photo in public domain.

As prescribed by section two of Chapter 75, Governor Roberts called for an election, to be held in September 1881, to choose a location for the new school. Numerous legislators lobbied for their respective districts over the summer months, but voters overwhelming chose Austin as the site of the main campus. Austin got 30,913 votes with Tyler coming in second place with 18,974 votes. Similarly, voters chose Galveston as the location of the medical branch with 20,741 votes, while Houston got 12,586 votes.[40]

    Sections five through ten of Chapter 75 details the provisions for appointment of regents and their role in governing the University of Texas. On April 1, the Senate confirmed Governor Roberts' appointees to the board of regents from among the most prominent citizens across the state. Appointees to the board included Thomas J. Devine of Bexar County, A. N. Edwards of Hopkins County, Richard B. Hubbard of Smith County, Smith Ragsdale of Parker County, Ashbel Smith of Harris County, James Starr of Harrison County, James W. Throckmorton of Collin County, and Elisha M. Pease of Travis County. Following objections over Pease' nomination, Roberts submitted the name of James H. Bell of Travis County. At the first meeting of the regents on November 14, 1881, members chose Ashbel Smith to serve as president of the board.[41] Although, they were the governing body of the University of Texas and were charged with overseeing spending of legislative appropriations from the AUF, the regents did not gain control over the disposition of the university lands for twenty-four years.

    Meanwhile, the effects of a severe drought in 1881 meant that groundwater resources had to be made exploitable to attract settlers to West Texas. Without

---

    [40] O. M. Roberts, "A History of the Establishment of the University of the State of Texas," <u>Southwestern Historical Quarterly</u> 1, no. 4 (April, 1898): 248; Lane, <u>History of UT</u>, 249-250.

    [41] Roberts, "History of the Establishment of UT," 248; Lane, <u>History of UT</u>, 250-251; Benedict, "Source Book," 254; Franz, <u>Forty Acre Follies</u>, 12-13.

available water sources, settlement of the region and increased sale of university lands was not likely. Cattlemen who arrived in the 1870s initially found sufficient surface water in creeks, springs, and playa lakes. Such sources proved sufficient during periods of normal rainfall but not during periods of drought. The introduction of the windmill to the Great Plains in the 1880s encouraged greater settlement in the arid western region of Texas.[42] Possibly the earliest water-well drilling contractor, C. B. Foote, is known to have operated in West Texas in 1882. Nonetheless, windmills proved essential for the settlement of ranchers and farmers and the establishment of towns in West Texas.[43]

During a special session of the legislature on April 6, 1882, Governor Roberts spoke to lawmakers about unresolved problems regarding the university lands. More specifically, he decried the injustice of the Constitution of 1876 that canceled the One-in-Ten Railroad Act of 1858. After depriving the university of 1,750,000 acres of prime land under the 1858 law, Roberts explained, the constitutional convention substituted 1,000,000 acres of marginal land in West Texas, which was far from equal to the railroad land in either quantity or quality. He advocated an additional 2,000,000-acre appropriation for university lands. The addition would generate sufficient revenue to

---

[42] Walter Prescott Webb, The Great Plains (New York: Grosset and Dunlap, 1931), 335- 6; Samuel D. Myres, The Permian Basin: Petroleum Empire of the Southwest, Era of Discovery, from the Beginning to the Depression, vol. 1 (El Paso: Permian Press, 1973), 17.

[43] Joe Pickle and Ross McSwain, Water in a Dry and Thirsty Land: The First Fifty Years of the Colorado River Municipal Water District (Big Spring: CRMWD, 2000), 8–9.

cover expenses of the establishment and maintenance of a first class institution of higher learning.[44]

Two days later, on April 8, 1882, State Comptroller W. M. Brown reported to the legislature on the financial situation of the PUF. He detailed all expenditures and withdrawals since 1860 from the older university fund, which existed before the creation of the PUF in 1876, and noted that the state still owed the fund, which became part of the PUF in 1876, $134,472.26. Lawmakers debated the merits of repaying the PUF, and introduced several bills to do so. Some of the bills suggested remedies that included monetary or additional land appropriations. For example, Senator A. W. Terrell introduced legislation to appropriate 2,000,000 additional acres for university lands. He gave to both houses an impassioned speech on April 19, and argued that the additional acreage would preclude the need for future appropriations from general revenues.[45] Despite the efforts of Terrell and others, nothing regarding university lands passed during the 1882 legislative session.

Throughout 1882, however, state and university officials continued with the construction of the University of Texas. Then, on November 17, about three thousand people turned out for the cornerstone ceremonies. Ashbel Smith, Governor Roberts, and Attorney General J. H. McLeary gave speeches to commemorate the occasion. Smith's speech contained a statement regarding university lands. "Texas holds embedded in its earth rocks and minerals which now lie idle because unknown, resources of incalculable industrial utility, of wealth and power," he proclaimed. "Smite the earth," he continued, "smite the

---

[44] Benedict, "Source Book," 268-269, 271.

[45] Lane, History of UT, 215-226, *passim*; Benedict, "Source Book," 283, 285-296.

rocks with the rod of knowledge and fountains of unstinted wealth will gush forth."[46] He had no way of knowing, of course, how true his words would ring forty-two years later.

In January 1883 the issue of university lands again caught attention. The outgoing executives, Governor Oran. M. Roberts and Lt. Governor L. G. Storey, gave impassioned speeches regarding public school and university lands before the Eighteenth Legislature. But, the new Governor, John Ireland, spoke of the "wicked folly," regarding the state land policies between 1865-1882.[47] Land Commissioner W. C. Walsh gave a report expressing his displeasure with Roberts' 1879 law to sell public lands at fifty-cents an acre, calling it "a misfortune rather than a benefit."[48] He further asserted that "The one million acres of university land situated in Tom Green, Crocket[t], Pecos, and Presidio counties, might be yielding revenue if there were any authority for their lease." Walsh also noted that after the repeal of the One-in-Ten Railroad Act (1858), the university lost five-dollar an acre land. It got fifty cents an acre land. He further reported that there were two million acres turned back by the railroads. It might be used, he suggested, for the benefit of education.[49]

---

[46] Roberts, "History of the Establishment of UT," 263; Lane, History of UT, 26-30; Franz, Forty Acre Follies, 3.

[47] Miller, Public Lands, 112-113.

[48] W. C. Walsh, Biennial Report of the Commissioner of the General Land Office of the State of Texas from August 1831, 1880, to August 31, 1882 (Austin: E.W. Swindells, State Printer, 1883), 4.

[49]Ibid., 8; Lane, History of UT, 134-135; Benedict, "Source Book," 618; Presidio County was incorrectly mentioned in Walsh's report.

Partly in reaction to Walsh's report, as well as the urging of newly elected Governor John Ireland, the Eighteenth Legislature, in the spring of 1883, passed four laws regarding public lands. First, "Chapter 6" removed all public lands from the market for ninety days or until they could be properly classified. Second, "Chapter 27" provided for the payment of $256,272.57 in past state debts to the PUF. Third, "Chapter 72" appropriated one million acres for public schools and one million acres for the university lands, referred to as the "legislative million." Finally, the legislature passed "Chapter 88," which created the State Land Board. The board included the governor, the comptroller, the treasurer, the attorney general, and the land commissioner. The mandate of the State Land Board was to classify public lands as, "agricultural, pasture, and timber lands and ascertain which tracts have permanent water on them, or bordering on them ..."[50] The land board was also charged with appointing an agent to dispose of the land on behalf of the respective state agencies. Of each of the aforementioned laws, the regents probably viewed Chapter 88 least favorably because it gave control over the disposal of university lands to the State Land Board, rather than allowing the regents themselves the authority to sell or lease property.

Besides the creation of the State Land Board, and that body's mandate to classify and sell the public domain, Chapter 88 also included the first provisions for the leasing of the public lands, including the university lands. Section sixteen of the law stated that any agricultural or rangeland which did not have timber could be leased for stock raising. Ranchers could lease the land for no less than four cents per acre, per year, for periods of ten years. The law further

---

[50] Chapter 88, Acts of the Eighteenth Legislature, Regular Session (1883), Gammel, Laws of Texas, IX, 391-392; Hendrickson, Chief Executives, 112.

prescribed that leases be executed by an agent of the State Land Board, under rules formulated by that body, and leasing must be conducted under a system of competitive bidding. The leases had to be executed in the county of locale, and when applications for both lease and purchase were made, preference would be given to the purchaser. At first, lease revenues remained low, amounting to $1,772.80 for 1884, but they totaled more than $76,812.20 over the next decade.[51] The new mechanism for capitalizing on university lands became an important income generator.

The regents wasted little time. They voted on a resolution to the land commissioner and pressed him to expedite the selection and survey of the legislative million acres. Land Commissioner Walsh, however, argued that he did not have the administrative capacity to complete the request in a timely fashion, having neither adequate staff nor a skilled draftsman. At the board meeting of June 4, 1883, Regent Thomas D. Wooten revealed that he had met with Governor John Ireland, and that Ireland agreed that additional help for the land office was needed to select the balance of the university lands. The following day, Walsh told the board that the additional assistance had been procured. Nonetheless, because of continued pressure from the regents over the following months, relations with the land office were tense throughout the process of selection of the legislative million acres. The legislature provided the funding, from the AUF, through an appropriations bill, "Chapter 116," which set aside $5,000 to pay expenses of the survey.[52]

---

[51] Ibid., 394-395; Lang, "Financial History of the Public Lands," 218-219.

[52] Chapter 116, Acts of the Eighteenth Legislature, Regular Session (1883), Gammel, Laws of Texas, IX, 433-435; Haigh, Land, Oil, and Education, 69-70.

When the regents convened on September 14, 1883, Thomas Wooten reported that the State Land Board had recommended Dennis Corwin for the job of selecting and surveying the legislative million. The regents were delighted. Corwin, one of the earliest land agents for the University of Texas for which information is available, served with Texas Confederate forces during the Civil War and, in what is generally described as a brilliant career, eventually achieved the rank of major. Later, he became county and district surveyor of Travis County. He worked there until he entered state service. The state land board employed him to classify the legislative million for sale or lease. He was a natural choice to carry out the assignment. Corwin was ill at the time, but he promised to depart for West Texas when he recovered.[53] Meanwhile, state revenues increased because Land Commissioner Walsh, Governor Ireland, and the Eighteenth Legislature all pushed for the classification of the land and for setting optimal market values based on their classification.

    An unforeseen consequence, however, was that cattle ranchers increased their holdings and began to enclose their property with barbed wire fences. Some ranchers fenced substantial amounts of public lands and the lands of their neighbors, land for which they held no legal title. Fencing advocates felt they were protecting their own property rights, especially access to grass and water. Opposition to fencing stemmed from the popularly held belief that foreign and eastern cattle ranching syndicates, which could afford to build extensive fences, did so to establish their dominance over free grass, as well as the cattle industry in general. Many small landowners advocated cutting fences

---

    [53] Ibid., 70; J. D. Freeman, "The Early Surveyors of Texas," in One League to Each Wind, ed. Sue Watkins (Austin: Texas Surveyors Association, 1964), 291.

to restore access to water and free grass on public lands. In 1883, a rash of fence cutting took place in the state, with a consequent rise in violence that reached a crisis stage by the end of the year.[54]

In January 1884, Governor Ireland called a special session of the Eighteenth Legislature to address the growing problem of illegal fencing and fence cutting. Lawmakers passed a fence law that made it a felony to cut fences, with a prescribed punishment of one to five years in the state penitentiary. They made an exception for farmers who were literally fenced in, so as to give them access to and from their own property. Still another act, "Chapter 33," prohibited fencing and unlawful stock raising on university, public school, and asylum lands. The law stated that it was illegal to prevent "the herding, or loose herding or detention of stock upon the lands of the state."[55] Despite Land Commissioner Walsh's earlier concern that some of the university lands had been illegally used by ranchers, there is no evidence that a case for violation of Chapter 33 made it into the courts. The law nonetheless had the effect of further strengthening the University of Texas' legal control over its lands.

The same legislative session also saw subsequent developments that had a direct impact on the investment of the proceeds from the leasing and sale of university lands. Governor Ireland sent a proclamation to the legislature that called for a change from investment of public school funds in state bonds. He also called for the transfer of the state bonds "to the university fund [PUF] at better rates than

---

[54] Hendrickson, Chief Executives, 112; Richardson, Anderson, Wintz, Wallace, Texas, 298.

[55] Chapter 33, Acts of the Eighteenth Legislature, Special Session (1884), Gammel, Laws of Texas, IX, 600-602; Miller, Public Lands, 187-188.

could be obtained from the market, and [thus] result in advantage to both funds; as the school fund could be easily reinvested in the county bonds at a better interest than it is drawing at present."[56] Ireland felt it was foolish for the state to buy its own high-cost bonds in an effort to pay off the debt. Although the Senate considered a bill to transfer bonds from the public school fund to the PUF, no action was taken in 1884 regarding the matter.

Meanwhile, Dennis Corwin went out beyond the line of settlement and began to select and survey the so-called legislative million, which was mostly situated West of the Pecos River. On September 15 and 16, 1884, he reported to the board of regents, offering his assessment of the land he had selected. He explained, in general terms, that the land was "good grazing land and that an abundance of wholesome water could in most places be gotten by digging wells from 25 to 100 feet deep."[57] The regents commended Corwin for his work. They also determined to have him meet with the State Land Board to certify his conclusions and to have the land he surveyed legally transferred to the University of Texas.

At the December 1884 meeting of the University of Texas Board of Regents in Austin, board members began preparing plans to lobby for control of leasing and sale of university lands. Regent Thomas Harwood related the details of a recent meeting he had with Governor Ireland on the subject. Ireland, unfortunately, felt strongly that the regents should not handle the sale of university lands. He argued that the State Land Board, of which he was a member, should handle the sale and lease of all public

---

[56] Benedict, "Source Book," 314.

[57] Minutes of the University of Texas Board of Regents, Meeting #14, September 18, 1884, 116.

lands to insure uniformity in their disposal. He refused to accept as valid the argument that the State Land Board could not possibly afford the university lands the attention that was necessary to optimize revenues for the PUF and the AUF, revenues which were sorely need by the school. Governor Ireland, however, agreed to introduce the idea of regent control over disposition of university lands during the next legislative session without offering an opinion one way or the other.[58] The legislature took no action on the matter during the next session, probably because it was focused on a controversial bill introduced by a supporter of the A&M College.

    The Texas A&M College problem arose during the regular session of the Nineteenth Legislature. On February 6, 1885, Senator George Pfeuffer, one of the directors of the A&M College, introduced "A Bill to Perfect the University of Texas." The bill suggested a general restructuring of the state higher education system. Following a series of attacks on him in newspapers throughout the state, Pfeuffer stepped up to defend his bill and himself in the final hours of the legislative session. He gave a lengthy oration regarding his earlier efforts to improve administration of the University of Texas. He admonished those who believed that the agricultural and mechanical arts had no place in higher education, and he attacked the notion that folks who supported such pursuits were enemies of the university. He pointed out that his only problem with the Austin-based school was that its governing body, the regents, spent AUF money exclusively on the main institution, ignoring the needs of the agricultural branch at Bryan. Pfeuffer explained that he simply wanted to restructure administration of the university, not to destroy it, as had been erroneously

---

[58] Haigh, Land, Oil, and Education, 71.

portrayed in the press, but to improve it. The result of his effort was two appropriations for the A&M College for support and maintenance for the next two years: $20,000 from general revenues and $10,000 from the AUF.[59] Pfeuffer's actions represent the first of many attempts over the next forty-plus years to obtain for the A&M College appropriations from the AUF, appropriations to which many prominent Texans believed the institution was constitutionally entitled.

The regents met in Austin in June 1885 and again addressed the disposition of the university lands. First, they passed a resolution approving Dennis Corwin's work and charged Regent Thomas Wooten with paying the expenses of the surveys. Corwin himself appeared before the board on the third day and reported on his progress in selection, survey, and classification of the legislative million. He displayed a number of maps and drawings and explained further that the land commissioner had already extended approval for the work completed. In a subsequent meeting in September, Regent Wooten reported that Corwin had submitted all drawings and field notes to the land office.[60] Despite the apparent completion of Corwin's survey, more survey work connected to the university lands was needed.

At the January 29, 1886, meeting of the board of regents, faculty chairman Leslie Waggener reported on his efforts to persuade the State Land Board to give control of leasing and sale of university lands to the regents. He explained that the State Land Board resolved to do so by making the board of regents an agent of the State Land

---

[59] Dethloff, History of Texas A&M, 107-110, 112; Benedict, "Source Book," 318-336, *passim*.

[60] Haigh, Land, Oil, and Education, 72.

Board. The resolution further stated that the regents could appoint their own agent to execute leases and sales of university lands. The resolution allowed the regents to set the term of service, payment, and duties of said agent. The regents responded by passing a resolution of their own, which formally accepted the resolution of the State Land Board.[61] For the first time a government agency affirmed the acceptibility of the regents controlling the disposition of the university lands.

At the same meeting, Regent Wooten offered a report regarding some of the land chosen by Dennis Corwin. Wooten pointed out that it was the opinion of Land Commissioner Walsh that some portion of the land chosen for the legislative million was of inferior quality and should be exchanged for land of higher quality. Wooten requested that an agent be appointed by the regents to select an equal amount of land from the unappropriated public domain and exchanged it for the inferior land. The regents agreed with the recommendation and on February 6, 1886, they appointed O. W. Williams of Fort Stockton to carry out the assignment.[62]

Williams wasted little time setting out for West Texas. Upon his arrival to the area in question, located in Andrews, Loving, Ward, and Winkler counties, Williams wrote that he was immediately struck by the worthless nature of the land. In July and August 1886, he surveyed lands in El Paso Country for the University of Texas to exchange for the inferior land, and he made recommendations on what portions of the Corwin surveys

---

[61] Minutes of Board of Regents, Meeting #19, January 29, 1886, 152-155.

[62] Ibid., 155-156; Samuel D. Myres, ed., Pioneer Surveyor, Frontier Lawyer: The Personal Narrative of O. W. Williams (El Paso: Texas Western Press, 1968), 217.

he felt should be turned back to the state. In a report to the regents in December 1886, Williams described the flora and fauna as well as the availability of water.[63] The regents accepted Williams' recommendations and began efforts to make the land exchange legal and binding.

Land policy figured prominently in the gubernatorial race of 1886, particularly the feasibility and effectiveness of the State Land Board. The candidates included William J. Swain, an advocate of the State Land Board, and Lawrence Sullivan "Sul" Ross, who hoped to abolish it. Following Ross' election, the Twentieth Legislature, in early 1887, passed "Chapter 99," which abolished the State Land Board and transferred its authority to dispose of the public domain to the General Land Office. The action passed in spite of a January 27, 1887, resolution from the University of Texas regents asking the legislature for sole control over the sale and lease of university lands.[64] Certain aspects of the Chapter 99 reflected some of Ross' positions during the campaign. In particular, the law stipulated that leasing and sale of the public domain would take place under an agency system accountable to the land commissioner and ordered that only settlers could purchase the land.[65] Despite the fact that lawmakers ignored their request for control over the university lands, the regents were pleased with the actions of the legislature.

Over the next several years, the sale and lease of university lands rose steadily. In 1887, revenues from land sales totaled more than $8,024.51. Lease revenues totaled

---

[63] Myres, Pioneer Surveyor, Frontier Lawyer, 217.

[64] Barr, Reconstruction to Reform, 83.

[65] Chapter 99, Acts of the Twentieth Legislature, Regular Session (1887), Gammel, Laws of Texas, IX, 881-889; Benedict, "Source Book," 343-44.

$3,686.28. Land Commissioner R. M. Hall in June 1887 urged the regents to focus on leasing because lease revenues went directly to the AUF; thus more money was available for appropriation. The following year, 1888, revenues from sales jumped to $11,971.03 and lease revenues dropped to $3,016.56. The 1888 sales revenues would prove to be the highest. Conversely, lease figures continued to climb, reaching $17,186.54 in 1893.[66] The 1893 figure was the highest amount before the regents gained control in 1895.

In a message before a called session of the Twentieth Legislature in late spring 1888, Governor Ross reopened the question of outstanding state debts to the University of Texas. At the request of the governor, the regents presented to the legislature an accounting of all money owed, plus interest, totaling $431,188.85. Following the failure of three separate bills, which offered various remedies, a compromise appropriations bill passed on May 17, 1888, entitled "Chapter 20." The law did two important things for the school. First, Chapter 20 made a loan of $125,000 to the AUF, to be paid back without interest before 1910. Second, Chapter 20 established the long anticipated medical branch of the University of Texas at Galveston. The measure stipulated that $50,000 of the above mentioned loan must be set apart for the construction of the medical school buildings. The citizens of Galveston were required to donate land for the institution and the executors of the John Sealy estate had to build a hospital building at a cost of $50,000, which was to be donated to

---

[66] Lang, "Financial History of the Public Lands," 218-219.

the University of Texas and administered by the regents.[67] Construction of the medical branch began within months.

Over the following months the regents continued to lobby lawmakers for control over the sale and lease of university lands. The effectiveness of their efforts is evident from Governor Ross's opening message on January 10, 1889, to the regular session of the Twenty-first Legislature. Ross addressed directly the suggestions of the regents they be given control of the lands. The governor, however, was non-committal on the issue of regent control of university lands, even though, he admitted, they offered compelling arguments for why the matter should have been given consideration. Ross stated:

> The proposition to turn over the lands belonging to this special interest has much connected with it which does not commend the suggestion to my judgment; and at the same time the history and the experience of similar interests in other States seem to show that it has proven wise and judicious in the States mentioned. The Legislature is the trustee charged with the duty of making all needful regulations for the disposition of these funds and the proper disposition and control of its lands, and your superior judgment and discretion I most cheerfully defer.[68]

---

[67] Chapter 20, Acts of the Twentieth Legislature, Regular Session (1887), Gammel, Laws of Texas, IX, 1017; Lane, "History of Education in Texas," 230-232.

[68] Benedict, "Source Book," 354-355.

Governor Ross's statement, and his refusal to take a position, indicates that he understood the political nature of the regents' request and all that it entailed.

Discussion of numerous issues regarding the University of Texas and its lands took place in the legislature throughout the spring of 1889. Senators introduced two separate bills to give the regents control of university lands, but neither made it out of committee. Most importantly, lawmakers amended parts of Chapter 99, modifying lease regulations on the properties. Section fourteen of Chapter 99 prescribed that all public land north of the Texas & Pacific railroad and east of the Pecos River be leased for a maximum period of six years, while lands south of the railroad and west of the river be leased for a period of ten years. The measure stated that public lands were to be leased for no less than four cents per acre per year, except university lands. Because they were located in huge contiguous blocks, the lands could be leased for no less than three cents per acre per year.[69] The measure was intended to make the leasing of university lands more attractive and competitive in relation to other public lands, which were normally in smaller blocks and seldom adjacent in proximity.

The regents, in June 1889, passed a resolution referring an El Paso County land dispute case to Attorney General James S. Hogg. They instructed the board secretary, C. A. P. Woolward, to forward a copy of the resolution and all pertinent information to the attorney general and requested that his office undertake the necessary measures to secure the university's title to the disputed land, known as the San Elazario grant. Presumably the attorney general took the request into

---

[69] Chapter 56, Acts of the Twenty-first Legislature, Regular Session (1889), Gammel, Laws of Texas, IX, 1078-1081.

consideration, but until 1894 nothing regarding the details of the land dispute appears in the historical record.

During the 1890 gubernatorial campaign, candidate James Hogg, on April 19, gave a speech to his hometown, Rusk, and hinted at his support for state funding for higher education. He specifically mentioned the need to insure the maintenance of both the University of Texas and A&M College. A week later, Leslie Waggner wrote the candidate to thank him for his advocacy on behalf of the university, indicating that he was the first prominent leader in Texas to do so in a campaign speech. Hogg's response was noncommittal regarding the issue of state funding for higher education. Nonetheless, his appeal to the common folk and his adversarial stance towards the railroads insured his election to the governor's office over his Republican opponent Webster Flanagan.[70]

In his speech before the Twenty-second Legislature, on January 21, 1891, Governor Hogg spoke about the importance of the university and its branches, pointed out that AUF appropriations were insufficient for maintenance of the institutions, and urged lawmakers to do all they could to come up with a remedy. In response, the legislature raised appropriations out of general revenues, but only slightly: from $5,000 to $7,500. In addition, it allocated a significant amount of money from a special indemnity fund from the United States. Governor Hogg and the legislature then focused their efforts on the establishment in 1891 of the Texas Railroad Commission, an agency that would have a profound impact on the university lands some years after the discovery of oil.[71] Incidentally, that same year, former Governor Sul Ross became president of A&M College, a move that added

---

[70] Haigh, Land, Oil, and Education, 102-103.

[71] Ibid., 103-104; Benedict, "Source Book," 367-368, 371.

greatly to the prestige of the institution, and, in the fall, the Medical Branch at Galveston opened.

The regents continued to lobby for control over the sale and lease of the university lands without avail, but in 1893 there were efforts to increase the number of acres. According to a report of the land commissioner, there were still 4,393,835 acres of unappropriated public domain. Governor Hogg, in a speech to the Twenty-third Legislature on February 21, 1893, proposed dividing the aforementioned unappropriated public lands equally among public schools and the University of Texas. Several such bills came before both houses of the legislature, but no such legislation passed.

Perhaps lawmakers were distracted by a heated tirade from Oscar Cooper. In a report of the Joint Committee on State Institutions of Learning, Cooper questioned the competency of the regents to manage the University of Texas and its branches.[72] Cooper's ideas got nowhere, but the resulting responses and debates consumed valuable time.

In a speech before the Twenty-fourth Legislature, outgoing Governor Hogg urged lawmakers to give the regents control over university lands. He argued that, although the land commissioner had done a commendable job, the regents could give greater attention to land income and thereby increase revenues for the PUF. Lawmakers answered his request with the passage of "Chapter 18," which did just that: it gave the regents exclusive authority over the leasing of university lands. The law stated that the land commissioner should provide the regents with all available information on each and every tract and render

---

[72] Ibid., 104; Benedict, "Source Book," 376-379, 380-386, *passim*.

any additional assistance as requested.[73] The legislation, however, was ambiguous regarding minerals, the importance of which would not become apparent for some years.

Following the passage of Chapter 18, the regents convened on March 26, 1895, "to consider the matter of managing the [u]niversity [l]ands." They formed a special committee to obtain information from the land commissioner pertaining to university lands. The following day, they requested $2,500 from the legislature to defray the cost of managing the lands for the fiscal year 1895.[74] They also discussed the possibility of employing an agent to obtain information on the land and make recommendations to the board, which would retain sole authority to act, or not act, on the agent's recommendations.

At a subsequent meeting on May 16, the minutes reveal that the regents received several applicants for land agent, but Regent Thomas Wooten suggested turning the land back to the state. Aghast, Regent Thomas S. Henderson said it would be ill advised to do so without first trying to dispose of the land themselves.[75] Finally, at a meeting held June 20, 1895, the board resolved to give the chairman of the land committee the authority to execute leases for a length of time that he determined optimal to university interests and to employ an agent as he saw fit. The resolution further called for the land committee to

---

[73] Chapter 18, Acts of the Twenty-Fourth Legislature, Regular Session (1895), Gammel, Laws of Texas, X, 749.

[74] Minutes of Board of Regents, Meeting #54, March 26-27, 1895, 34-35.

[75] Ibid., Meeting #55, May 15-16, 1895, 40, 44.

draw up blank lease contracts and instructed the chairman to report to the regents all applications for the purchase of university lands over which the entire board retained authority.[76]

By 1895, a new era in the history of the university lands had begun. Over the preceding two decades lawmakers accomplished a great deal. The Constitution of 1876 called for the foundation of a state university, the establishment of permanent and available university funds, and the appropriation of one million acres of the public domain for the endowment of the institution, the so-called "constitutional million. " At the same time, the constitution canceled the One-In-Ten Railroad Act of 1858. In 1881, lawmakers finally established the University of Texas, which opened to students in the fall of 1883. Advocates of the university, including former Governor O. M. Roberts, pushed the legislature to make an additional appropriation to make up for the estimated 1,700,000 acres denied the school after the cancellation of the railroad act. The legislature responded with the appropriation of the so-called "legislative million." At the same time, lawmakers established the State Land Board to handle the lease and sale of all public lands, including the university lands. Over the following years, the University of Texas regents pushed for exclusive control over the sale and lease of the lands, almost achieving their goal with the abolition of the State Land Board in 1887. Finally, in 1895, at the prompting of Governor James Hogg, the Twenty-fourth Legislature passed Chapter 18, which invested in the board of regents, the authority to sell and lease the university lands. Thus, the regents entered into the land business. A new chapter in the history of the university lands had begun.

---

[76] Ibid., Meeting #56, June 17-20, 1895, 46, 54 ; Haigh, Land, Oil, and Education, 105-108.

CHAPTER III

SURFACE LEASING, 1896-1996

From 1896 to 1996 the University of Texas Board of Regents exercised nearly exclusive control over the sale and lease of the university lands. In 1896 the regents implemented an agency system to conduct sales and execute leases on their behalf. Although the sale and lease of university lands had taken place over two decades with modest revenue first under the State Land Board and later the General Land Office, income increased dramatically after the regents took over. Land sales slowly decreased, but surface leasing very quickly became an important and immediate income source for the Available University Fund (AUF) and attracted some of the earliest settlers to those areas of West Texas where the land was located.

Nonetheless, as time passed, the regents played a diminishing role in the affairs of the university lands, as more and more of the power and initiative shifted to a university lands' staff. In addition, as the source of initiative reversed, the organizational structure altered. In 1896 for example, the regents played a very active role in the management of the university lands; they were the ones who dominated the decision making process. But in 1996 the regents merely approved or disapproved the activities and spending of the staff of University Lands West Texas Operations.

Similar changes occurred regarding surface use. Initially, in 1896, surface users of university lands were primarily ranchers who leased for grazing purposes. Over the next century surface usage became increasingly diversified as ranchers gave way to oil men, a variety of businessmen, and even the federal government.

When they began to look at how to best utilize the university lands for the benefit of the university, the regents looked to the Texas cattle business. Big cattle operations needed grazing land in West Texas and some of the university lands became an affordable source. Cattlemen used university property and, despite numerous droughts and harsh winters in the late nineteenth and early twentieth centuries, as well as volatile cattle prices, they persevered. Ranching remained the primary economic activity in West Texas until the discovery of oil.

Almost immediately after taking control over university lands in 1896 the regents appointed an agent to execute contracts of sale and leases on their behalf. At their January meeting in Austin, Regent William L. Prather recommended the appointment of Thomas J. "Tom" Lee of Waco as the first "university land agent." The regents agreed, and they appointed Lee for one year, at a salary of $125 per month, with an additional appropriation of $500 for travel and correspondence expenses.

Lee worked under the three-member land committee of the board of regents. The land committee spelled out the specific duties of the land agent:

> to investigate and ascertain the actual condition and the character of the holdings of all lands belonging to the University of Texas, and to obtain all possible data and report the same in systematic form to the Land Committee for submission to the [b]oard, and at all times be subject to the direction of the Land Committee and the Board of Regents.[1]

---

[1] Minutes of the Board of Regents of the University of Texas, Meeting #58, January 14, 1896, 71-72.

Lee's primary duty was to execute the sale and lease of university lands. All sales and leases were subject to approval by the board of regents. Budgetary designations on university books and letterhead used in official correspondence indicate that the land committee and Lee worked under the name "University Land Department." The expected workload was extensive enough that the regents also adopted a resolution that added $500 to the salary of the board secretary, John J. Lane, placing him at the disposal of the land committee and the land agent. Lee, the board expected, would increase lease revenues by as much as $10,000 over the next year.[2]

Lee exceeded expectations. Over the following year, he executed more than thirty leases and at least one sale of university lands. The leases included lands in Andrews, Crockett, Crane, Irion, Shleicher, Tom Green, and Upton counties. Each was for grazing purposes and varied in size from 5,760 to 61,440 acres. The smaller of the tracts leased for three cents per acre, while the larger tract leased for two and a quarter cents per acre.[3] The contracts stated that payments were to be made to the state treasurer and delinquent payments were assessed a late charge of ten percent. If, after sixty days, payment was not received, the regents could cancel the lease and assess a fee of one year's payment as penalty for breach of contract. Leases could also be canceled if a lessee transferred his lease to another party without the express permission of the regents.[4] For a wide variety of reasons, as many as a quarter of such early

---

[2] Ibid.

[3] Lease #12, University Grazing Leases, Texas General Land Office, September 1, 1896, 1-4

[4] Ibid.

81

leases were canceled before the specified contract period ended. The regents set the term of all leases and approved them after Lee executed the lease. The regents stipulated that all lease agreements were for a term of ten years, with annual rental payments due on the first of each year.

Although individual ranchers entered into many of the early leases, corporations leased some land. The Western Union Beef Company of Colorado in 1896 was the first such corporation to enter an agreement. The agent of the Western Union Beef Company, N. T. Wilson, originally had leased university lands through the General Land Office in Pecos County in 1892 and 1893 under lease numbers 7370 and 6704, respectively. When the regents gained control, the leases were canceled by agreement of both parties. Then in 1896, George W. Baxter, the president of the Western Union Beef Company, entered a new lease for Blocks 30 and 31 of university land in Crane and Upton counties, land northeast of the earlier leases. The contract stated that the area under lease contained forty-eight sections totaling more than 61,440 acres. The initial payment of $460.80 was made on September 1, 1896, with an annual payment of $1,382.40 paid on January 1, 1897, and each successive year on that date. A final payment, to cover rentals to the expiration date, of $921.60 was made on January 1, 1906.[5]

Other contemporary leases contained similar provisions, although figures varied depending on the amount of land leased and the quality of grass and water. The Western Union Beef Company's lease, however, was never completed. The company stopped paying on the lease and the regents canceled it on May 1, 1900, citing non-payment of rental as the reason.[6]

---

[5] Ibid.

Some of the first settlers in West Texas counties were among the early lessees. Clint Owens arrived in Crockett County, Texas, in 1887, and was one of the first to settle southwest of present-day Barnhart. In 1896, Owens leased 5,760 acres from Tom Lee at a cost of $0.03 per acre for grazing Hereford cattle and Ramboulette sheep. Because they were expensive, fences were not immediately built. Livestock in the area generally grazed free and lessees got to use more land than they actually leased. Every spring area ranchers hired cowboys to assist in a round up and it was not uncommon for Owens to find some of his cattle as far south as the Pecos River, over sixty miles distant.[7]

In the early decades of surface leasing there was no limit on the number of animals that could be kept on the land. After a few years, much of the surface area was severely overgrazed, but nothing was done to remedy the matter. Few ranchers in turn-of-the-century West Texas were aware of the negative aspects of overgrazing or the need to manage range use.

During his first year as the university land agent, Tom Lee increased lease revenue to $11,693.33, an amount slightly higher than the previous year. Revenue in 1897, however, more than tripled, totaling $34,814.21. Conversely, land sales of remnants of the original fifty leagues dropped to a low of $475.14 in 1896 and in the following decades amounted to a fraction of the revenue brought in by leasing. The regents re-appointed Lee in 1897 and 1898; his aggregate total acreage leased at that point was 1,384,362 acres at an average of 2.89 cents per

---

[6] Ibid.; Letter from R. E. L. Saner to Land Commissioner Charles Rogan, July 5, 1900, Berte R. Haigh Collection, Permian Basin Petroleum Museum, Midland, Texas.

[7] Buck Owens, university lands lessee, interview by author, May 21, 2003, tape recording.

acre. The century closed with lease revenue of $57,693.80 for the year 1899, despite a severe winter that saw herds reduced by twenty to fifty per cent throughout the plains states.[8] Clearly, by the end of the nineteenth century the agency system of leasing university lands had gotten off to an auspicious start.

Extant leases and the regents' minutes indicate that Lee's tenure as land agent was not without problems, although they were not his fault. In late 1896 the land commissioner suggested that the board of regents give Lee more discretion in executing leases, and he further advised that they modify the lease agreement. The modifications included a provision that permitted the lessees to remove all improvements, such as fences and windmills, from the land if rent and fees were paid in full. The provision was intended to make leasing of university lands attractive to settlers and to encourage improvements. There was also a provision for a lien on cattle for all rent in arrears, a provision that protected the interest of the university. The board minutes further indicated that some of the lessees were delinquent in their payments and the regents considered launching lawsuits.[9] By responding to problems as they arose, rather than trying to prevent them, the regents slowly developed leasing policies.

In 1897 the regents settled an old land title dispute between the University of Texas and certain private parties in McLennan and Hill counties. The land was part of the original fifty-league grant for a state university dating back

___

[8] Aldon S. Lang, "Financial History of the Public Lands in Texas," The Baylor Bulletin 35, no. 3 (July, 1932), 219; Berte R. Haigh, Land, Oil, and Education (El Paso: Texas Western Press, 1986), 109; Schleebecker, Cattle Ranching, 9.

[9] Minutes of the Board of Regents, October 30, 1896, Meeting #63, October 29, 1896, 117.

to 1839. A man named Joachin Moreno, whose interest dated before Texas independence, also had a legal claim. The disputed land totaled more than 14,255 acres, some of which was sold by the state as part of the university lands. Berte Haigh explains that it took the work "of four governors, three State attorney generals, a private law firm, $3,500 in legal fees and much debate, with pages of resolutions and laws in six legislatures" to settle the matter.[10] When a compromise was reached, the Twenty-fifth Legislature "ratified and confirmed" the settlement. The state gained title to 6,533 acres and the defendants settled for 7,022 acres of the disputed land. The other seven hundred acres was relinquished to purchasers of university lands that had already settled and improved upon the land.[11]

Emboldened by the outcome of the McLennan and Hill counties dispute, the regents focused their efforts on the San Elazario land dispute in El Paso County. O. W. Williams had first surveyed the land in 1886 to exchange it for certain marginal lands previously selected and surveyed by Dennis Corwin as part of the legislative million. Williams believed the 25,000 acres he chose for the university southeast of El Paso was outside of the so-called "San Elazario Grant," which had been awarded to settlers in the upper Rio Grande Valley when Texas was under Spanish rule and was upheld by the Texas legislature in 1853. The regents were aware in the early 1890s that some of the land in El Paso County was being claimed by other parties. Not until their September 18, 1897, meeting in

---

[10] Haigh, Land, Oil, and Education, 205.

[11] Harry Y. Benedict, ed., "A Source Book Relating to the History of the University of Texas: Legislative, Legal, Bibliographical and Statistical," University of Texas Bulletin, no. 1757 (Austin: University of Texas, 1917), 215-216.

Austin did the regents resolve that the land committee should "secure the services of a reliable person to supervise the cutting of timber and prevent depredations by squatters and others."[12] As the agent of the land committee, the task fell to Lee, who was authorized to pay the person ten per cent of the proceeds from the sale of the wood. There is no evidence, however, that Lee ever hired any such help.

The regents moved closer to initiating legal action in January 1898. They instructed the land committee to confer with the attorney general about their claims to the land dispute with the San Elazario claimants, and if he deemed it necessary, to obtain legal counsel in El Paso. The regents allocated $1,000 for a retainer and an additional $1,500 for counsel fees. The regents stipulated that payment of the fee was contingent upon a successful outcome of the suit. In May, the regents ordered "that an assistant land agent be appointed in El Paso County to secure information concerning said lands, and put it in available shape."[13] There is no mention in the minutes for subsequent months that an assistant land agent was hired at that time, but the regents' actions indicate that Lee needed assistance, which, in turn, would allow him to focus on the leasing and selling of the university lands. Another year passed before significant developments occurred in connection with the San Elazario case, and Lee never got his assistant.

Lee faced a variety of problems as land agent in 1899 ranging from the mundane to the serious. For example, the minutes of the board of regents for January 18 indicate that

---

[12] Minutes of the Board of Regent, Meeting #68, September 18, 1897, 197.

[13] Ibid., Meeting #70, January 18, 1898, 213; Meeting #72, May 14, 1898, 232.

Lee told the assembled officials that he had borrowed a saddle that was subsequently stolen while he was conducting university business. He had paid the owner, a Mr. F. Payne, the sum of twenty dollars for the saddle. The regents voted to reimburse Lee for the cost. A much more serious difficulty involved an attempt by certain regents to reduce Lee's salary from $1,500 to $1,200 per year. At the July 10, 1899, meeting, Regent Prather asked that the matter be reconsidered and Lee's salary remained fixed at $1,500 per annum, but their reasons for doing so is unclear.[14] Lee subsequently resigned in December 1899 and although there is no explanation for his resignation, the attempted salary reduction might explain his departure.

The regents wasted very little time replacing Lee. In January 1900 they hired Dallas native R. E. L. Saner, a recent graduate of the University of Texas Law School. The fact that he had a law degree made Saner an excellent candidate for the job. The intricacies of land leasing and selling practically required such expertise. Often referred to as "Judge" Saner, he officially began his duties in Austin on January 27, 1900, at a salary of $1500 per year. Like Lee before him, Saner and the land committee still worked under the title of "University Land Department."[15] Saner operated out of Austin until June 1901 when he moved his office to Dallas. He had access to West Texas along the Texas & Pacific Railroad. Saner oversaw the university

---

[14] Ibid., Meeting #75, January 18, 1899, 257; Meeting #77, July 10, 1899, 316.

[15] Dallas Newspaper Artists Association, R. E. L. Saner, Makers of Dallas (Dallas: Dallas Newspaper Artists Association, 1912), 40; Minutes of the Board of Regents, Meeting #89, January 26, 1900, 376; Meeting #92, June 13, 1901, 440; Letter from R. E. L. Saner to Land Commissioner Charles Rogan, July 5, 1900, Berte R. Haigh Collection, Permian Basin Petroleum Museum, Midland, Texas.

Figure 5: Robert Edward Lee Saner, called "Judge" Saner. Seved as land agent for the University of Texas system 1900-1929. He was President of the American Bar Association during the 1920s. Photo in the public domain.

lands for almost thirty years, and he had a long and illustrious career as the land agent.

About the time Saner was hired, Land Commissioner Charles Rogan reported that certain lands in Brewster, El Paso, and Presidio counties likely contained copper, silver, and cinnabar. He explained that the lands were being sold at the same price as grazing lands. He asked for an appropriation from the legislature to conduct a mineral survey on all state lands to ensure that potential minerals were not sold too cheaply. At the same time, a professional geologist named Robert T. Hill also suggested to the regents that the university should conduct a mineral survey of its lands. Moreover, the regents were aware of the mineral-bearing possibility of some of its lands, for in 1899 a man named Henry Gavnan approached them with a request to prospect for minerals on land in El Paso.[16] Thus, in their December 1900 annual report to the legislature, the regents asked for a survey to evaluate mineral potential of all state lands. At the bidding of Governor Joseph Sayers, the Twenty-seventh Legislature in March 1901 responded with "Chapter 28," which called for the regents of the University of Texas to make provisions for a mineral survey of all state lands. The legislature stipulated that the work be completed in two years and appropriated $10,000 per year for the expenses of the survey.[17] The regents appointed William Battle Phillips to head the survey at a salary of $2,500 per year and conferred upon him the title "professor of field and economic geology."[18] After the Spindletop discovery in 1901 the possibility of petroleum reserves became a consideration.

---

[16] Walter Keene Ferguson, Geology and Politics in Frontier Texas, 1845-1909 (Austin: University of Texas Press, 1969), 114-115.

[17] Chapter 28, General Laws of the State of Texas Passed at the Regular Session of the Twenty-Seventh Legislature (Austin: Von Boeckmann, Schultz & Co., State Printers, 1901), 736-737.

[18] Minutes of the Board of Regents, Meeting #91, May 4, 1901, 425-426.

Policies continued to evolve. In July 1901 R. E. L. Saner transmitted to the regents a request to buy lands in El Paso County. The El Paso land was part of the legislative million grant, dated 1883, which the regents had not yet begun to sell. All land sales since 1883 had only been remnants of the original fifty leagues, which were mostly located in northeast Texas. The regents decided, for the time being, to decline the offer. Although they did not pass a resolution or take official action, the regents continued to follow the policy of selling only the remaining fifty-league land and only leasing the constitutional and legislative grants. Saner's sales revenues during 1901 totaled $3,252.95. They climbed slightly in 1902, but declined to no revenue for 1906.[19] The decline in sales between 1902 and 1906 was partly due to the mineral survey, the purpose of which was to prevent the sale of state lands at unrealistic prices and thus to avoid great monetary loss to the public school and university funds.[20] Another reason for the decline in sales may have been Saner's focus on leasing and legal matters.

In June 1900 the regents finally took action regarding the San Elazario land dispute in El Paso County. After conferring with Governor Sayers, they hired William Burgess of El Paso to assist Attorney General Thomas S. Smith with the suit. From the available university fund, the regents paid Burgess a fee of $500 for his services. In 1901, Assistant Attorney General T. S. Reese traveled to El Paso County to gather information on the case. He also contacted O. W. Williams at Fort Stockton and asked him to resurvey the land and provide evidence in the pending litigation. The regents paid Williams $300. Reese also

---

[19] Lang, "Financial History of the Public Lands," 219-220.

[20] Ferguson, Geology and Politics, 117.

deposed Stephenson Archer, who had surveyed the region in 1855. Court proceedings began in 1902 in the Twenty-sixth State District Court at Travis County, and despite Williams' testimony, Judge R. L. Penn decided against the university.[21] The judge said the area Williams surveyed in the valley fell within the boundaries of the San Elazario grant. Judge Penn's decision followed then-existing case law that gave precedence to earlier surveys. The university got 11,500 acres of lesser quality land on a nearby mesa. The terrain was sandy with gravel and supported only scrub vegetation. The land also contained a wide and exceptionally dry arroyo.[22] The whole episode illustrated that the university's legal title to its lands would have to be secured.

During their February 1903 meetings the regents discussed a variety of issues pertaining to university lands and referred several issues to the land committee. First, they hoped to make it a permanent policy not to lease land for town sites, for they did not like the idea of lessees subletting university lands. The policy was never made a permanent one. Second, the regents wanted the land committee to look into the feasibility of contracting for accurate surveys of university lands. The San Elazario dispute left the regents less than confident in the accuracy of earlier surveys and thus the university's claim to the land.[23] A call for new surveys was constant over the next three decades.

---

[21] Samuel D. Myres, ed., Pioneer Surveyor, Frontier Lawyer: The Personal Narrative of O. W. Williams (El Paso: Texas Western Press, 1968), 217, 219.

[22] Haigh, Land, Oil, and Education, 208-209.

[23] Minutes of the Board of Regents, Meeting #103, February 12, 1903, 16.

Despite the legal diversions and the need for new surveys, Saner's primary responsibility remained the sale and leasing of university lands. Lease revenues increased dramatically under Saner's guidance with his efforts resulting in receipts totaling $57,166.62. Revenues increased every year over the following decade, totaling $127,864.95 in 1911.[24] Saner deserves credit for the increases, but his success owes something to the influx of settlers moving into West Texas after the turn of the century. The market demand for grazing land had increased.

In the early twentieth century, some West Texas families with their own sizable land holdings leased university lands adjacent to their property. Very often they rotated pastures, using the leased land for grazing and water. John and Clarence Scharbauer of Midland first leased university land in 1903 in Andrews, Dawson, Gaines, and Martin counties. The agreement indicates that the Scharbauer brothers leased some 106,240 acres at $0.07 per acre per annum for a period of ten years. They agreed to "protect the said lands from trespass and use same only for farming and grazing purposes, and use the timber thereon only as may be necessary to carry on the business of farming and grazing."[25] The Scharbauers also agreed to allow access to agents or representatives of the regents for the purpose of prospecting or mining. At the end of the lease, the lessees were allowed to remove wire from fences and windmills from wells, but were liable for any damage to fence posts or well casing. Other ranching families that entered into similar leases on university lands were the

---

[24] Lang, "Financial History of the Public Lands," 219-220.

[25] Lease #122, University Grazing Leases, Texas General Land Office, 1-4.

Noelkes and the Cowdens, both of whom held large holdings of their own.

Saner's success and the increasing revenue led to a change in the length of appointment of the university land agent. The regents summoned Saner before the board in January 1906 and renewed his appointment for the next two years at $1,500 per year. One-year appointments were the norm during the employment of Tom Lee.[26] The regents were pleased with Saner and his work.

Saner continued to execute leases, but like Lee, he also had to terminate them. The aforementioned Scharbauer lease (#122), for example, replaced three earlier leases, including that of the Five Wells Cattle Company originally executed in 1896. Saner and the land committee also canceled leases for non-payment of rent and for the assignment of a lease to another party without regent approval.[27] Sub-leasing was strictly prohibited, and the regents wanted to be involved in the transfer of surface leases.

In 1906 the ten-year lease period for the 1896 lessees was expiring. Clint Owens renewed his Crockett County lease that year at a cost of $0.07 per acre, and with additional acreage his lease totaled 10,240 acres. Owens had made improvements on the land over the preceding decade, including construction of a house. The house originally had two rooms, but as his family grew he had continued to add on, eventually reaching ten rooms. He had two wells dug near his home, one was sixty feet deep, the other seventy-five feet, and he had installed windmills on both of them. One well supplied the house; the other

---

[26] Minutes of the Board of Regents, Meeting #120, January 16, 1906, 285.

[27] Lease #122, University Grazing Leases, Texas General Land Office, 1-4.

filled a stock tank. He continued to run Hereford cattle and Ramboulette sheep and would often plant sorghum in low-lying areas to supplement the diet of his stock. Like most other ranchers of his day, he continued to run more animals than the land was able to carry, causing damage to the range that would lead to a variety of problems in following years. Buck Owens, the grandson of Clint Owens explained that like other ranchers in the late nineteenth and early twentieth centuries, his grandfather was unaware that overgrazing would damage the range, lead to soil erosion, and spread undesirable weeds.

In addition to grazing contracts, the regents and Saner began to lease university lands for an increasingly wide variety of uses. At the December 11, 1909, meeting of the board of regents, Regent George Brackenridge discussed a contract, dated November 15, 1909, between the university and the Big Bend Manufacturing Company to buy *guayule*. Indigenous to northern Mexico and Western Texas, *guayule* is a plant that was used to produce a crude rubber. It was apparently present in abundant quantities on university lands. William H. Staton, president of the Texas Rubber Company, guaranteed the contract in the event the Big Bend Company did not. The regents ratified the contract for a term of five years and the Big Bend Company agreed to pay $30,500. During a July 1910 meeting, Saner told the regents that the company had paid $30,625.[28] Without warning, Saner appeared before the regents in April 1911 and reported that the Big Bend Company was bankrupt and asked the board for instructions regarding the disposition of the *guayule* contract. The regents told him to go to San Antonio and obtain all information on the Big Bend

---

[28] Thomas Lloyd Miller, The Public Lands of Texas, 1519-1970 (Norman: University of Oklahoma Press, 1971), 211.

Company and report back to the board.[29] The records of Saner's reconnaissance are no longer extant, but we know the Texas Rubber Company was not forced to fulfill the contract because the money had been paid.

Another use for the surface involved the granting of rights-of-way for transportation and communication. In 1904 the regents, under an 1895 statute that promoted railroad building and gave free access across public lands, granted a right of way to the Panhandle & Gulf Railway Company. The proposed line was never constructed. The Kansas City, Mexico & Orient Railroad (KCM&O) reached San Angelo in September 1909, and railroad officials had plans to continue westward to Presidio. In June 1910 they requested a conveyance of the previous right-of way of the Panhandle & Gulf Railway Company across portions of university property in Irion, Reagan, Upton, and Pecos counties, totaling thirty-eight and one half miles. Saner reported that the railroad company requested access to build without compensation. The regents voted a resolution to deed to the railroad company a right-of way one hundred feet wide through the aforementioned counties. Nothing was done, however, to carry out the board's resolution until April 1911 when Saner inquired about the status of the railroad right-of-way, pointing out that the conveyance had never been executed.[30]

The regents resolved that the land committee should study the law and ascertain whether or not the right-of-way should be granted without compensation. If the committee determined that it was legal to charge for the right-of-way,

---

[29] Minutes of the Board of Regents, Meeting #140, December 11, 1909, 2.

[30] Ibid., Meeting #143, June 11, 1910, 5; ibid., Meeting #147, April 6, 1911, 97.

then both sides must reach an agreement on reasonable compensation. If an agreement could not be reached then the land committee was authorized to seek proper legal remedies to secure compensation.[31] No agreement was reached with the University of Texas concerning the right-of-way for several years. Nonetheless, construction on the line began in 1911 and the railroad reached Girvin, on the Pecos River, in February 1912.[32] The railroad had an immediate impact on each of the communities it passed through, but the railroad company was beset with financial difficulties and went into receivership twice, once in 1912 and again in 1917. Despite the loss of compensation, the railroad made university lands more marketable because it gave ranchers access to transportation facilities.

In September 1911 Saner reported an offer to buy 311,000 acres in Andrews County for five dollars an acre. The regents resolved to carry out an investigation of the matter. The episode provides evidence that the regents were highly involved in the affairs of university lands. Land committee chairman and Regent George Littlefield, chairman of the board of regents Clarence N. Ousley, and land agent R. E. L. Saner met in Fort Worth and traveled to Andrews County to inspect the property. Littlefield described how sandy the land in the western part of the county was and where conditions made automobile travel impossible. He also noted that wells were drilled to 500 feet with no water found. He then discussed the poor quality of the land for farming and ranching and recommended that the regents sell it. The following

---

[31] Ibid., Meeting #143, June 11, 1910, 51; ibid., Meeting #147, April 6, 1911, 97.

[32] John Leeds Kerr, Destination Topolobompo: The Kansas City, Mexico & Orient Railway (San Marino, Ca.: Golden West Books, 1968), 86.

month, despite recommendations of the land committee, a majority of the board rejected the purchase offer.[33]

A second request to buy land, this time in El Paso County, resulted in the sending of Saner to the locale, where he examined the area, and reported back to the board. The regents also turned down this offer to buy university lands. Both instances signal the emergence of the unwritten, but fairly consistent policy of "lease only" for the legislative and constitutional millions. Then, on November 15, 1916, the regents approved a motion of George Littlefield that specifically forbade the sale of university lands. Aldon S. Lang's accounting indicates that some sales continued, but only of land that was part of the original fifty leagues. The regents reaffirmed their policy not to sell university lands at their May 24, 1921, meeting.[34]

As revenues increased, the collection of money became a cumbersome matter for the small staff of the General Land Office. Money for the leases on university lands had been collected in the land office, but the agency was struggling to keep up a proper accounting. In November 1912 the regents instructed Saner to confer with the attorney general to see about having lease money paid to the auditor of the University of Texas rather than the General Land Office. In June 1913, the chairman of the land committee also received instructions to discuss the matter with the attorney general. The regents wanted to know if legislative action was in order. Eventually, the parties agreed that payments would be made to the

---

[33] Haigh, Land, Oil, and Education, 114-15; Minutes of the Board of Regents, Meeting #157, November 11, 1912, 280-281.

[34] Lang, "Financial History of the Public Lands in Texas," 219-220; Minutes of the Board of Regents, Meeting #202, May 24, 1921.

university auditor's office. In 1919 leases began to state that payments must be made to the auditor of the University of Texas.[35] Copies of leases still had to be submitted to the General Land Office, but the office no longer accounted for rental payments. The action was a big relief for the perpetually over-worked staff.

During World War I, the federal government expressed an interest in university lands. In September 1917 Washington officials offered to purchase university land near San Angelo for military purposes. The regents stated that "it was the spirit of the board that the request be granted."[36] Apparently the matter ended there. No record of a sale of university land to the federal government exists, and federal interest in university lands does not appear in extant records until 1926, when it is concerned with potash prospecting.

During the 1920s R. E. L. Saner, although active in work with the state Democratic Party and in a term as President of the American Bar Association, continued to serve as land agent of the university. He set the university lands on a course for pragmatic solutions to potential legal problems, especially after revenue from surface usage and petroleum production on university lands increased. For example, on January 13, 1923, he addressed the regents and suggested that the university should voluntarily make property tax payments in each county where university land was located. In those counties, the University of Texas was usually the owner of the greatest amount of surface area. County officials decried the injustice of lost revenue because the university, as a state agency, was not legally

---

[35] Lease #251, University Grazing Leases, Texas General Land Office, January 1, 1919, 2.

[36] Board of Regents' Minutes, Meeting #184, September 14, 1917, 109.

obligated to pay property taxes. The regents agreed to take the matter under advisement and give it full consideration. Tax payments did not begin until 1929, but it was an astute move on the part of Saner and the regents.

Revenues from surface use continued to rise through the 1910s and 1920s. In 1910 lease revenue totaled $122,604.49 and climbed each year afterward, reaching $169,057.11 in 1915. High agricultural prices during World War I kept lease rentals high. In 1918, lease money surpassed $200,000 and continued to increase until 1920, when it was $210,555.67. The following year revenue decreased by $30,000 because of post-war economic problems, but it rebounded in 1922. Revenues continued to climb because of increased surface activity related to petroleum production.[37] Ranchers who weathered fluctuating beef prices and survived periodic drought in the 1910s and 1920s continued to ranch on university lands. They accounted for a major portion of the surface usage before the 1920s.

After the discovery of oil in 1923, however, surface usage related to the petroleum industry began to increase dramatically. Although it had been a deliberate policy of the regents to avoid leasing land for town sites, the policy changed after the success of the oil field worker's camp at Texon. The Texon site grew and developed as part of the mineral lease but with no extra compensation to the university. The policy changed again for town sites in the vicinity of oilfield activity after the Santa Rita, the discovery well on university lands, blew in on May 21, 1923. R. E. L. Saner and the land committee devised a separate surface lease for the town sites of Best and Santa Rita, among others, to insure all possible revenues for university coffers.

---

[37]Lang, "Financial History of the Public Lands in Texas," 220-222.

The town site at Santa Rita was the first from which the university generated revenue. On August 16, 1923, a rancher named P. L. Childress leased two sections along the Kansas City, Mexico & Orient railroad for the Santa Rita Townsite Company at Best, Texas. Childress wanted to use some of the land for grazing, but he also wanted to sub-let town lots to people who moved to the region because of the increased oil field activity. He leased Sections 33 and 34 of Block 9 at a cost of fifteen cents per acre per year. He made an advanced payment of $1,248 at the lease signing, and agreed to pay the auditor of the university one-fifth of the proceeds from the townsite on the first day of January every year until the lease expired on July 1, 1930. Because of extensive petroleum activity in the vicinity, the regents also stipulated that the Santa Rita Townsite Company could not sub-let any part of the land within two hundred feet of drilling or pumping activity.[38] Santa Rita prospered during the following decade, with a fine school, a small hospital, and a busy railroad.

In the spring of 1924 an agent of the railroad approached the regents with an offer to lease a strip of land adjacent to the line in Reagan County. The agent indicated that the railroad wanted to build a siding, petroleum storage facilities, and related commercial structures. The regents quickly saw the benefit of having railroad facilities built adjacent to Santa Rita, and on July 31, 1924, they, Childress, and the railroad reached an agreement. Childress gave the railroad a strip of land 150 feet wide on the north side of the track, and gained the benefit of rail facilities for his bustling little town at Santa Rita. In exchange, the railroad agreed to build similar siding and storage facilities on university land at Best. Along with

---

[38] Lease #256, University Grazing Leases, Texas General Land Office, May 7, 1924.

expanding petroleum activity, the populations of Santa Rita and Best continued to increase.[39]

With increased petroleum activity in Reagan County and with Saner's Dallas office being so far removed from the activity, the regents, in September 1924, asked the land commissioner if there was a way to check production numbers on wells in Reagan County.[40] The regents took steps to insure the university was paid the full royalty amount. In October 1924 they authorized the president of the board to hire a "royalty oil gauger" to measure oil production at Texon and the surrounding vicinity.[41] The gauger had other responsibilities, and he served as Saner's man on the ground in West Texas. In November the regents appointed Haywood Hughes to the position, at a salary of $130 per month. The following month the regents allocated $591.92 "for purchase of a Ford roadster, fully equipped for the use of Mr. Hughes, the oil gauger in the oil field."[42] The gauger used the car to travel to oil collection and storage facilities and to monitor surface leases.

The following year, the regents created another position. They initially called it the "oil inspector" and later the "oil supervisor." The regents then hired a man named

---

[39] Santa Rita Townsite Company Contract with the Kansas City, Mexico, & Orient Railway Co., July 31, 1924, University Lands Administrative Records.

[40] <u>Minutes of the Board of Regents</u>, Meeting #232, September 15, 1924, 302.

[41] Ibid., Meeting #233, October 27, 1924, 306.

[42] Ibid., Meeting #234, November 26, 1924, 308; It should be noted that there was not yet an organizational division between surface and geology, Saner worked for the regents, and Hughes worked for Saner.

L. G. Graves to oversee Hughes' field activities from an office in Best, where the regents allocated $4,000 to build him a house. With help in the field, Saner now focused on other problems.

After he got the field help, most of Saner's activities focused on legal matters. Saner and the regents knew that survey problems existed on university lands. On occasion one of the regents would suggest a resurvey of the problem areas, but cost usually precluded progress. The failure to act proved costly in 1927 when a Fort Worth oilman named Ed Landreth identified a vacancy between two surveys on parts of university land in Crane County. He quickly filed on the vacancy with the state of Texas, but it turned out to be land already claimed by the University of Texas. After Landreth struck oil, the regents filed suit to assert title to the land and the minerals. The court ultimately sided with Landreth, and the regents took the defeat as a good reason to remedy the situation.[43]

A good example of the diverse use of university lands was gravel and caliche permits, a use that began in the 1920s. In 1924 Saner negotiated the first of many contracts with private parties to remove gravel from university land. Although the exact details of the contract are no longer extant, revenue for 1924 totaled $178.75. It was deposited in the AUF. In 1925, revenue from gravel sales only totaled $20.15, but in 1926 the amount climbed to $173.50. There was no revenue for gravel sales reported in 1927, but in 1928 gravel sales totaled more than $2,221.15.[44] In July 1930 Dick Dillard contracted to remove sand and gravel from university land in Andrews County. The term of the contract was for one year, and Dillard agreed to pay $0.25

---

[43] Haigh, Land, Oil, and Education, 220-228.

[44] Lang, "Financial History of the Public Lands," 222-223.

per cubic yard of sand and gravel removed. The regents required Dillard to give them a monthly report accounting for all material removed and all material sold. He was to put up a $1,000 bond, which he would forfeit if he failed to provide the monthly report.[45] The regents executed similar contracts over the following decades. The proceeds went to the AUF.

    A change in personnel took place at the end of September 1926 when regents relieved the oil supervisor and the gauger, Graves and Hughes, respectively, from their duties. Possibly accounting problems resulted in their release. The next month, the regents hired Elliot J. Compton of Crawford, Texas, as the new oil supervisor. They set Compton's salary at $200 per month until January 1, 1927, when they raised it to $225 per month. Compton was Saner's representative in West Texas, and he was responsible for gauging production and monitoring surface leases. He slowly began to assume many of Saner's responsibilities, and in 1927 the regents ordered the house at Best moved to Texon, where Compton would live for the next thirty years.

    R. E. L. Saner continued to develop new surface leases. In 1927 he negotiated a town site lease with C. A. Brooke for 640 acres in Ward County. It adjoined a railroad stop on the Texas and Pacific at Pyote, Texas, which the lease actually designated as an industrial site. Following the approval of the regents, Saner executed a lease on May 27, 1927. Because of the availability of ground water, Saner executed a water development contract

---

[45] Lease #387, University Grazing Leases, Texas General Land Office, January 1, 1930, 1-2.

at Pyote with Frank Pickrell, the promoter behind the Santa Rita #1, for the sum of $1,600.[46]

Compton and his gaugers continued to ensure compliance with surface leases and to gauge oil production. But the continued expansion of petroleum activity in West Texas in the 1920s caused a deficiency in manpower in the management of university lands that required thoughtful remedy. The regents needed to devise a better management system for what had become a sizable land leasing operation.

By 1929 Compton and his field staff had become overwhelmed by the work they were required to perform. In response, the regents moved to reorganize the management system. They began the process of reorganizing by identifying root causes of problems associated with the increased revenue. When causes were identified and solutions devised, the regents began lobbying the legislature to codify them. As a result of their efforts, the Forty-first Legislature, in April 1929, established management organizations for the university lands, dividing them into the surface, geology, and survey offices, as well as the Board for Lease of University Lands to conduct mineral lease sales.

With the legislative changes going into effect, Judge Saner decided to retire. He had worked with university lands for twenty-nine years, from 1900 to 1929. He was the lone, full-time employee dealing with the lease and sale of university lands until 1924. During his years as land agent, he laid a solid foundation for the management of university lands, and he contributed significantly to legal activities connected to them. His departure at the time of the establishment of the various university lands management organizations signals the end of an era.

---

[46] Ibid., Lease #308, May 27, 1927, 1-3; Lease #317, October 11, 1927, 1-3.

With the departure of Saner the regents promoted Elliot J. Compton, the current oil supervisor, to head the newly established University Lands Surface Office. He carried out his duties, including leasing of land for grazing and supervising oilfield gaugers, from an office at Texon. The surface office remained responsible for leasing surface area and tasks related to the petroleum activity, such as gauging production and ensuring compliance to lease rules.

Compared to Saner, Compton had a reduced workload and some additional help carrying it out. Compton focused on leasing to ranchers and checking on activities of the oil companies. He arrived at his office at the crack of dawn, completed his duties with expedience, and went to the local domino hall, reaching it about 3:00 PM. There he socialized with area ranchers and oil field workers.[47] Compton was a forceful steward for university interest, and he served with university lands for some thirty years. His promotion signals the beginning of a second era in the history of surface management of university lands.

At the same time that it established the surface office, the legislature also created University Lands Geology Office. It placed the new office under the control of the board of regents. The board hired Dr. Hal Bybee, the former director of the Bureau of Economic Geology, to head the new organization. The regents originally hired Bybee in 1914 as a geology professor, but he left in 1925 to take a better paying position with the Dixie Oil Company. The Forty-first Legislature also created the Board for Lease

---

[47] Steve Hartmann, Executive Director of University Lands West Texas Operations, interview by author, January 28, 2002, tape recording.

of University Lands. It was to handle the sale of mineral leases, and it proved quite important for raising income.[48]

Another management organization, also created in 1929, was the University Lands Survey Office. Under the direction of Frank Friend, on June 15 it opened an office in San Angelo. The board of regents instructed Friend to put together an estimate of cost to re-survey all 2.1 million acres from the 1876 constitutional grant and the 1883 legislative grant. His estimate for the cost of the survey, explaining that it would require eight men, was $21,015.15 per year. Friend knew he faced a monumental undertaking. It required fieldwork and heavy research into prior surveys and land records. Friend's survey techniques included two methods: transit orientation and chain measurement and triangulation that required a number of people to conduct.[49]

Friend's survey crew consisted of five people, each of whom as part of the team had a specific job. The crew initially consisted of Friend as the surveyor, J. A. Conklin as the "transit man," W. P. Conklin as the "rear chainman," Gibbons Poteet as the "front chainman," Lee Binyon as the cook and the truck driver, and C. E. Grimmer as the "flagman." On July 1, 1929, Friend hired Ruby Snodgrass as a part-time secretary and stenographer. Fieldwork began late that year. In June 1930 Friend hired a young man named Norris Creath to clear brush lines for the chains and carry the instruments. He quickly promoted Creath up the ranks of the crew, and Creath remained with the agency until it was disbanded in 1947. The crew spent the next

---

[48] Chapter 282, General and Special Laws of the State of Texas Passed by the Forty-Second Legislature at the Regular Session (1921), 616-629; Haigh, Land, Oil, and Education, 177-183.

[49] Haigh, Land, Oil, and Education, 184-202, *passim*.

Figure 6: Frank Friend, far left, and survey crew resurveyed all 2.1 million acres between 1931-1937 out of an office in San Angelo, Texas Photo courtesy of The Permian Basin Petroleum Museum, S. D. Myres Collection.

eight years weathering the elements while carefully measuring and re-surveying the entire body of university lands.

When Friend and his crew completed the fieldwork of the surveys in 1937, the regents hired former Land Commissioner J. H. Walker as a special university land officer and Scott Gaines to head University Lands Legal. Walker was to help Friend complete field notes and data regarding the new survey. In 1941 Friend moved the survey office from San Angelo to Austin. Conklin and Creath remained in West Texas to handle any unfinished fieldwork. Later that year Conklin and Creath also moved to Austin and the regents merged the surveying office with the legal office under the budgetary designation "University Lands Legal and Surveying." When the maps, notes, and pertinent data were completed and turned in to the General Land Office in 1947 and with the university's legal authority established over its land, the legal and survey office disbanded. J. H. Walker and Scott Gaines began to operate out of the Office of Investments, Trusts, and Lands.[50] Nonetheless, the survey had been a necessity for many years and its completion was a major accomplishment in connection with the regents' efforts to secure the university's legal claim to its land.

Also in 1929 the University of Texas and Texas A&M College reached an agreement on A&M's claim to a portion of the university lands and a part of the proceeds from the PUF. After many years of stalling and haggling over constitutional intent, and a renewed threat by A&M officials to sue, the University of Texas Board of Regents and the A&M Board of Directors agreed to work out a compromise. A joint committee of the two boards discussed the division of revenues, originally recommending that A&M get $100,000 per year for four years and one-third of revenues from the PUF in perpetuity. The University of Texas regents rejected the proposal but agreed to continue negotiations. Per the agreement reached on April 21, 1929, Texas A&M got one-third of legislative appropriations from the AUF, excluding revenues from the surface leases that were reserved for the university. The university retained its two seats on the newly created Board for Lease of University Lands. The land commissioner became the chairman of the Board for Lease, which was statutorily charged with selling mineral leases on university lands. Texas A&M got a stake in a most lucrative resource. Money from mineral leases, which were not considered a renewable resource, went into the PUF.[51] After the agreement was finalized, the university had a new partner

---

[50] Ibid., 200-201.

[51] Henry C. Dethloff, A Centennial History of Texas A&M University, 1876-1976 vol. 2 (College Station: Texas A&M University Press, 1975), 418-419.

in helping to stave off future claims to the PUF from other Texas colleges.

Drier than normal weather in the early to mid-1930s led to soil erosion problems and a consequent reevaluation of ranching practices. Compton and the regents knew that overgrazing was damaging the range, prompting them to implement early conservation efforts on university lands. Leases from the latter half of the 1930s reflect the changes that were necessary for better management of the land and to insure minimal damage to range. For example, J. E. Hill of Midland, on December 18, 1937, leased thirty-nine sections of university lands in Andrews County totaling 25,075 acres. The duration of the lease was ten years at an average cost of fourteen cents per acre per year, with the aggregate sum over the course of the lease totaling $35,105.28. The lease, however, allowed Hill to set a limit on the number of animals that he would run at no more than eight hundred cattle and fifty horses, with no sheep and no goats. The lessee, with Compton's approval, set the number of animal units to be grazed per section of land, provided that it would not damage the range, and the lessee further agreed to pay a flat fee per animal. Although the lessee was allowed to set animal limits himself, Compton or his staff had the right to inspect the number of livestock at any time. Failure to abide by the self-set limit would result in cancellation of the lease or the assessment of a fine. The lessee could apply to the land agent for an increase in the number of animals and if the he was satisfied that such an increase would not damage the range, the agent could grant the request. The lease also prohibited the lessee from making pasturage contracts for animals other than his own without the permission of the university land agent.[52] Because of the size of his staff, Compton and

---

[52] Lease #445, University Grazing Leases, Texas General Land Office, January 1, 1938, 1-3.

his field men, to assure adherence to contractual obligations, could only do random checks on a sampling of university lands. They simply could not check them all, but the system worked pretty well.

Conservation efforts also became a means of bringing in additional revenue to the AUF. Geophysical exploration required access to surface area to use seismic technology in the search for subsurface petroleum reserves. Geophysical crews drilled holes on the surface and filled them with explosive charges. Seismic cable was stretched across a specified area. When the explosives were ignited, the crew measured the sound waves that bounced back toward the surface. The collection and analysis of the seismic data helped to determine possible petroleum reserves. Surface department staff also determined if the permit holder caused any damages. Compensation for damages were paid into accounts for each lease and could be used for improvements on the lease.

During the 1940s, surface leasing for cattle ranching continued, but there was continued interest in university land for other reasons as well. Following the U.S. declaration of war against Japan on December 8, 1941, the federal government once again took an interest in university lands for military purposes. By December 22, the federal government had signed easement #159 on fifteen thousand acres of university lands in Andrews County. The land was for a bombing range for the nearby bombardier school at Midland. Army engineers used bulldozers to build dirt mounds shaped like enemy ships on the ground and students dropped dummy bombs made of concrete. Later in the instructional cycle, as trainees became more proficient, live munitions were used. The regents insisted that because of "the present national emergency" the federal government only need pay the university one dollar per year for no more than a term of ten years.[53] They added, however, that the federal government must also compensate current lessees for the money they had paid towards their respective leases. In June 1942 Colonel William M. Garland, on behalf of the U. S. government, leased university land in Crockett, Irion, Reagan, and Scleicher counties for additional bombing ranges.[54] By early 1943 several ranchers with leases had complained that the bombing caused fires and damaged valuable grazing land. The regents declared that "the Comptroller of the University is the officer charged with the duty of the management of university lands for grazing purposes," meaning he should determine if payment for damages was in order.[55] Subsequently, the comptroller determined that the damage was not permanent and the university had no claim to damage payments. The comptroller began by determining a value and discounting the surface lease by that amount.

Another important instance of federal use of university land during WWII began in August 1942 when the regents received a request from the United States Engineer's Office in Albuquerque to lease land near Pyote, in Ward County, for the construction of a military airport. The regents granted an immediate right of entry agreement, which allowed the military to store material and begin construction. In the meantime, the regents and government representatives began negotiations over the amount of

---

[53] Minutes of the Board of Regents, Meeting #417, December 22, 1941, 168.

[54] Ibid., Meeting #427, June 27, 1941, 367; University Lands Easement #159, December 1941, University Lands Administrative Files.

[55] Ibid., Meeting #428, August 1, 1942, 485.

acreage and the terms of the lease.[56] The following week, the land committee reported that the military had drilled two water wells and had begun construction on a pipeline to connect the wells to a new Army Air Corps training base.[57] Construction of buildings on the new air base began on September 5. Crews encountered so many rattlesnakes that the base became widely known as the "Rattlesnake Bomber Base." The regents approved on December 29 a lease for additional acreage for sewage disposal facilities. The university, the federal government, and the grazing lessee were all party to the contract. The government paid the university $529 per year for 2,645 acres, which was renewable annually until six months after the end of the war. The Pyote Air base housed over 2,500 airmen and women at its peak.[58] The base remained under federal control until it closed in 1965, after which the state used some of the buildings, including the officer's quarters, for a juvenile detention facility. The land reverted back to the university in 1966.

During the war, an increase in oilfield related surface usage kept Elliot Compton and his gaugers busy. Pipeline easements and leases for storage facilities became more common. Compton worked closely with oil companies to ensure minimal damage and compliance with accounting procedures. Humble, Shell, Gulf, and Magnolia, represented the primary companies operating on university lands during the war, all of which held several easements on university lands in West Texas. Eventually, the university auditor's office took control of accounting oil

---

[56] Ibid.

[57] Ibid., Meeting #429, August 8, 1942, 506.

[58] Ibid., Meeting #430, September 25, 1942, 31.

production, freeing Compton and his gaugers to focus on increased surface activity.

In 1949 the legislature transferred management authority over all minerals on university lands, except for oil and gas, from the General Land Office to the board of regents. The regents, in turn, handed the matter over to their respective management organizations. The law opened up new possibilities to generate revenue on university lands in the second half of the twentieth century. The development of other minerals and other sub-surface resources stirred up considerable interest in subsequent years.[59]

Ranching in the post-war period remained a generally secure economic pursuit, and as surface lessees continued to add improvements to their leases, the value of the leases rose. Once, when families decided not to renew their grazing leases, the rules stated that they were allowed to remove improvements, such as barbed wire from fence posts and windmills from wells, as long as the families avoided property damage. When improvements like homes and barns were constructed, however, the buildings could not be removed if the lease were not renewed.

In response, the regents developed a policy of using bonuses to help lessees recoup some of their investment. The bonus was a one-time payment above and beyond the annual per acre rental. When a lease-holder decided not to renew his lease, he usually found interested parties to take over. Because the rental amount was already determined, the parties bid an amount for a bonus, and whoever was highest bidder was awarded the lease. The bidder paid half of the bonus to the previous lessee and half to the AUF. The exact year that bonuses were first used on university

---

[59] Chapter 186, <u>General and Special Laws of the State of Texas Passed by the Regular Session of the Forty-First Legislature</u> (1949), 362-363.

lands is difficult to trace because surface leases did not switch hands very often, and the bonus amount was not reported in lease agreements. Many families simply passed surface leases on to their children, without taking bids and without using the bonus.[60]

In 1959 the surface office at Texon, still under the leadership of Elliot J. Compton, moved to Midland to share facilities with the geology office. After the move Compton announced his retirement. He had served as head of the surface office since 1929 and was responsible for implementation of range conservation efforts such as limiting the number of animals per acre and assessing of damages. Compton set the tone for relations with the surface lessees and he generally got along well with them. His primary responsibility, however, was to take care of the land, which sometimes necessitated policies that ranchers did not like. Compton felt his responsibilities as steward were more important than making friendships with surface lessees.[61] With his retirement, the second era of surface leasing on university lands came to an end.

The regents appointed one of Elliot Compton's employees, Billy Carr, to head the University Lands Surface Office. Carr's father was an old friend of Compton's and Billy grew up at the Texon Camp. After a brief stint at Texas A&M College, the younger Carr dropped out of school and returned to Texon to work for Compton. After Carr's promotion, the surface office increased its staff and made it a deliberate policy to develop a long-term management plan for the university lands that required the cooperation of the lessees. Initially, the surface staff focused on voluntary compliance of lessees,

---

[60] Hartmann, interview, June 10, 2003.

[61] Owens, interview, May 21, 2003.

but in a decade conservation programs were mandatory for all university grazing leases.

Billy Carr is most responsible for the focus on diverse use and range management that began in the late 1960s. He played a significant role in the establishment of the Texas A&M Agricultural Experimental Station situated on university lands at Barnhart. At Carr's behest, the regents approved a policy that required grazing leases executed after October 1, 1969, to participate in federal conservation programs. An important example was lessee participation in the Great Plains Conservation Program.[62] Following the severe drought of the mid-1950s, the federal government allocated funds for ranchers to receive federal aid to develop water supplies to help re-seed depleted range lands. Other cost-sharing items under the Great Plains program were land terracing and controlling certain weeds and undesirable shrubs.[63] Lessees used federal money to improve land management.

Another way the regents sought to improve upon university lands was charging fees for damage to the property, a practice much like that used for geophysical exploration in the 1930s. When a pipeline or telephone company took out an easement, the company paid damages for each "rod" they set. A rod is sixteen-and-one-half-feet long, and three hundred twenty rods equaled one mile. The damage money was placed into accounts, which were assigned to each lessee. Payment was proportionate to the

---

[62] Billy Carr, "Report on Surface Leasing on University Lands in West Texas, December 1973" (Midland, Texas: University Lands Surface Office, 1973), 2-6, 24-25, photocopied.

[63] Douglas Helms, "Great Plains Conservation Program, 1956-1981: A Short Administrative and Legislative History," in Great Plains Conservation Program: 25 Years of Accomplishment, SCS Bulletin no. 300-2-7 (November 24, 1981), 10.

number of rods on that particular lease. The lessee, in turn, could ask for his damage money to construct fences, dig wells, lay waterlines, and other improvements by submitting a written request. The staff determined which requests were granted, exercising influence over where and when the improvements would be made on the land. Because some leases had greater easement traffic than others, most of the damage money was confined to those leases.[64]

The increased influence of the university lands staff in land operations is evident from the "Tour of West Texas Lands" they conducted to educate the regents in 1965. The staff took the board of regents out to West Texas where it gave information about the lands and the management organizations. It showed them the land, the offices, and the ways that lessees used the land. The tour was a major one, and it was not limited to regents. State and local politicians participated as well. State Senator W. E. "Pete" Snelson of Grandfalls, Texas, for example, was present.[65] The tour suggested that a shift in the flow of authority from the regents to the staff had occurred. No longer did an omnipotent board of regents take the initiative. Rather, a professional staff informed the regents about conscientious land management and suggested policy changes. Following his participation in the tour, Senator Snelson in 1966 helped the university lands management system acquire the funds to build its own office building in downtown Midland.[66] The Hal P. Bybee Building ensured

---

[64] Hartmann, interview, January 28, 2002.

[65] Long, Laddie F., Charlie Timberlake, Jr., and James B. Zimmerman, "Tour of West Texas Lands," (Midland, Texas: University Lands Geology Office, 1965), 1-25, *passim*, photocopied.

[66] State Senator W. E. "Pete" Snelson, interview with author, March 25, 2002, tape recording.

that the university lands management organizations would remain in Midland, removed from constant regent influence.

In 1965 with changes in national military priorities, the federal government closed the Rattlesnake Bomber Base at Pyote. The military used the facility, situated along Interstate 20, for the storage of WWII surplus aircraft. The facilities included two 8,400 foot runways, six large hangars, numerous administrative buildings, and housing for officers and enlisted men. There was also a well-developed water field in the vicinity of the base, which made it a leasable property. Before 1965, however, the government ordered the planes chopped up and erected a smelter to process the scrap. In 1965, when the base closed, the land and buildings reverted to the University of Texas. In 1983 and 1984 the University of Texas regents transferred a water lease held by the Duval Corporation to the Colorado River Municipal Water District (CRMWD). The CRMWD began to operate the Pyote water field as a single entity, as a closed system, and it raised the potential production of 26 millions gallons per day. Various communities served by the CRMWD used the water.[67]

Another important development during Carr's term as head of the surface department related to the issue of hunting rights on university lands. With increased labor problems and lower agricultural prices, many ranchers in Texas began to look to for additional sources of income. Deer and bird hunting became an important source for the AUF, as well as for the surface lessees, during the late 1960s. For many years the surface lessees got to

---

[67] Joe Pickle and Ross McSwain <u>Water in a Dry and Thirsty Land: The First 50 Years of the Colorado River Municipal Water District</u> (Big Spring: CRMWD, 2000), 86.

harvest wildlife at their will, and very often they used hunting to barter for goods and services. Land attorney Scott Gaines first addressed the question in 1950. He stated that hunting on university lands was confined to surface lessees. As hunting for sport became increasingly popular and because care was taken of range and habitat, wildlife numbers proliferated. The University Lands Surface Office looked at lease rates on surrounding land, as well as wildlife numbers, to determine a fair market value for hunting on university land. The university received one half of the income from hunting leases on its land, and the surface lessee got the other half. The surface lessee also had the option to pay the fee himself and thus reserve hunting rights for himself and his family. Lessees always had the option to keep outsiders off of their ranches. The rancher with the grazing lease, not university lands, would advertise for hunters and negotiate lease rates. The rancher provided the hunters with campgrounds, and might charge extra for firewood or cooking and cleaning services. The surface lessee became the agent of the university and was responsible for hunter compliance with all lease rules and state laws. In the 1990s many ranchers in West Texas saw hunting as a way to keep their ranching operations solvent.

Carr followed up his policy on hunting with an especially important policy regarding the management of university lands. He wanted to insure sound conservation of the resources. In November 1971 Carr and his staff revised their policies for grazing leases, now requiring lease-holders to use Soil Conservation Service personnel to improve their range management plans. The new policy called for an addition to the lease called "exhibit B." Soil Conservation Service staff members worked with university lands lessees to devise and implement a variety of measures that became part of the standard exhibit B section of a grazing lease."[68] The cooperation of University Lands Surface Office and the Soil Conservation Service was largely due to the relationship between Billy Carr and his friend D. B. Polk of the Soil Conservation Service. Polk taught Carr a great deal about range conservation, and once converted, Carr translated conservationist principles into sound management practices on the university lands.[69]

An important example of Carr's commitment to conservation was the implementation in 1974 of the flexible grazing lease program. Carr and his field people evaluated the rangeland, and the lessees set a fixed number of animal units per section of land. Different animals had different values, a horse was one-and-one-quarter units, a cow with an unweaned calf was one unit, and six goats or five sheep also equaled one unit. Any combination of such animals could graze a given piece of land as long as their total did not exceed the self-prescribed number of animals per section.[70] The amount paid per animal unit was determined by livestock market prices. A lease would have an animal unit price that changed annually, based on livestock market prices. The surface lessees generally found the system fair and reasonable, and the new grazing rules led to better maintenance of valuable grazing land.

To evaluate properly range needs and handle the responsibilities of implementing his policies, Carr hired people with expertise in range and wildlife management, resulting in a professionalization of the surface staff. In the late 1960s and early 1970s, Carr hired two range management specialists, Gary Condra and Guy Goen, and a

---

[68] Carr, "Report on Surface Leasing," 6.

[69] Hartmann, interview, January 28, 2002.

[70] Owens, interview, May 21, 2003.

wildlife biologist, Mike McMurry, to conduct fieldwork on surface leases. The experts aided in the development of range management plans of individual lessees, and they performed random checks to insure that grazing leases were in compliance.

In 1976 Carr hired Steve Hartmann, a Texas A&M University trained range management specialist, to work for the surface department. Hartmann was raised on a Hill Country goat and sheep ranch and brought to his new job a lifelong appreciation for the concerns of ranchers. At first, Carr put him to work in the oilfield. Hartmann was to check on petroleum production, which was still measured by hand as the old gaugers did under Saner and Compton. After Hartmann became familiar with the petroleum duties, Carr put him in charge of some agriculture experiments designed to develop new ways to capitalize on university lands.

The agricultural experiments occurred in the 1970s. The University Lands Surface Office, upon the advice of University of Texas professor, Dr. Charles McKinney, who noticed that Texas was on the same latitude as the Mediterranean, planted two experimental vineyards and an experimental orchard in Culberson and Pecos counties. Workers planted the first vineyard in 1974 in a draw East of Van Horn in Culberson County. The following year they planted another vineyard and orchard in the Escondido Valley near Bakersfield in Pecos County. The staff planted the orchard with jojoba, pistachios, and pears to determine if such crops were commercially viable. In 1977 Carr told Hartmann to hire someone to run the vineyard and plant another one southwest of Fort Stockton. Hartmann hired Gene Drennan, but later Jim Evans replaced Drennan.[71]

---

[71] Hartmann, interview, January 28, 2002.

Of the experiments, only the Bakersfield vineyard showed any promise, and in 1980 Hartmann and Drennan planted 160 additional acres of grapes there. In the first years, Evans experimented with wine making in a Midland warehouse, but it was never the intent of the university lands staff to enter into the commercial wine business. Staff members had, however, become a sort of extension service for the fledgling Texas wine industry. They shared information with other grape growers. Hartmann contends that they learned important information from their agricultural experiments. After two offers to lease for commercial purposes fell through, the giant French wine company, Domaines-Cordier, began to express an interest in the vineyard. Carr agreed to plant more grapes the next year, 320 acres the following year, and another 320 acres the year after that. In four years there was over 1,000 acres planted west of Bakersfield.[72]

By the mid-1980s Domaines-Cordier's Texas subsidiary, Cordier Estates, Inc., had begun to produce wine under the "Ste. Genevieve" brand. Per the agreement with the regents, Cordier paid a rental for the land and the university received six percent of sales. The money went to the AUF. The operation continued to grow and Ste. Genevieve wine became better with each passing year. The quick expansion, however, was not free of problems. In 1985 migrant laborers threatened to sue if the "piece wages" they were paid were cut. They also claimed there were inadequate restroom facilities for the large number of laborers at harvest time. When the company did not respond, the workers threatened to sue the University of Texas. Before the situation got any worse, the regents and

---

[72] Ibid.

Cordier management resolved the situation.[73] In 1996 the winery produced an award-winning wine and had become the largest producer in the state.

Because of booming production in the West Texas oil industry and the increasingly high revenues, in September 1979 the Sixty-sixth Legislature gave the regents responsibility for accounting for revenues from university lands. In response, the regents created the University Lands Accounting Office, which was located in downtown Austin. The accounting office handled all university lands lease revenues, previously handled by accountants that worked in the General Land Office. The university kept an independent accounting before 1979 in an office called the "Audit of Oil and Gas Production." The accounting office staff audited oil and gas production numbers, but also it handled all grazing lease revenues. The accounting office, like the surface and geology offices, was responsible to the regents, but not to each other.[74] The necessity of the office was revenue from petroleum, which eclipsed revenue from all other uses combined.

Despite the fact that oil revenues were exponentially higher than those generated for surface usage, Hartmann and his staff continued to aid surface lessees through collection of payments for damages to non-renewable resources. Lessees spent damage account money for improvements to their respective leases, thereby increasing the value of the land. Some lessees spent the money on developing water resources or building pipelines

---

[73] Barbara Linkin, "Vineyard Workers Threaten to File Suit," The Daily Texan, July 16, 1986.

[74] Patsy Neidig, University Lands Accounting Office Lands Records Supervisor, personal communication, December 2, 2003.

and storage facilities, while some used the money to build better fences or barns. The last barn built using damage money was on Buck Owens' Crockett County lease. There were certain leases, however, that had a much higher concentration of easements and rights-of-way for which there was a commensurately higher damage account. Some other surface leases had little or no damage money and the lessees were forced to pay for improvements on their own.[75] The system did not seem fair and Hartmann set out to devise a more equitable system for distributing damage money.

With a focus on conservation and environmental protection during the 1970s, the University Lands Surface Office, in conjunction with Marathon Oil Company and the Soil Conservation Service, undertook a soil reclamation experiment on an 11,000-acre area of saltwater damaged land in Reagan County called the "Texon Scar." For many years a high volume of salt water, a bi-product of petroleum production, was allowed to drain into ditches and fields north of Texon. High salt content caused a decrease in vegetation, which left topsoil vulnerable to erosion. An impermeable layer six feet below the surfaced kept natural processes from removing the saline content. Wind caused dust to blow with nearly zero visibility on the highway towards Big Lake to the east. Some effort was made earlier to build syrup pan burms and plant salt leaching vegetation, but erosion problems persisted. Aerial photography showed the extent of the scar and the parties designed a drainage system to leach salts from the soil.[76]

---

[75] Hartmann, interview, June 10, 2003; Owens, interview, May 21, 2003.

[76] Ibid.

The specific goals of the project were to reduce both salt content and topsoil erosion on a 0.5 acre part of the scar that served as a sample area. The drainage system consisted of a series of surface dikes and 125,000 feet of perforated pipe set on a precise grade that drained into a series of cisterns. When it rained, water drained through the topsoil to the pipe and drained the salt along with the water. When cisterns filled, saltwater was pumped by pipeline to a nearby injection well. In 1994, staff geologist Michael "Doc" Weathers, range management specialist Kenneth R. Moore, and two other individuals published an article on the project in a professional journal. More recent aerial photography shows that vegetation has increased on the test area and provides clear evidence that the Texon Scar is on the mend.[77] Like other ventures undertaken by them since he has been involved, Hartmann argues emphatically that despite the high cost, the university lands personnel learned some things from the experience.

Another major problem for university lands surface lessees was predators. Hartmann noted that after he was hired the primary predators were coyotes, but mountain lions and golden eagles increased steadily. Buck Owens said he has had problems with eagles for many years. In the old days, ranchers shot predators without a second thought. In more recent times, however, endangered species statutes protect certain predators. University land officials encouraged compliance with the law. Non-lethal measures had to be used to control predators, which required cooperation of lessees to be successful. Many times when his goats and sheep were giving birth, Owens

---

[77] Michael "Doc" Weathers, Kenneth R. Moore, Donald L. Ford, and William E. Black, "Surface Reclamation in the Big Lake Field," AAPG Division of Environmental Geosciences Journal 1, no. 1 (June, 1994): 50-56.

said he and his sons had to go out and chase away the majestic birds by yelling and flailing their arms.[78] Anyone who killed a protected species could expect to be prosecuted under state and federal laws, and compliance of lessees was crucial to success. Further evidence of the prevailing attitude of stewardship at University Lands Surface Office resulted from the agency's response to the Texas Antiquities Code. Originally passed in 1969, the legislature revised the code in 1977 and 1983. The law also created the Texas Antiquities Committee, which gave out permits to conduct a number of field investigations on state lands between 1974 and 1980.[79] At the same time that the surface department was planting vineyards and attempting to reclaim the Texon Scar, Billy Carr hired Gordon Bronitsky, an archeologist at the University of Texas of the Permian Basin, and his assistant Sandy Grice, to conduct the first cultural antiquity survey. The survey area in 1979 covered 160 acres of university lands in Pecos County at the site of the Ste. Genevieve Winery. Bronitsky and Grice reported the recovery of eight lithic artifacts, but their survey was never completed.[80]

Carr subsequently hired Eunice Barkes, a Midland archeologist, to survey the area directly north of the

---

[78] Hartmann, interview, June 10, 2003; Owens, interview, May 21, 2003.

[79] J. Barto Arnold III, "Texas Antiquities Committee," The Handbook of Texas Online. <http://www.tsha.utexas.edu/handbook/online/articles/view/TT/mdt5.html> [Accessed Mon Aug 11 21:29:49 US/Central 2003].

[80] Eunice Barkes, Report on Archeological Survey of Parts of sections 8, 9, 12, and 13 of Block 19, University Lands, Pecos County, Texas, Texas Antiquities Permit no. 257 (Midland, TX: Author, 1980), 6.

Bronitsky and Grice survey in Block 19 of Pecos County. She identified the location as south of Interstate 10, a few miles west of Bakersfield, Texas. Barkes found stage tracks of the old mail route from San Antonio to El Paso and rock points dating to about 12,000 years ago along an old creek bed. The site had been an ancient watering hole for early humans. Barkes published her findings in the form of a report to the Texas Antiquities Commission.[81] A third survey of the area, in 1983, for a pipeline easement noted the importance of Barkes' survey.

Additional cultural survey work continued on university lands from the late 1980s through the 1990s. Hartmann commissioned Solvieg Turpin, who had conducted extensive work in Trans-Pecos archeology, to carry out an archeological survey on university lands. In 1995 she looked for ancient sites in Terrell County.[82] Hartmann viewed such sites as valuable resources to be preserved and trained his surface staff to identify possible sites before an easement of right of way is granted.

In 1986 Hartmann took over management of University Lands Surface Office. Carr did not retire until 1992, but Hartmann's promotion signaled the beginning of the final period in the history of the university lands. Hartmann's office, during the mid-1980s and 1990s, continued to explore several interesting possibilities in relation to surface use of university lands. There was serious talk in 1985 about using university lands for a low-level radioactive waste disposal site. In 1988, the Department of Defense brought a proposal to the

---

[81] Ibid., 8-9.

[82] Solvieg A. Turpin, West of the Pecos: A Cultural Reconnaissance on University Lands, Terrell County, Texas, Texas Antiquities Permit no. 1414 (Austin: Borderlands Archeological Research Unit, 1995), iv, 1-3.

University of Texas regents to use university lands near Fort Stockton for a rail gun test. The Department of Defense had committed $21.9 million for the development of such an electromagnetic gun before it approached the regents. The rail gun was tested in a lab at Balcones Research Center, but the fieldwork would be conducted on university land. Hartmann pointed out to the press that the testing would not preclude other uses for the surface because the tests were scheduled for specific times. The military liked the topography because there were cliffs to stop projectiles. Safety was important for all parties concerned.[83] The project, however, never made it past the laboratory stage.

In the 1980s the staff of University Lands Surface Office reached its maximum number of employees, but by the 1990s the organization had shrunk from streamlining for more efficient administration. Ken Moore and Don Cox worked in the field with lessees to formulate range management plans. Jim Evans and Tommy Gray monitored surface activity related to ranching and petroleum production. Surface office personnel continued to conduct random checks of grazing leases to ensure compliance with animal limits and to tally wildlife numbers. Carr hired Leslie Smith in 1984 to oversee annual operating budget of the organization and to coordinate all the leasing and payment activities connected to grazing lessees.[84]

Although there had been a secretary on staff since 1929, very little is known about most of the early office

---

[83] Laura Beil, "Regents Expected to Approve Rail Gun Testing in West Texas," The Daily Texan, February 9, 1988.

[84] Hartmann, interview, June 10, 2003; Leslie Smith, University Lands West Texas Operations Senior Accountant, personal communication, August 4, 2003.

personnel. Budget designations in the board of regents' minutes indicate that the surface office did not hire more than one secretary until the 1960s, when Carr was in charge. In the 1970s, there was a growing need for additional administrative help. Officials hired such new help as the need arose, but the numbers of administrative personnel were not equal to that of the field employees until the 1980s. During that period Melba McKandles handled and filed easements for surface area of university lands. Sharon Burkes, hired by Carr in 1981 and Hartmann's secretary after 1986, supervised all administrative operations.[85]

In the 1990s the regents moved to overhaul parts of the University of Texas System, including the university lands management agencies. In 1996 the regents integrated the management organizations and placed University Lands Surface Office, University Lands Oil, Gas, and Mineral Interests, and University Lands Accounting Office under a single executive director, Steve Hartmann. The new organization, called University Lands West Texas Operations, was still headquartered at the Bybee building in Midland and the accounting office remained in Austin.[86] The re-organization took place one hundred years after the regents had taken control over the sale and lease of university lands.

Cattle ranching continued to be an important use for university lands in 1996, but it too was changing. Ranchers, like Buck Owens, no longer used horses to traverse their leases and gather their cattle; now they relied on gas-powered dune buggies, pick-up trucks, and "four

---

[85] Ibid.; Sharon Burkes, University Lands West Texas Operations Administrative Coordinator, personal communication, August 4, 2003.

[86] Hartmann, interview, June 10, 2003.

wheelers." Also, in the 1990s university lands had over two thousand surface easements. Hunting continued to be an important revenue generator for ranchers, who got fifty percent of the hunting fees. For many years, the right to harvest wildlife was a free perk for university lands lessees, who would allow hunting in exchange for goods and services. Hartmann devised a system for lease by which the ranchers became agents of the university for leasing hunting rights. In the 1990s, some ranchers cut back on stock numbers to focus instead on managing the range to increase wildlife numbers. As the livestock business became more precarious, the demand for well-managed hunting land increased.

    In the century from 1896 to 1996, surface operations on university lands developed from the employment of an individual agent to an office staffed by specialists in range management, wildlife biology, and administration. In 1896 leases were predominantly held by ranchers, but in following decades surface usage diversified. Easements became a common instrument for lease of university lands for everything from railroads to pipelines to utility lines. The use of the bonus component of surface leasing discouraged speculation in university grazing leases and insured that lessees were serious about remaining for long periods of time. Certain members of the board of regents were quite active through the mid-century, but initiative and expertise began to originate more and more from staff members of university lands. The regents became less involved in land matters as various experts in the field took increasingly more control of university lands operations.

    Clearly, from 1896 to 1996, income from surface leasing of university land increased. Likewise, the level of technical management improved, and more and more university lands personnel have come to manage the land with policies and regulations that ought to ensure successful use for the foreseeable future.

CHAPTER IV

MANAGING SUB-SURFACE RESOURCES, 1896-1996

Between 1896 and 1996 the Board of Regents of the University of Texas controlled the utilization of university lands. For many years after 1896 the regents and their land agent, "Judge" R. E. L. Saner, promoted exploration for sub-surface resources on university lands, but their attempts to gain control over the capitalization of the mineral estate proved fruitless. In 1929, however, lawmakers gave the regents limited control over the exploitation of minerals, including oil and gas. That year the Forty-first Legislature created the Board for Lease of University Lands to conduct sales of oil and gas leases. The same law also established the University Lands Geology Office, later called University Lands Oil, Gas, and Mineral Interests, to aid the Board for Lease with oil and gas sales and to monitor the production of minerals from university land. The regents through the Board for Lease and the successive heads of University Lands Geology Office developed operational procedures and policies for capitalizing on subsurface resources on the lands during the next six decades.

In 1895 Texas' Twenty-fourth Legislature passed a mineral prospecting law that stirred interest in mining on university lands. Called the "1895 mineral law," it lowered the price of mining land from $20 and $10 an acre to $15 and $10 an acre, the amount determined by distance of the land from the railroad. The purchaser of a prospecting permit had ten years to pay at four percent interest annually. Article 4041 of the law gave land owners mineral rights, and in Article 3495 the state reserved the minerals of all future land sales.[1] The law proved short-sighted and wasteful, but it precipitated regent interest in the mineral potential of university lands, and during the same 1895 session the legislature finally gave the regents control of the university lands.

The regents wasted little time in setting up a system to manage the lands. They hired Thomas J. "Tom" Lee of Waco to sell and lease university lands for grazing purposes, but they were also interested in the property's potential for minerals. In 1893, John Galey discovered oil in commercial quantities at Corsicana, Texas. Plus, significant mining activity in Brewster County in far west Texas, including the mercury mines near Terlingua, led to increased inquiries from private parties regarding the possibility of mineral wealth on state lands, including land owned by the University of Texas.

The earliest documented request regarding minerals on university lands dates from 1899. The regents' minutes for January of that year indicate that land agent Lee reported on an application received in the General Land Office from Henry C. Gavnan to prospect for minerals in El Paso County. The regents referred the matter to the land committee with the power to execute a contract with Gavnan.[2] If the parties reached an agreement, it is no longer extant, and there is no evidence that Gavnan ever found anything. There were no further inquiries related to minerals in 1899, and Lee inexplicably resigned his position at the end of the year.

At their January 1900 board meeting, the regents hired "Judge" R. E. L. Saner as university land agent.

---

[1] Thomas Lloyd Miller, The Public Lands of Texas, 1519-1970 (Norman: University of Oklahoma Press, 1971), 162.

[2] Minutes of the Board of Regents of the University of Texas, Meeting # 75, January 17, 1899, 251.

Saner, an Arkansas native and recent UT Law School graduate, proved an ideal choice. He was a very capable attorney who later served as president of the American Bar Association and held several leadership positions in the state Democratic Party. With state laws regarding mineral rights becoming increasingly complex, Saner's legal expertise proved vital in the early years of mineral development on university lands. He kept an office in Austin until 1901 when the regents approved his request to move his office to Dallas.[3]

During Saner's first year as land agent several people began to express an interest in the mineral potential of the university lands. In December 1900, for example, Regent George W. Brackenridge, who at an early date had advocated the development of minerals on university lands, and the eminent geologist William Battle Phillips, called for a state mineral survey. One month later, Land Commissioner Charles Rogan urged lawmakers to fund a mineral survey on public school and university lands. The same day, January 10, 1901, Captain Anthony Lucas' Spindletop well near Beaumont blew in and touched off an unprecedented search for oil in Texas.[4]

In response, on March 28, 1901, during a special session of the legislature, lawmakers passed the Moore McInnis Bill, which gave the regents the authority to conduct a mineral survey. Lawmakers appropriated $10,000 per year for two years, requiring that the work be completed within two years. Then, in May 1901 the regents hired William Battle Phillips as a geology professor

---

[3] Dallas Newspaper Artists Association, R. E. L. Saner, Makers of Dallas (Dallas: Dallas Newspaper Artists Association, 1912), 40; Minutes of the Board of Regents, Meeting #82, January 26, 1900, 369.

[4] Walter Keene Ferguson, Geology and Politics in Frontier Texas, 1845-1909 (Austin: University of Texas, 1969), 114-116.

at a salary of $2,500 per year and placed him in charge of the survey. They also hired Benjamin F. Hill as assistant geologist. The regents required Phillips to teach geology while conducting the survey, which meant he carried out field-work when school was not in session.[5]

The mission of the survey was to turn out a state geological map for deposit in the General Land Office. Field-work began in the summer. It started on university lands in northeastern Pecos County, and later that year Phillips published his first report on the mineral survey, a bulletin entitled Texas Petroleum. During the following years Phillips spent most of his time conducting field work, writing additional bulletins, studying the growing petroleum industry, and lobbying legislators for continued funding so that the mineral survey might be continued.[6]

Besides seeing that the mineral survey focused first on university land, the regents stayed busy with a land dispute in El Paso County. The university, and certain private parties who held legal title since Spanish rule, each claimed title to land southeast of the city of El Paso. The possibility of mineral wealth in the Rio Grande valley near San Elazario made the need to insure university title all the more urgent. Court proceedings began in 1902 in Travis County. Despite the testimony of former university surveyor O. W. Williams, the court decided against the university, leaving it with marginal land on the mesas surrounding the valley. At a meeting of the board the following year, the regents instructed the land committee to address three issues: "One, the matter of condemnation of land for town sites.... Two, more accurate surveys of

---

[5] Minutes of the Board of Regents, Meeting #91, May 4, 1901, 428-433.

[6] Ferguson, Geology and Politics, 117-118, 126, see note #38.

university lands.... Three, the sale of university mineral lands."[7] The regents were aware, even at this early date, that more accurate surveys were crucial for optimal capitalization of resources on university land.

With funding for the mineral survey about to end in 1903, Governor Joseph Sayers recommended that legislators extend it for two years. Land Commissioner Charles Rogan supported Sayers, noting continued mining activities in the far western part of the state. Commercial operators mined copper, silver, and cinnabar in significant quantities in El Paso, Presidio, and Brewster Counties. Sayers and Rogan, along with the regents, believed that minerals were being stripped from reserved lands, that is land reserved for the various state agencies, without fair compensation to the respective funds. In response, the Twenty-eighth Legislature, led by a group of representatives from the trans-Pecos region, passed a law that extended the mineral survey to include private and public lands for two more years. Opponents of the mineral survey offered an amendment to withdraw the lands from use until their value could be ascertained. Lawmakers responded with an extension of survey funding for the next two years, and the amendment to withdraw lands was quickly defeated.[8]

Although the survey got its funding in 1903, the university regents and Phillips continued to speak of the need for legislation to protect the mineral interest of reserved lands and their respective funds, including especially university lands and the Permanent University Fund (PUF). Phillips continued to teach geology and

---

[7] Minutes of the Board of Regents, Meeting #103, February 12, 1903, 16.

[8] Ibid., 118-119.

collect geological data when school was not in session. As the 1905 legislative session approached and with the biennial survey funding ending, Phillips pointed to the importance of his work in trans-Pecos water resources. He wanted the legislative appropriations to continue. In response the Senate passed a bill that extended appropriations for the mineral survey for two more years. It also approved a bill dealing with the protection of the state's mineral rights. The bill to extend the survey, however, provoked opposition from Land Commissioner John J. Terrell, who thought the cost was a waste of taxpayer money. Terrell pointed out that loopholes in existing laws allowed companies to remove minerals without extra compensation. He asked for money to conduct a proper classification of mineral bearing lands, which were naturally priced higher than land without minerals. Terrell argued that a new mineral law was more important than extending appropriations for the state mineral survey. The survey had failed to produce a state geological map, which back in 1901 was a central aspect of its purpose. Terrell also noted that it had not produced any benefits for either the university or the school fund.[9] Despite very public pleading from all sides, a vote on the survey bill was postponed until the end of the session.

Ultimately, the Twenty-ninth Legislature voted to end appropriations for the state mineral survey, but it passed a new mineral prospecting law, "Chapter 99."[10] The law required purchasers of prospecting permits to begin making payments on patented claims during the first year and a

---

[9] Ibid., 120-122.

[10] Chapter 99, Laws of the State of Texas Passed at the Special Session Twenty-Ninth Legislature (Austin: Von Boeckmann-Jones Co., 1905), 148-150; Galveston Daily News, April 12, 1905.

payment on one-fifth of the land value each year afterward, with interest accruing to the unpaid balance. The act was specifically passed to prevent stripping of minerals without compensation to the state. It proved to be much more effective than the state mineral survey at promoting mineral development for the benefit of the school funds.[11]

No significant activity towards mineral development took place on university lands until 1909. That year, the board of regents seized the initiative and created the Bureau of Economic Geology. Because it was part of the University of Texas, the agency depended upon funding from the legislature. The regents basically institutionalized the state mineral survey under the umbrella of the University of Texas, evident from the appointment of William Battle Phillips as the agency's first director. The establishment of the bureau signaled the end of geological research in the political realm and allowed Battle to pick up where the mineral survey left off. The idea was not to keep secret any information obtained, but rather to promote development of mineral resources through publication of bulletins and presentation of public lectures.[12] The Bureau of Economic Geology enabled the regents to control the state geological research agenda and maintain a focus on the mineral development of its university lands.

Meanwhile, grazing leases continued to bring in revenues to university coffers. When income reports were delayed in the General Land Office, however, inquiries were met with a message from the commissioner that his staff was inadequate to keep up. In 1910, Land Commissioner Rogan suggested that payments should be made directly to Judge Saner, but no legislation to relieve

---

[11] Ferguson, Geology and Politics, 122-123.

[12] Ibid.; Berte R. Haigh, Land, Oil, and Education (El Paso: Texas Western Press, 1986), 111.

the land office of the duty of collecting rental payments was forthcoming. The backlog of work connected to university lands continued to grow as Saner leased more and more surface area for a wider variety of purposes. The regents instructed Saner and land committee chairman Clarence N. Ousley to ask the attorney general if a legislative remedy were in order. Although the exact date of the change of payments to the university auditor's office is not available in the board minutes, lease contracts dated 1919 reveal that by that time the university auditor collected lease revenue.[13]

Despite the problems with payment collection, the regents continued to consider other possible sources of income, including subsurface resources. In January 1911, the regents acquired the services of C. H. Winkler and J. A. Udden to explore the possibility of exploitable groundwater resources on university lands.[14] In April of the same year, the Kansas City, Mexico & Orient Railway Company requested an easement to build a line along a prior easement the regents in 1904 had granted to the Panhandle and Gulf Railway Company. They took the matter under consideration. Finally, in May 1911, the regents received their first specific inquiry to prospect for oil on university land. A man named Truxell approached the regents with a request to drill a prospect well in El Paso County. They, in turn, referred the matter to the land commissioner, Charles Rogan, with a request that the commissioner report his findings at the next board meeting. There is no evidence that the land commissioner acted on the request, and the

---

[13] Minutes of the Board of Regents, Meeting #144, October 22, 1910, 77; Lease #251, University Grazing Leases, Texas General Land Office, 2.

[14] Minutes of the Board of Regents, Meeting #145, January 9, 1911, 13.

existing records contain no further references to a Mr. Truxell.

In 1913 the Thirty-third Legislature passed a law that had an indirect, though significant, impact on mineral development on university lands. With growing interest in developing Texas' petroleum potential, lawmakers created the State School of Mines and Metallurgy at El Paso and placed it under the direction of the University of Texas Board of Regents. The establishment of the school of mines is essentially the beginning of the University of Texas System. The city donated the campus of the recently closed El Paso Military Institute, which provided immediate facilities, and the school opened in 1914.[15] The regents gained access to additional geological expertise. Geologists trained at the school of mines in El Paso played a significant role in ongoing exploration of the geology of the western part of the state.

During the same period that the it created the State School of Mines and Metallurgy, the legislature passed the so-called "permit law of 1913," or "Chapter 173," to facilitate and stimulate petroleum exploration on state lands. The law instructed the land commissioner to issue permits for prospecting for oil and gas and removed authority to dispose of minerals from the regents. It is unclear why lawmakers removed authority to sell minerals from the regents. Legislators probably believed that the regents, hoping to raise money more quickly, would sell the minerals too cheaply. The law said the land commissioner could make provisions for disposing of the minerals so long

---

[15] Chapter 178, General Laws of the State of Texas Passed by the Thirty-Third Legislature at its Regular Session (Austin: Von Boeckmann-Jones Co., 1913), 427; Harry Y. Benedict, ed., "A Source Book Relating to the History of the University of Texas: Legislative, Legal, Bibliographical and Statistical," University of Texas Bulletin no. 1757 (Austin: University of Texas, 1917), 492-493.

as the provisions were not in conflict with existing laws.[16] The section of Chapter 173 that removed regent authority over minerals made little sense from their viewpoint. The university clearly led the state in mineralogical expertise, and the land commissioner already made known his concerns about his small staff being overworked. Despite the objections, the legislature designated the General Land Office to handle leases for mineral exploration, which it did for the next sixteen years. Saner, the university land agent, played no direct role in leasing university lands for minerals, but he continued to lease to ranchers and to manage legal matters connected to university property.

The General Land Office in turn, implemented provisions under Chapter 173 for mineral sales on public school and university lands. The land office made permits available in county seats, with a filing fee of $1 to the county clerk and a $1 fee to the General Land Office. The acreage could not exceed 1,280 acres, or 200 acres if the well was located within ten miles of a producing oil or gas well. The permit holder had six months to begin drilling, and when production began, the permit converted into a production lease for $2 per acre for a period of ten years. Additionally, the lease holder had to pay one year rental in advance and agreed to pay a royalty of one-eighth of the sale price on oil and one-tenth on gas. The stringent payment conditions had a negative effect. They priced the state out of the petroleum land market. Not a single prospecting application was filed for university lands under the 1913 permit law, and there was no development of petroleum resources until after lawmakers changed it.[17]

---

[16] Chapter 173, <u>General Laws of the State of Texas Passed by the Thirty-Third Legislature at its Regular Session</u> (1913), 409-413; Benedict, "Source Book," 491-492.

[17] Miller, <u>Public Lands</u>, 162-163.

In 1914, William Battle Phillips resigned as director of the Bureau of Economic Geology to take the post of President of the Colorado School of Mines. J. A. Udden, Phillips' assistant, took the helm of the bureau amid renewed calls for survey of university lands for minerals, specifically oil and gas. In October 1915, Udden requested a meeting with the regents, which took place the following April when Regent Will C. Hogg asked for Udden to report on any of the current or future mineral surveys on university lands. On June 12, 1916, Udden gave a report before the board of regents. In it he discussed his belief that an oil-bearing formation called the "marathon fold" was present beneath certain parts of university lands. He also furnished the regents with an additional report about other potential minerals on university lands.[18] Armed with Udden's information, the regents began to lobby for changes to the mining law to make prospecting for oil and gas more attractive.

    The calls for a new permit law led in spring 1917 to amendments to Chapter 173, known as the "permit law of 1917." The Thirty-fifth Legislature passed "Chapter 83," and Governor James Ferguson signed it into law on March 16, 1917. The amendment to section one of the law listed thirty-four minerals that state officials deemed commercially exploitable. Only four of the minerals were known to be present on university lands: oil, gas, salt, and sulfur. Lawmakers also doubled the lease size from 1,280 to 2,560 acres, but stated that a single permit could not contain more than 1,000 acres of university land in an oil or gas producing area. The applicant had to pay a $1 filing

---

[18] <u>Minutes of the Board of Regents,</u> Meeting #173, October 26, 1915, 499; ibid., Meeting #174, April 25, 1916, 534; ibid., Meeting #176, June 12, 1916, 601.

Figure 7: Texon Oil and Land Company Office, date unknown. Photo courtesy of The Permian Basin Petroleum Museum, Abell-Hanger Collection.

fee to the county clerk and $1 to the land office. To spread out the areas under exploration, the law required that multiple permits held by the same party had to be spaced two miles apart. Drilling had to begin within one year, and if nothing was produced within that year, the lessee had to pay an additional ten cents per acre and provide proof that he was making an effort toward production. If the well was a producer, and the permit holder provided proof in the land office, the drilling permit converted to a production lease for $2 per acre per year for a term of ten years. Lessees made payments in advance and paid an additional one-eighth royalty on oil production and one-tenth royalty on gas annually. The permit holder also accepted responsibility for insuring that the lease was not drained from an offset well not on university property. The land office issued more than 3,000 permits under the 1917 law, and the sale of permits contributed almost $500,000 to the Permanent University Fund.[19]

Under the 1917 permit law, Frank Pickrell and Haymon Krupp obtained 171 permits on 670 sections covering 431,360 acres on university lands in West Texas. The pair raised money by selling shares of their corporation, the Texon Oil and Land Company, organized under the corporate laws of the state of Delaware. While Pickrell and Krupp put together their drilling project, a discovery one hundred miles northeast of their leases made prospects look even brighter. In 1921, the Texas & Pacific Abrams No. 1 well became the first commercially producing oil well in the Permian Basin when it blew in ona dusty Mitchell County ranch near the little crossroads community of Westbrook.[20] Quickly afterward, with time running out to commence drilling under their permits, Pickrell and Krupp hired Carl Cromwell as the driller.

Pickrell also hired a San Angelo geologist named Hugh Tucker for five days at a cost of $100 per day to help him locate the best spot to drill. Tucker chose a site within yards of the Kansas City, Mexico & Orient Railroad (KCM&O) in southwestern Reagan County, and Cromwell began drilling the well known as the Santa Rita #1. Work went slowly, but after two years of toil and uncertainty, the Santa Rita #1 blew in on May 23, 1923.[21]

---

[19] Chapter 83, General Laws of the State of Texas Passed by the Thirty-Fifth Legislature at its Regular Session (1917), 158-163.

[20] Samuel D. Myres, The Permian Basin: Era of Discovery, from the Beginning to the Depression, vol. 1 (El Paso: Texas Western Press, 1973), 152-155.

[21] Martin Schwettmann, Santa Rita: The University of Texas Oil Discovery (Austin: Texas State Historical Association, 1958), 24-27;

The potential for wealth on university lands became immediately apparent to all parties involved. The media coverage of the discovery was unprecedented. Numerous regional and national newspapers ran the story. The KCM&O railroad scheduled a special train from San Angelo out to the well near the steadily growing oil camp at Texon. Upon arrival, workers opened the valve on the well and the sightseers witnessed oil gushing out of the flow line. In July, the Rio Grande Oil Company bought the first production, 1,672 barrels for $1.25 per barrel. Rio Grande shipped the crude by rail to refining facilities in El Paso.[22]

In the early stages of production the proximity of the railroad to the Santa Rita #1 proved invaluable for transporting petroleum out of the region, but the need for additional infrastructure, such as pipelines and collection facilities, was evident. Pickrell and Krupp did not have the financial resources to commence such an operation. They needed capital and Pickrell eventually approached Transcontinental Oil Company owner Michael Late Benedum, who initially turned down the proposition. After a second meeting, however, Benedum made a counter offer. He would take 10,000 acres and drill eight test wells with the Big Lake Oil Company, an operating subsidiary, before committing further investment. In exchange, Pickrell and Krupp got one-quarter of the Big Lake Oil Company's stock. Benedum created an additional corporation, the Plymouth Oil Company, to handle the

---

Berte R. Haigh, "Santa Rita, The Oil Well," The Permian Historical Annual 17 (December, 1977): 58-59; Joe B. Franz, The Forty Acre Follies: An Opinionated History of the University of Texas (Austin, Texas Monthly Pres, Inc., 1983), 123.

[22] Diana Davids Olien and Roger Olien, Oil in Texas: The Gusher Age, 1895-1945 (Austin: University of Texas Press, 2002), 150-153.

other three-quarters of the Big Lake Company's stock, which he alone controlled. He wanted to insure that he could operate other prospects that might develop outside his partnership with Pickrell and Krupp. Levi Smith, a native of the Desdemona field in north-central Texas, became President of the Big Lake Oil Company and oversaw operations in West Texas. With eastern capital pouring in, production numbers soared in the following years.[23] The increased capital also helped remedy the infrastructure problems in the aftermath of the Santa Rita discovery.

The oil field camp at Texon, built just south of the Santa Rita #1, is an important example of how petroleum development contributed to the settlement of the western part of the state. It also illustrates the symbiosis between independents and the majors in developing the oilfields of the Permian Basin.[24] Levi Smith made the camp at Texon his pet project and wanted to make it a model community with all of the modern amenities. Texon had a hospital, a school, a baseball park, and a golf course. The Texon town site, however, did not contribute any additional money to the Available University Fund (AUF), because a separate lease for the surface land did not exist apart from the drilling permit. The original drilling permit allowed for quarter-section blocks of surface access and the little community grew in that area. The regents and Saner saw the possibility of additional revenue in the future and quickly executed a number of leases specifically for

---

[23] Sam Mallison, The Great Wildcatter: The Story of Mike Benedum (Charleston, West Virginia: Education Foundation of West Virginia, 1953), 331-337, 343-345, *passim*.

[24] Olien and Olien, Oil in Texas, 164-165.

town sites. Petroleum operators increasingly held surface leases of university lands and used lease rights to build infrastructure, such as roads and utilities.

After the Big Lake Oil Company sunk additional wells in the vicinity, the amount of production at Texon began to exceed rail transport capacity and on-site storage facilities. Pickrell and Krupp eventually sold out to Benedum because they did not have the resources in capital, much less the expertise or manpower, to keep a proper accounting of royalties. The remaining Texon stock holders plus Benedum's Plymouth Oil Company and the New York-based Marland Oil Company partnered to construct gathering facilities. They organized under the name Reagan County Purchasing Company. The new company bought oil from the Big Lake Company at a reduced price, paying the university's royalty on that amount. Then, it sold the oil at normal market price, essentially cheating the university out of the proper royalty amount.[25] Such entangled corporate arrangements and their natural tendency to try to reduce financial obligations created mistrust between the regents and the Reagan County Purchasing Company.

Keeping an accurate accounting of production became increasingly difficult because the Dallas office of land agent R. E. L. Saner was too far removed from the activity in Reagan County to monitor the activity. In 1924, the regents moved to remedy the situation. They hired Haywood Hughes, Saner's first full-time employee, to gauge production and monitor surface usage for a salary of $130 per month.[26] The regents bought Hughes a Ford roadster, which he used to travel to production locations

---

[25] Ibid., 151-153.

[26] Minutes of the Board of Regents, Meeting #233, November 26, 1924, 308.

and storage sites. He used a tape measure with a weight on the end to gauge the amount of oil in a tank battery. The method was crude and required regular checks to insure that oil was not hauled off before the amount could be recorded. As production continued to increase, one gauger proved inadequate to insure that all royalties were being paid. The regents hired an additional gauger, knowing full well that a better system had to be devised.

In spring 1925, the Thirty-ninth Legislature enacted a law that stated that oil royalties from university lands were to be paid to the AUF rather than the PUF. Governor Miriam A. Ferguson quickly signed the measure into law. The regents favored the law because the money from oil royalties did not become part of the endowment, the PUF, the investment of which they controlled. Instead, oil royalties became part of the AUF, and were immediately available for legislative appropriation to the regents for construction and permanent improvements.[27] The attorney general and the state treasurer expressed the opinion that the law was unconstitutional, and the Texas Supreme Court agreed. In State v. Hatcher, on March 10, 1926, the court ruled that petroleum was not renewable and thus a permanent part of the land that could not be replaced. Petroleum royalties were therefore payment for part of the permanent endowment and must be deposited in the PUF.[28]

To further alleviate accounting problems the regents in 1925 created another position they initially called the

---

[27] Norman D. Brown, Hood, Bonnet, and Little Brown Jug: Texas Politics, 1921-1928 (College Station: Texas A & M University Press, 1984), 260 .

[28] State v. Hatcher, Texas Supreme Court, No. 4506, March 10, 1926, 1-2; David F. Prindle, "Oil and the Permanent University Fund: The Early Years," Southwestern Historical Quarterly 86, no. 2 (October, 1982): 287.

"oil inspector," later called the "oil supervisor." They also hired an additional gauger. The regents employed L. G. Graves to oversee field activities from an office in Best, Texas, just up the road from Texon. The regents allocated $4,000 to build Graves a house at Best. At the same time, they also hired Judge Charles Black of Austin to advise them about legal solutions to the royalty problems. In 1926, they acquired the services of independent auditors Ernst and Ernst to conduct a thorough audit of all royalty payments. In their report, the oil auditors concluded that there were possible problems and referred the matter to Attorney General Dan Moody. Moody was to undertake legal action, if that was necessary, to recover university money.[29]

Even though the increase in petroleum production created new problems for them, the regents looked at their own system to begin making changes. Personnel changes were among them. At the end of September 1926, they released the oil supervisor and one of the gaugers from their duties. No reasons for the terminations were recorded, but it is possible that the pair were released because of the accounting problems. Within a month, the regents hired Elliot J. Compton of Crawford, Texas, as the new oil supervisor. They set Compton's salary at $200 per month until January 1, 1927, when they raised it to $225 per month. Compton was responsible for gauging production and monitoring surface leases, but he slowly

---

[29] Haigh, Land, Oil and Education, 145-147; Minutes of the Board of Regents, Meeting #252, November 23, 1926, 416-417; Prindle, "Oil and the PUF,"287.

began to assume many of Saner's responsibilities. In 1927 the regents ordered the house at Best moved to Texon.[30]

The adjustments in personnel, however, did little to alleviate the growing accounting irregularities. With subsequent discovery of the Church Field in Crane County in 1926 and the Taylor-Link Field in Pecos County in 1929, the problems worsened.[31]

The accounting problems facing UT officials during the post-Santa Rita 1920s were indications of the need to establish an agency to manage its university lands. First, the results of the Ernst and Ernst audit prompted the regents to initiate a suit against the Texon Oil and Land Company and the Reagan County Purchasing Company for $2.7 million in unpaid royalties. When it appeared the court would side with the regents, the parties reached a settlement. The defendants agreed to pay the University of Texas $1 million and a higher royalty over the next three years.[32] The settlement, however, did not ensure against future accounting problems.

Despite the increase in accounting problems the regents and Saner continued to develop other ways to utilize university lands. Besides oil and gas, another sub-surface resource of interest, water, possessed value. In October 1927, Frank Pickrell entered into one of the earliest water development contracts on university lands. Pickrell paid $1,600 cash for a ten-year lease of 640 acres, Section 20 of Block 16, in Ward County. Pickrell intended to drill water wells and build a pipeline to supply the town

---

[30] James B. Zimmerman, "Dollars for Scholars: University Lands' Contribution to the Permanent Fund of the University of Texas System," The Permian Historical Annual 7 (December, 1967): 43.

[31] Ibid.

[32] Prindle, "Oil and the Permanent University Fund," 285.

of Pyote with drinking water. By the following year Pickrell, with regent approval, assigned the lease to the Pyote Water Company.[33] If Pickrell collected a fee from the Pyote Water Company is unclear, but it is doubtful he gave up the lease for free.

Another problem facing the regents was a vacancy in Crane County known as the "Landreth strip." Poorly conducted surveys in the 1870s and 1880s led to "vacancies," or land spaces between adjacent surveys. A Fort Worth oilman named Ed Landreth located such a vacancy adjacent to university lands in Crane County. Four miles long, the strip of unclaimed land was almost 607 feet wide on one end, and 135.8 feet on the other. Landreth discovered huge amounts of petroleum, prompting the regents to sue for the university's share of royalties. The court sided with Landreth stating that the faulty surveys of Dennis Corwin and Robert Estes did not give the university the right to the minerals. The mineral rights therefore reverted to the Public School Fund (PSF).[34] The case made it clear that the university could not rely on the courts to uphold its rights. Thus, it refocused attention on the need for a re-survey of its entire land holdings.

A foreshadowing of the potential for oil and gas at greater depths, called "deep pay," began in Reagan County. The University 1-B deep well test, begun in 1926, was

---

[33] Lease #317, University Lands Leases, Texas General Land Office, October 1, 1927, 1-3 ; Letter from Frank Pickrell to R. E. L. Saner, October 10, 1927; Letter from R. E. L. Saner to Land Commissioner J. T. Robison, October 19, 1927; Letter from J. T. Robison to R. E. L. Saner, October 22, 1927; Contract Assumption of Lease #17, October 5, 1928, 1-2; Letter from Land Commissioner J. H. Walker to R. E. L. Saner, October 23, 1928, University Lands Administrative Files, Midland, Texas.

[34] Ibid., 289.

completed in 1929 when operators after two years and ten months reached a depth of 8,525 feet. It was at that time the deepest oil well drilled with a cable tool rig in the world, and it was the first drilled into the Ordovician, or Ellenburger, formation. The well is significant because it was the first of many in what proved to be a very prolific pay zone. After the record depth was surpassed, the University 1-B received heavy coverage in newspapers around the region and contributed to the general optimism of the industry in early 1929. A subsequent report by geology professor Elias H. Sellards helped to disseminate the story of the deep well and the possibility of deeper pay.[35]

During this period of rapid development in the industry, the regents moved to strengthen its title to university land holdings, both legally and physically. In so doing, they prompted the legislature to devise a system to manage the lands for the benefit of future generations.

The year 1929 was a watershed year in the history of petroleum development on university lands. Following intense lobbying by the regents, the Forty-first Legislature codified measures to end the problems of ownership and royalties. On March 29, 1929, the legislature passed "Chapter 282," which made several changes in the management of university lands. The law created four management organizations: the University Lands Geology Office, the University Lands Surface Office, the University Lands Survey Office, and the Board for Lease of University Lands. The law further appropriated money to finance the

---

[35] Haigh, Land, Oil and Education, 152; Olien and Olien, Oil in Texas, 200; Elias H. Sellards, "The University Deep Well in Reagan County, Texas," University of Texas Bulletin no. 2901 (October, 1929): 175-179.

re-survey of the entire 2.1 million acres of university lands.[36]

On July 1, 1929, the regents appointed Hal P. Bybee, then Director of the Bureau of Economic Geology and a former student of Udden, to head the University Lands Geology Office, as the "geologist in charge." Bybee set up an office in San Angelo in 1931 "to secure the best possible return from the mineral development of the land belonging to the University."[37] Because the University Lands Geology Office was essentially a state agency, Bybee had to take bids on office space to get the lowest price. Unlike the University Lands Surface Office, professional geologists staffed the geology office from its inception. Under Bybee's leadership geology office personnel began collecting geological data and lease rates for land surrounding the university lands to insure the university got the best market rates. Evaluation of this data helped determine which tracts might bring the highest return in a given market situation. Over the next seven decades the University Lands Geology Office staff collected a sizable library of geological data.

Chapter 282 also established University Lands Surface Office. The regents promoted oil supervisor Elliot J. Compton to head the new office. The surface office was

---

[36] Chapter 282, General Special Laws of the State of Texas Passed by the Forty-first Legislature at the Regular Session (1929), 616-629.

[37] Berte R. Haigh, The Story of University Lands (Midland: unpublished manuscript, 1937), 8, Berte R. Haigh Collection, The Permian Basin Petroleum Museum, Midland, Texas.

Figure 8: Hal P. Bybee, Ph.D. headed the University Lands Geology Department 1929 – 1954. Photo courtesy of The Permian Basin Petroleum Museum, Abell-Hanger Collection.

primarily charged with leasing for grazing purposes, but it continued to employ gaugers to track petroleum production and monitor petroleum related surface use.[38] Although the it had no role in management or sale of minerals, the surface office insured that operators complied with all rules and regulations of the lease, as well as state laws.

The Board for Lease of University Lands proved important. Lawmakers established it to conduct lease sales for minerals on university lands and to make policy in regard to the sales. The law stipulated that the membership of the newly created Board for Lease would consist of the land commissioner and two UT regents, with the chairman selected by the members.[39] By its very establishment, the Board for Lease was conservationist in nature. The focus on reduction of waste and protecting the university's mineral rights bears this out. The Board for Lease selected and named the tracts eligible for bids, but it could withhold any tracts it desired based on market values and other factors. The board had access to geological expertise of Bybee and his staff. In this way, the regents wielded considerable control over oil and gas leasing on university lands.

An equally important aspect of Chapter 282 was an appropriation for the re-survey of university lands. It was a way to insure the university's physical and legal control of the property. Lawmakers approved the resurvey because of the potential for large sums of money from petroleum production and the resulting benefits of a reduced burden on Texas taxpayers. The regents met on June 7 and 8, 1929, and created the University Lands Survey Office.

---

[38] Chapter 282, General Special Laws of the State of Texas Passed by the Forty-First Legislature at the Regular Session (1929), 616-629.

[39] Haigh, The Story of University Lands, 8-9.

They accepted several applications for a surveyor, settling on Frank Friend of San Angelo. Within two weeks, Friend had a staff of six and a field office in a San Angelo office building. The actual survey work began later that year and continued until November 24, 1936. The following year the regents hired former Land Commissioner J. H. Walker as a special land agent to help prepare maps and field notes for submission to the General Land Office. Walker's employment is evidence of the importance the regents gave the resurvey. The survey office moved to Austin in 1937. It disbanded in 1949 when all maps and survey notes were completed and placed in the General Land Office.[40]

A primary obstacle for the regents in securing a tight hold on the endowment funds gained from its lands was Texas A&M's claim to a share of the PUF and AUF. The Constitution of 1876 provided the impetus for the PUF, which served as the endowment of the university and the repository for proceeds from the use of the university lands. The AUF represents interest income from the PUF and revenue from surface use. The Board of Directors of the A&M College at Bryan claimed their school was entitled to a portion of AUF appropriations. The 1876 Constitution stated explicitly that proceeds from university lands were also intended to support the Agricultural and Mechanical "branch" at College Station. In August 1929, A&M officials asked the attorney general for an opinion on the matter, and thus UT officials were faced with a serious legal challenge.

Following something of a clandestine meeting of officials from both schools in a Houston hotel, UT and A&M reached an agreement, but no record of the hotel meeting is extant. The absence of official minutes conjures up images of a 'corrupt bargain' in Texas higher education. Per the settlement, however, Texas A&M was to receive

---

[40] Ibid., 184-198.

one-third of the money from the AUF, while the University of Texas would retain the other two-thirds of AUF appropriations. Texas A&M did not get a seat on the Board for Lease of University Lands and the university retained its two seats. The University of Texas also retained exclusive title on grazing lease revenues, which were deposited in the AUF to the credit of the university. The simplest and most likely explanation for the settlement: it was pragmatic for the university to join with Texas A&M to keep other institutions of higher learning from claiming a share of the AUF.[41] The claims of other schools for such a share remained an important political issue in Texas for the remainder of the century.

In 1930, another state agency, the Texas Railroad Commission, began to figure into the increasingly complex process of exploiting oil and gas. That year, the Railroad Commission issued its first order to limit oil and gas production, which many industry people viewed as government meddling and price fixing. Operators were unsure if the courts would uphold the constitutionality of the order, and compliance was minimal as they waited to see what the outcome would be. When the court upheld its order in 1935, the Railroad Commission's status as the regulatory agency of the oil and gas industry in Texas was firmly established.[42] University Lands Geology Office and University Lands Surface Office staff members then had the added duty of insuring that oil and gas operators

---

[41] Henry C. Dethloff, A Centennial History of Texas A&M University, 1976-1976, vol. 2 (College Station: Texas A&M University Press, 1975), 418-420.

[42] David F. Prindle, Petroleum Politics and the Texas Railroad Commission (Austin: University of Texas Press, 1981), 26-31.

complied with rules and regulations of the Texas Railroad Commission.

In 1931, the Forty-second Legislature steered state land policy toward conservation. It removed all minerals and resources on university land, except oil and gas, from the market until their potential could be ascertained.[43] There was a real concern among officials that state lands in general were losing money from such minerals that were not properly classified and priced. Additionally, the law made no mention of water, which the regents continued to develop through leasing.

By this time too, the ill effects of the depression were being felt. So-called "hot oil," illegal oil produced and sold beyond the Texas Railroad Commission (RRC) prescribed production limits, flowed in the eastern part of the state, flooding the market, and causing the price of petroleum to plummet.

While the market effects of hot oil stymied production in the Permian Basin, the University Lands Surface Office was busy with increased petroleum-related surface use and development of potable groundwater sources. Surface activity included building infrastructure for civil and industrial purposes as well as pipelines and utility rights-of-way. Petroleum related surface activities contributed no small amount to overall revenue figures deposited in the AUF from 1929-1996.

With production in West Texas at a low point in the first half of the 1930s, the regents began to push for a major policy shift in the sale of leases on university property. In 1935, J. R. Parten, a member of the board of regents, began lobbying the Board for Lease of University Lands to switch

---

[43] S. C. R. 8., General and Special Laws of the State of Texas Passed by the Forty-Second Legislature at the First Called Session (1931), 93.

methods for auctioning mineral leases. Pointing to the successful example of mineral leasing on Osage Indian land in Northeastern Oklahoma, Parten pushed for oral auctions of mineral leases rather than sealed bids. Parten argued that through competition public auction would increase bids. He also pointed out that people in the industry believed that sealed bidding favored the major oil companies.[44] Because royalties were standard and based on production amounts, bidders actually bid an amount called the "bonus." The party that bid the highest bonus amount obtained the right to operate that mineral lease.

The Board for Lease was receptive to Parten's recommendations and even hired the same auctioneer used by the Osage Tribe. It also made provisions to compensate him with a one per cent fee on bidding, to be paid by the winning bidder. The first public auction of university mineral leases took place on July 20, 1936, and raised twice the average revenue of the sealed bid auctions held between 1929 and 1935.[45] This method of conducting sales proved quite successful over the years as revenue climbed fairly steadily from the late 1930s until the 1980s.[46]

Under Hal P. Bybee's leadership, the University Lands Geology Office promoted new methods for finding oil. One such method was geophysical exploration, which could lead to increased petroleum production at deeper and deeper depths throughout the Permian Basin. The regents on August 3, 1933, received their first request for a

---

[44] Haigh, Land, Oil and Education, 255-257.

[45] Miller, Public Lands, 183; Prindle, "Oil and the Permanent University Fund," 297.

[46] Laddie Long and Wallie Gravitt, University Lands Geology Office geologists (retired), interview by author, March 11, 2002, tape recording.

geophysical prospecting permit. It was from the Amerada Petroleum Corporation for land in Andrews County. The regents postponed a decision until the following January when Amerada agreed to pay $6.40 per section, or one cent per acre, on eight blocks in Andrews County. Subsequently, Amerada's crews drilled shot holes for setting off explosive charges and took readings on an instrument called the seismograph. The method enabled evaluation of deeper strata that were not discernible from the surface geology. Amerada's geophysical operations were conducted with such care that there was not a single complaint about the company, and the regents assessed no surface damages over the next twelve years.[47] All geological data collected by operators was submitted for deposit in the data library in the University Lands Geology Office.

Within one year of the first permit the per acre rate for geophysical prospecting was over ten cents per acre, a one thousand per cent increase. Geophysical activity became commonplace, but damage claims from the explosions mounted. By 1937 the regents had begun to assess damage fees for renewable resources. Damage fees were usually earmarked for improvements to the surface lease. Similarly, when surface lessees complained that geophysical operations caused a decrease in lamb production, the regents restricted operations in sheep country during the lambing season.[48]

With the increasingly complex nature of oil and gas law the regents created the University Lands Legal, under the Office of Investments, Trusts, and Lands. In 1937, they appointed Scott Gaines to head the legal office. Gaines

---

[47] Haigh, Land, Oil and Education, 247-252.

[48] Carl Coke Rister, Oil! Titan of the Southwest (Norman: University of Oklahoma Press, 1949), 380.

brought badly needed legal expertise, lacking from the system since R. E. L. Saner's retirement in 1929. Gaines worked closely with Hal P. Bybee and Elliot J. Compton to insure that the legal rights of the university were protected in every instance. Gaines remained the attorney for university lands until his death in 1957.

At a September 25, 1937, meeting of the board of regents, George D. Morgan reported that state representative R. Ewing Thomason was seeking the assistance of the War Department to conduct an aerial photographic survey of the entire 2.1 million acres of university lands. Thomason and others believed that an aerial survey would help the search for potential minerals. Two years later, in late October 1939, J. R. Parten, as chairman of the board of regents, contracted with Edgar Tobin of Austin to conduct the aerial photographic survey. Tobin agreed to furnish the regents with two sets of photographs, which he did. The first set was printed horizontally at a scale of one inch to one thousand feet, and the second set's scale equaled one inch to two thousand feet. The regents paid Tobin $15,568 upon receipt of the prints. During 1940 and 1941, survey office employees Jess Conklin and Norris Creath drew the lines of the Frank Friend survey onto the prints.[49]

As exploration activity decreased in the Big Lake Field, and efforts focused on production, the University Lands Geology Office moved in 1937 from San Angelo to Midland. Emerging as the *de facto* division headquarters for several of the major oil companies, Midland served as the administrative center for petroleum related activity in the western part of the state. Moving the office to Midland

---

[49] Haigh, Land, Oil, and Education, 203.

Figure 12: Oilmen and UT leaders at Santa Rita #1. Front Row, L-R: W.M. Griffith Big Lake Oil Co.; Jess Conklin University Lands (UL) surveyor; Ed Warren, Texon Oil & Land Co.; Frank Friend, UL surveyor; J.S. Posgate, Big Lake Oil and Land Co.; Charles I Frances, UT regent; K.H. Aynesworth, UT regent; Beauford Jester, UT regent; Hal P. Bybee, UL geologist in charge; D.R. Johnson, Big Lake Oil Co.; back row, L-R: H. Lutcher Stark, UT regent; V. Stell UL guager; Nalle Gregory, UL geologist; Charles E. Bayer, Big Lake Oil Co.; H.Y. Benedict, UT President, E.J. Compton, UL land agent. Photo courtesy of The Permian Basin Petroleum Museum, Abell-Hanger Collection.

enabled the staff members to network with the industry representatives and to improve the collection of data.[50]

---

[50] Richard R. Moore, West Texas After the Discovery of Oil: A Modern Frontier (Austin: Jenkins Publishing Company, 1971), 79, 82, 86; Steve Hartmann, Executive Director of University Lands West Texas Operations, interview by author, January 28, 2002, tape recording.

Although the Board for Lease of University Lands' biennial sales of mineral leases were held in Austin, the sales became a common aspect of the West Texas oil industry. Sales revenue soared in the following years, and after 1936 bonus revenue climbed from $671,700 from three separate sales in one year, to a high of $703,651 for one sale in 1938. Bonus revenues reached an all-time low in 1939, but in 1940 rebounded to $1,312,375. The increase occurred despite Conservation Order M-68, which set wartime priorities for fuel and discouraged exploration.[51] The postwar period, however, saw revenues going increasingly higher.

In the 1930s and 1940s, petroleum related surface usage continued to increase. Companies and individuals alike leased surface area in the vicinity of oilfield activity for town sites, bars, and cafes. Likewise, the regents granted dozens of easements for pipelines. For pipeline rights-of way the lease contract stipulated that the lessee pay a flat fee per joint of pipe per year.[52] Oil companies operating on university lands also sought leases for the construction of storage and transportation facilities, which helped update infrastructure in the still sparsely inhabited western part of the state.

In 1948, the Texas Railroad Commission, in an effort to conserve the resources of the state, required operators to stop flaring residual gas. The commission wanted companies to build pressure plants to return the gas to the field. A university lands mineral lease holder in Crane County, the Atlantic Refining Company, moved first.

---

[51] Haigh, Land, Oil, and Education, 328-330; Olien and Olien, Oil in Texas, 222, 230.

[52] Misc. University Lands Easements, University Lands Administrative Files.

Atlantic Refining Company established at Block 31, a large unit to comply with the order. A unit, or the "unitization" of the field, meant the entire oil and gas reservoir was pressured and developed as a single entity. Block 31 was unique as a means of maximizing overall production because it was the first unit to inject its own bi-product gases back into the field.[53] The system necessitated the cooperation of multiple producers.

Scott Gaines, head of University Lands Legal Office, thought that the mineral lease holder should be required to obtain a separate surface lease for construction of such a plant. Income from the separate lease would go directly to the AUF. Increased production and revenues were the primary reason for voluntary compliance for participants. Bybee and the geology office staff supported and promoted participation in the project.[54]

Despite the increased work the University Lands Geology Office remained basically the same size throughout the period. Bybee remained the geologist in charge. His assistant, Berte R. Haigh trained at the State School of Mines and Metallurgy in El Paso, and who was hired in 1929 when the regents established the geology office, served as field geologist. Other employees of the geology office in the 1940s included an oil scout and a secretary, whose work was shared with the surface office, named Ruby Snodgrass.

Expansion of the petroleum industry contributed to settlement of the Permian Basin. Continued discoveries in the post-World War II boom led to an increase in

---

[53] Haigh, Land, Oil, and Education, 340-342.

[54] Letter from Scott Gaines to C. D. Simmons, Comptroller of the University of Texas, August 27, 1948, University Lands Administrative Files, 1; Haigh, Land, Oil and Education, 341.

Figure 10: Berte R. Haigh, probably on a geological field trip, date unknown. Photo courtesy The Permian Basin Petroleum Museum, Berte R. Haigh Collection.

settlement of West Texas and the resulting growth of oil field infrastructure in the 1950s. Midland and other towns along Highway 80 (later Interstate 20) became the focal points of the growing service activity in the basin. National trends to purchase cheaper foreign petroleum kept West Texas oil prices at an equilibrium that fostered steady growth. President Harry Truman's Fair Deal price fixing program, however, left little incentive in the late forties to prospect for gas. But as the economy stabilized and federal price fixing ended, the gas market expanded and operators continued to drill deeper tests.[55]

Between the 1950s and 1990s, the staff of the University Lands Geology Office, renamed University Lands Oil, Gas, and Mineral Interests in the 1970s, turned over very little, allowing some people to rise through the ranks of the organization. The hierarchy of the geology office was simple. The "geologist in charge," eventually titled "manager," was the manager of the office, the "supervising geologist, later called "senior geologist," was second in command, and the "geologist" was the low man in the group. From the 1950s to the 1970s, the geology office generally employed three geologists and at least one oil scout. Bybee was geologist in charge from 1929 until he retired in 1954, but he remained on as a consultant until 1957. The regents promoted his assistant, Berte Haigh, to head the geology office in 1954. Both Bybee and Haigh played important roles in the development of the agency's organization and procedures.[56] They were both present when the agency began in 1929, and Haigh was the last manager of the geology office to hold that distinction.

After Berte Haigh retired in 1962, senior geologist Harward Fisher became the geologist in charge, and he served until his death in 1964. The regents quickly promoted James B. Zimmerman from supervising geologist to geologist in charge, which changed to "manager of University Lands Oil, Gas, and Mineral Interests in the 1970s. He remained in that position until 1979 when his senior geologist, Laddie Long, took the title "manager of

---

[55] Samuel D. Myres, The Permian Basin: Petroleum Empire of the Southwest, Era of Advancement, from the Depression to the Present, vol. 2 (El Paso: Permian Press, 1977), 399-403.

[56] Zimmerman, "Dollars for Scholars," 44.

University Lands Oil, Gas, and Mineral Interests." Senior geologist Wallie Gravitt, hired in 1971, followed Long up the ranks to the top-spot in 1986. Clearly, then, the record indicates that most employees of the University Lands Geology Office stayed in the employment of the organization for numerous years.[57] The regents tended to promote from within the ranks of the agency, a practice that provided continuity and stability to the organization and to fundamental administrative procedures in the office.

The organization, or division of labor, within the University Lands Geology Office, a system developed under Bybee's leadership, remained basically the same from 1929 to 1996. During the 1950s the regents increased the number of staff geologists to three. The geologists had oversight in of exploration and development activities in specific regions, usually handling operations by county. In addition, each geologist carried out a specific activity on the university lands related to leasing for water rights, brine production, underground storage, and various minerals other than oil and gas, and supervising disposal wells. As petroleum-related activity became more technical, so did the expertise of the geologists. Besides the staff of geologists, the regents in the late 1950s hired Ernest Weichert, a petroleum engineer, the first one employed by the University Lands Geology Office.[58]

The geology office advised the Board for Lease on the presence of sufficient interest shown by the oil and gas industry to justify a call for nominations of lease tracts and on the selection of tracts to be offered. The Board for Lease determined each lease auction sale date. The nomination process was very involved, and the geology

---

[57] Long and Gravitt, interview, March 11, 2002.

[58] Ibid.

staff considered many factors in making recommendations. It looked at geological and petroleum marketing data to determine which tracts would bring the most return. Bybee required university lands geologists to compare their methods and revenue numbers with that of federal offshore oil and gas leases in the Gulf of Mexico or with mineral lease sales on state and federal lands in New Mexico. Of increased importance, however, was seeing that operators were compliant with the terms of the lease and with all Texas Railroad Commission rules. Such action meant that more time had to be spent in the field, and it eventually led to the hiring of an oilfield representative.

In monitoring surface operations for compliance and damage the geology office also had the help of Elliot Compton's field personnel. As late as 1965, Billy Carr, Compton's successor as head of the surface office since 1959, still used the title "oil supervisor" in certain official correspondence.[59] The extent of production activity, the distances involved, and the lack of manpower, limited the ability of the staff to monitor activity. The surface office resorted to random checks of selected leases in order to ensure compliance with lease agreements.

An important development on university lands that began in the 1950s during Bybee's and Haigh's leadership was the issuance of permits to prospect for minerals other than oil and gas. There was sporadic interest until 1931 when the legislature removed those minerals, which included sulfur, brine, and potash, from the market. In 1949 the Fifty-first Legislature transferred control of all minerals on university lands, except oil and gas, to the

---

[59] Letter from Billy Carr to William M. Stewart, Endowment Officer of the University of Texas, May 7, 1965, University Lands Administrative Files, 6.

board of regents.[60] Although the legislature's actions elicited praise from the regents, only a handful of minerals known to be present in the state were available on university lands. Demand in another subsurface resource, water, increased as the population of West Texas grew in the post-war years.

The exploitation of potable water had proved to be a reliable revenue generator since the 1950s. The city of Midland signed the first municipal contract with Berte Haigh's University Lands Geology Office in 1957 and officially developed the Paul Davis water field to supplement Midland's water supply. The City of Andrews and Andrews County Independent School district also entered into a contract to drill for water on university lands. Both agreements started as exploration permits, which once production commenced changed into royalty-for-use agreements. The Midland contract was for a period of ten years with options to renew for ten years at a minimum royalty of $40,000 annually. The Andrews contract, extending for the same duration, was for a minimum royalty of $10,000 annually. Haigh and his geologists determined that the area exploited by Midland produced four times the water as did the area exploited by Andrews. In fact, both were using the same water field in the area near the border of Andrews and Martin Counties.[61] Over the following years, the regents developed other water resources, including additional potable and non-potable

---

[60] Chapter 186, General and Special Laws of the State of Texas Passed by the Fifty-First Legislature at the Regular Session (1949), 362-363.

[61] Minutes of the Board of Regents, Meeting #559, January 11, 1957, 443-444; Water Exploration and Development Contract No. 70, University Lands Administrative Files, January 11, 1957.

water contracts. The geology office remained in control of water leasing through 1996.

The university lands staff also promoted and leased land for the production of brine that came out of subsurface formations. Companies entered into brine production lease contracts to mine the ten-pound brine, thereby creating additional royalty revenue for the AUF. Drilling operators utilized ten-pound brine as an additive to increase the weight of drilling fluids. The brine solution and subsequent production washed out caverns in subsurface salt formations. The regents also executed contracts with operators to wash out caverns not for the production of brine, but to create underground "jugs" for the storage of liquefied natural gas products such liquefied propane and butane.[62]

When Bybee retired as head of University Lands Geology Office in 1954, the regents promoted his longtime assistant Berte Haigh to the top job. Haigh took over the geology office during a very dynamic period in the Permian Basin petroleum industry. He was geologist in charge when the regents announced a sizable royalty increase. In 1960, the Board for Lease sent an unwelcomed ripple through the industry when it increased the standard royalty for crude oil from one-sixth to one-quarter. The royalty increase angered many operators at the time, but the figure soon became an industry norm. Other increases in the standard royalty took place from the 1960s to the 1990s and the petroleum industry simply passed the cost on to the consumer.

By the mid-1950s, oilfield activity was booming and companies continued to drill into deeper pay zones. Several companies drilled record wells on university lands. One such well was the Phillips Petroleum Company's University EE No. 1, drilled near Fort Stockton in Pecos

---

[62] Long and Gravitt, interview, March 11, 2002.

County. In September 1958, the crew, employees of Parker Drilling Company, reached a record depth of 25,000 feet. They drilled the well to a total depth of 25, 340 feet. When the they determined that the hole was dry, the operators plugged and abandoned the well.[63] The activity received invaluable press coverage, which created interest in mineral sales on university lands.

Throughout the 1950s, Haigh and the University Lands Geology Office staff found Midland an ideally centralized locale to conduct both administrative and field activities. Because of access to air, rail, and interstate highway travel, every major oil company kept a division office in Midland. In 1959, when Elliot Compton retired from the University Lands Surface office, Billy Carr moved the operation from Texon to Midland to share offices with Haigh and the geologists. In 1966, State Senator Pete Snelson of Midland pushed an appropriations bill through the legislature. The bill provided for the construction of a permanent facility for University Lands Geology Office and University Lands Surface Office near downtown Midland. The Hal P. Bybee Building had a geological laboratory, a vault, a large conference room, numerous offices, and a big room for a library at its center.[64] Staff of the two organizations no longer had to take bids on office space and move every few years.

Major oil companies drilled additional wells on university lands in a number of counties during the 1960s and 1970s. These operations reflected a general trend in the West Texas oil industry. The discovery of the Gomez field in 1963 foretold of deeper gas pay, and a stream of

---

[63] Myres, The Permian Basin, 391.

[64] Senator W. E. "Pete" Snelson (retired), interview by author, March 25, 2002, tape recording.

subsequent discoveries took place in Pecos County over the next few years. Most of the deep gas activity was in the area south of Fort Stockton. In 1971 and 1972, the Parker Drilling Company drilled the Ralph Lowe Estate No. 1 University well to a depth of 28,500 feet, a record-breaking depth at the time. Ironically, it proved to be the deepest dry hole in the world.[65] Publicity associated with the deep well proved invaluable for promoting petroleum development on university lands.

Growing interest in other subsurface resources during the 1960s and 1970s is reflected in the name change from "University Lands Geology" to "University Lands Oil, Gas, and Mineral Interest." The name change did not alter the operations of the office, but merely signified a recognition that its mission was somewhat broader. During their respective periods of leadership, James Zimmerman, Laddie Long, and Wallie Gravitt, promoted and developed prospecting for minerals other than oil and gas.[66]

Sulfur was one of those minerals that was previously known to be present on university land. It began to create interest in the mid-1960s. From 1964 to 1968, sulfur prices increased by as much as sixty to sixty-five percent. There were small amounts of sulfur in a gypsum surface exposure in Culberson County, and geologists found other indications of its presence in well cuttings from east-central Pecos County. The discoveries were enticing, but extraction of the sulfur was a complex and expensive process.[67] A more cost-effective process was needed to make production possible.

---

[65] Myres, The Permian Basin, 406.

[66] Long and Gravitt, interview, March 11, 2002.

[67] Haigh, Land, Oil and Education, 293-294.

In 1967, the Duval Corporation began operating a sulfur mine in Pecos County, with the "Frasch-process." The method, first devised in 1894, used steam to remove the sulfur from the host rock. The Frasch process was cheaper to operate than conventional mining and enabled the exploitation of deposits on university lands. When the Midland office received numerous inquiries for sulfur leases, the regents then announced they would accept sealed bids for leases on twenty tracts in Pecos County. The total bonus received was $766,124.43 and the highest bonus bid for a single 640-acre tract was $333,333.33, an average of over $520 per acre. Each lease provided a rental payment of $2 per acre was due in advance each year and a substantial royalty was to be paid on each ton of silver produced.[68] Although operators carried out extensive prospecting, none of the tracts was developed. The leases simply expired.

The regents held a second sealed bid lease sale for sulfur on December 2, 1973. The Texas Gulf Sulfur Company submitted the only bid for a 7,680-acre tract, a bid of $1,152,222.22. After a brief period of exploration, Texas Gulf built a Frasch-process plant that began operations in January 1975. By December 1980, royalties from sulfur had contributed $8.5 million to the PUF.[69]

The Texas A&M College System, created in 1948, underwent additional changes during the 1960s and 1970s. In August 1963, the legislature approved a bill that changed the official name of the school from the Agricultural and Mechanical College of Texas to Texas A&M University. Not all tradition-oriented Aggies approved, but their displeasure was short-lived. Similarly, in 1975 the Texas

---

[68] Ibid., 294-295.

[69] Ibid., 295.

A&M Board of Directors became the Texas A&M University System Board of Regents.[70]

From the 1970s to the 1980s two members of the board of regents and the Board for Lease demonstrated more than a passive interest in the development of petroleum resources on university lands. Regent Dan C. Williams, the first regent to have training as a petroleum engineer, was appointed to the Board for Lease of University Lands in 1972. Regent Sterling Fly, who joined Williams on the Board for Lease in 1976, was another regent with a keen interest in petroleum developments. The two men served on the Board for Lease during the most profitable period of oil and gas development on university lands. In 1975, they were responsible for moving the location of mineral lease sales from Austin to Midland to be closer to the center of the petroleum industry. Their tenure was marked by a discernable increase in lease sales revenues, and in 1980 they were instrumental in raising the standard royalty amount for university production leases to one-quarter of overall production. Williams served on the Board for Lease until his regency expired in 1980. Fly remained until 1983.[71]

The University Lands Oil, Gas, and Mineral Interests staff in 1979 was finally relieved of some of its responsibility for tracking production on mineral leases. That year, the Sixty-sixth Legislature gave the regents the responsibility for accounting for royalties derived from petroleum production. The regents pushed for the measure because they believed General Land Office personnel were

---

[70] Dethloff, History of Texas A&M, 500, 573, 584.

[71] Long and Gravitt, interview, March 11, 2002.

slow to deposit mineral lease revenues in the PUF.[72] In turn, the regents, created the University Lands Accounting Office. The accounting office, located in downtown Austin, was independent of the surface and geology offices, and answered directly to the board of regents.

Naturally, revenues from mineral leases on university lands remained high as long as oil and gas prices were high. The Board for Lease held several record sales from the 1950s to the 1980s. The sales were legendary for their suspense and entertainment. Bonus revenue totaled several million dollars at each sale. Banner sales included 1953 and 1956, each of which netted over $16 million in bonuses. Bonuses remained around $11 million per year for several years, finally topping $13 million in 1977. The all time high bonus generated at a single mineral lease sale was $44.2 million in 1980. The record was surpassed on March 11, 1981 when bonuses totaled $52.9 million. The auction was held at the Midland Hilton, and the atmosphere was charged with excitement as independent oil men gouged those bidding for the major oil companies, driving the average price per acre to $634.62.[73] But the "doo da days," as Gravitt warmly recalled that time, did not last. Annual royalties from oil and gas production declined steadily from a high of $262 million in 1981 to just $57 million in 1996.

Land Commissioner Gary Mauro saw the market slump as an opportunity to modify mineral lease policy in

---

[72] Patsy Neidig, University Lands Accounting Office Land Records Supervisor, personal communication, January 21, 2003, and December 2, 2003; Lynward Shivers, University of Texas Office of General Counsel Senior Attorney (retired), personal communication, January 14, 2004.

[73] Haigh, Land, Oil, and Education, 328-331; Miscellaneous annual revenue statistics, University Lands Administrative Files, computer printout in possession of the author, August 31, 1998.

order to conserve university interests. He believed that low oil prices and the decreasing number of bidders at the lease sale auctions would insure low bonus revenues if oral auctions continued. As chairman of the Board for Lease, Mauro reasoned that sealed bid auctions would work to the advantage of the PUF, with parties bidding higher because of the uncertainty of a competition for each nominated tract. Mauro lobbied state Senator Bill Sims of San Angelo to sponsor a bill to give the Board for Lease of University the option to offer sealed bid auctions. Most industry folk, however, believed that sealed bids favored big oil companies who could weather the tough times and operate through the low market period. Laddie Long and Berte Haigh objected, while Wallie Gravitt believed the move was prudent because many nominated tracts only had a single company bidding on them. Despite objections, Mauro and Sims in 1986 pushed for a change to sealed bid auction.[74] With the drama of the oral auction missing from mineral lease sales, the sales, after the change back to sealed bidding, became relatively inert affairs.

During Long's tenure as manager of University Lands Mineral Interests there were continued efforts to develop additional sub-surface resources. In 1982, senior geologist Gravitt negotiated three prospecting permits for low-level uranium in Andrews County. One company's officials, referring to an out of date map, incorrectly believed that rail facilities ran across parts of university lands in Andrews County and continued to the Texas & Pacific in Midland. However, the Midland Northwestern Railroad, which ran from Midland to Seminole in Gaines County, had been abandoned in 1925. Despite the setback

---

[74] Long and Gravitt, interview, March 11, 2002; The Eagle, Bryan, Texas, April 26, 1983 ; Minutes of Board for Lease of University Lands, November 10, 1986.

prospecting began and numerous test holes were drilled. The project was ultimately abandoned when the bottom dropped out of the uranium market.[75]

Also during the period of declining oil and gas markets, organizational reshuffling occurred. In the mid-1980s, Land Commissioner Gary Mauro, a graduate of Texas A&M University, was instrumental in getting the school a seat on the Board for Lease of University Lands. The University of Texas maintained its two seats on the board, but the change gave the Texas A&M regents a stake in policy-making regarding oil and gas leasing. Relatedly, Mauro convinced lawmakers, through the action of the Sunset commission, to approve legislation that made the land commissioner the permanent chairman of the Board for Lease.[76]

Since the late 1960s, the University of Texas Board of Regents employed former geologist in charge Berte Haigh to write about his experiences with the organization. Haigh spent many years collecting information on the legislative and administrative history of petroleum developments on university lands. He passed away in 1986 just weeks before the University of Texas El Paso's Texas Western Press published his manuscript entitled Land, Oil, and Education. The book offers a history of the evolution of university lands from the Texas Republic years to 1981, and it is a firsthand account of Haigh's years with university lands, 1929 to 1962. The book also provides valuable insight into important events related to the University Lands Geology Office during Haigh's employment.

Another portent of the ending era in the history of petroleum and university lands took place in May 1990

---

[75] Long and Gravitt, interview, March 11, 2002.

[76] Shivers, personal communication, January 14, 2004.

when Marathon Oil Company, the operator in the Big Lake field, plugged the Santa Rita #1. The legendary well had made the University of Texas the second wealthiest institution of higher education in the country. For the better part of the twentieth century it also played a significant role in development of the Permian Basin as the preeminent petroleum producing region in the continental United States. A steel derrick, an old wooden pumping mechanism, and a monument erected on the site remind visitors not only of the importance petroleum played in the region but also the impact it had on higher education in Texas.

By the late 1980s and early 1990s, the staff size of University Lands Oil, Gas, and Mineral Interests slowly declined. In 1996, there were four geologists on staff: Jim Benson, Michael "Doc" Weathers, Tim Hunt, and Rick Doehne. Dave Campbell, the staff petroleum engineer, was the third person to hold that position. The office also employed a production analyst group and a host of administrative help.

During the first half of the 1990s, the regents and lawmakers undertook a general reorganization of the University of Texas System, and in the spirit of efficiency, integrated its administration, including the management structures for the university lands. For university lands operations the changes in policy included the acceptance of crude oil for royalty payments, the management of revenues from university lands, and the management of the surface, minerals, and accounting offices under a single director.

The first change was the acceptance of crude oil payments. For many years petroleum production leases contained a clause that the regents could accept their royalty payments in crude oil if they chose. In 1990 the regents gave approval for a test trial by university lands staff to market oil in small quantities of five hundred barrels. The trials showed that by marketing the crude themselves higher profits were achieved, which led to the development of the so-called "Royalty in Kind" program. Tinsey Bradley, a production analyst with the University Lands Accounting office, was given responsibility for marketing university crude oil. Bradley received purchase statements from operators and compared their sales prices with the prices she received for the university's product. Bradley showed an increase of sixty to sixty-five cents more per barrel than if she received royalties based on the operators' sale prices. The program proved to be a success and continued beyond 1996.[77]

The second change related to revenue management. In November 1995 the legislature created the first investment corporation formed by a public university system, the University of Texas Investment Management Company (UTIMCO). It contracted with the regents to manage the investment of the PUF on behalf of the University of Texas System. UTIMCO was incorporated as a 501(c)(3) tax entity, non-profit corporation. It operated like the investment companies used by such private institutions as Harvard and Princeton. UTIMCO's board of directors consisted of three University of Texas regents, the Chancellor of the UT System, a Texas A&M regent, and four people with investment management expertise. The organization's "governance structure," according to the UTIMCO website, "was designed both to preserve ultimate regent control of investments for fiduciary purposes and to increase the level of expertise in

---

[77] Steve Hartmann, University Lands West Texas Operations Executive Director, interview by author, January 28, 2002, tape recording.

the governance of investments."[78] On March 21, 1996, the regents dissolved their Office of Asset Management and transferred investment responsibility to UTIMCO. David Prindle's 1982 argument that declining oil revenues from university lands would necessitate a change in focus to investment of the PUF to produce additional revenues turned out to be prophetic and may have even influenced the regents' actions.

The third change occurred in 1996. The regents placed the University Lands Surface Office, University Lands Oil, Gas, and Mineral Interests, and University Lands Accounting Office under a single director, Steve Hartmann. The united organizations operated under the name "University Lands West Texas Operations" and remained based in Midland at the Bybee Building. As Executive Director, Hartmann appointed managers to head each of the departments, which were directly responsible to him. Under Hartmann's leadership, University Lands West Texas Operations (WTO) continued the tradition of stewardship and efficient management policies that had developed *ad hoc* over the preceding century.[79]

The success of resource exploitation on university lands from the Santa Rita discovery in 1923 to 1996 is starkly evident when annual revenues are given careful consideration. From 1923 to 1996, the total contribution of oil and gas revenues to the PUF exceeded $3 billion dollars. In 1996, operations on university lands included over 8,100 oil wells, 500 gas wells, and more than 2,000 easements.

---

[78] Ibid.; Amy Strahan, "UT Investments to be Managed by New Company," The Daily Texan, July 1, 1996; "UTIMCO: About Us," UTIMCO Website, <http://www.utimco.org/scripts/internet/about.asp> [Accessed Sat Nov 15 20:15:32 US/Central 2003].

[79] Hartmann, interview, January 28, 2002.

The 2.1 million-acres of University of Texas land called "university lands" figures prominently in the history of petroleum development in West Texas. The Santa Rita #1 well and the semi-romantic tale of its drilling were instrumental in bringing interest to the Permian Basin and potential economic opportunities on university lands. In 1929, the legislature created management organizations to develop the economic potential of the land, and over the next seven decades the management organizations developed into important components of a larger integrated corporate structure, the University of Texas System.

CHAPTER V

THE PERMANENT AND AVAILABLE UNIVERSITY FUNDS,

1896-1996

From 1896 to 1996, the University of Texas Board of Regents capitalized on resources to fund construction using a constitutionally established system with three distinct parts: the university lands, the Permanent University Fund (PUF), and the Available University Fund (AUF). The management of university lands and utilization of the resources contained therein provided income for the PUF and the AUF. The PUF was the permanent endowment of the university, established under the Constitution of 1876, the principle of which could not be spent. Income from the investment of the PUF was placed in the AUF. The Constitution gave the legislature the power to appropriate AUF money for construction and permanent improvements. The PUF moneys amounted to very little before regent control over the sale and lease of university lands began in 1896, and the PUF grew moderately in the following years. Only after the discovery of oil in 1923 did its value climb quickly, totaling nearly $5.5 billion in 1996. The board of regents oversaw organizations within the University of Texas System that managed the university lands and the investment of money derived from them.

In the 1890s public funding for higher education became an increasingly important political issue in Austin, and it continued to be for over a century. After the Constitution of 1876 established the PUF, first the legislature, then the ill-fated State Land Board, and finally the General Land Office did a poor job of raising capital from university lands. Most of the income for the period 1876-1896 was from land sales and was deposited in the PUF. For nearly twenty years, despite constant appeals from the regents, the legislature refused to invest the board with the power to sell and lease its lands.[1] Only after reform-minded Democrat James S. Hogg seized on the issue of increased funding for higher education out of general revenues did the legislature finally acquiesce to the regents' overtures.

The Constitution of 1876 also set out the process for turning land and land-use into money. The simple act of selling and leasing university lands, however, did not immediately translate into bricks and mortar. According to Article Seven, Section Eleven of the Constitution of 1876, all revenue derived from the university lands along with, "all grants, donations, and appropriations that may hereafter be made by the State of Texas… shall constitute and become a permanent university fund."[2] The university lands were, therefore, only one of many sources for the PUF. Like all endowments, the principal could not be spent, only invested. Some legislators interpreted Section Eleven to mean that any money given the university, even by the legislature or private individuals, had to be invested and the proceeds placed in the AUF. Politicians who opposed public funding for the university in the 1890s often cited this interpretation as their justification.

The constitution provided specific guidelines for investing the PUF and designated the state comptroller's

---

[1] Harry Y. Benedict, ed., "A Source Book Relating to the History of the University of Texas: Legislative, Legal, Bibliographical, and Statistical," University of Texas Bulletin No. 1757 (Austin: University of Texas, 1917), 343-344.

[2] Article 7 Section 11, Constitution of Texas (1876), H. P. N. Gammel, ed., The Laws of Texas, VIII, (Austin: H. P. N. Gammel, 1900), 811-812.

office as the agency primarily responsible for handling the investments. The PUF could only be invested in bonds issued by the State of Texas, or if none were available, then bonds of the United States would suffice.[3] All proceeds from PUF investments were deposited into the AUF.

Section Eleven of Article Seven further prescribed that the legislature was responsible for appropriation of the AUF for "the establishment and maintenance" of the university. Section Fourteen, Article Seven stated that the lawmakers could levy no taxes or appropriate no general revenue for "the establishment and construction of the buildings of the University of Texas."[4] The AUF, it was generally agreed, was intended for construction of buildings and permanent improvements to existing facilities. In the first twenty years of its existence, the AUF amounted to very little because it was funded by investment income from the PUF, and it was therefore of no significant benefit to the cash-strapped university.

The public's general knowledge of the existence of the PUF sometimes hindered university officials' efforts to obtain additional appropriations from general revenues. Many lawmakers also believed the resources given the university, meaning the land, were not being fully utilized. The inability of university officials to complete the main building until 1900 is clear evidence of the school's financial situation during the 1890s. The regents' only recourse was to get control of university lands to increase the PUF themselves.

In early 1896, the regents hired Thomas J. "Tom" Lee of Waco to sell and lease university lands to generate more revenue for the PUF. When Lee took the job, the PUF

---

[3] Ibid.

[4] Ibid.

totaled a little more than $500,000, and it was only partly invested. Lee sold a little land but most of his activities focused on leasing for grazing purposes. Because grass was considered a renewable resource, the income from grass leases went straight into the AUF. Lee's efforts provided badly needed money for the AUF, but the PUF did not grow as quickly. State and federal bonds did not pay more than 1% to 2%, with interest on the PUF accruing very slowly. By August 1898, the AUF contained $22,477 to the credit of the University of Texas and $2,074 for the A&M College.[5] As prescribed by law, officials from both schools could only spend the money after the legislature appropriated it for a specific purpose.

Lee departed the land agent position in late 1899, and the regents in early January 1900 hired "Judge" R. E. L. Saner, a recent graduate of UT Law School. Under Saner, revenue for the PUF and AUF continued to increase but not as quickly as some lawmakers thought it should. Attempts to diversify use brought in more revenue, but the PUF continued to increase slowly.[6] Saner oversaw leasing and selling of university lands for almost thirty years.

From the 1890s through the 1920s, the regents tried to gain control over the use of minerals on university lands. In 1901, the Twenty-seventh Legislature authorized the regents to "sell, lease, and otherwise control" mineral interests, but the measure was quickly replaced by another law that gave control over leasing for minerals back to the

---

[5] John J. Lane, "The History of Education in Texas," United States Bureau of Education Circular of Information, no. 2 (Washington D.C. : Government Printing Office, 1903), 43.

[6] Minutes of the Board of Regents, Meeting #86, January 26,1900, 440.

land office.[7] Income for the AUF continued to increase through grazing leases and other surface use, but the PUF was not growing and, therefore, neither was its income. To encourage exploration the university in 1913, 1917, and 1919 prodded the legislature into amending mineral prospecting laws, but, nonetheless, until the 1920s there was no significant mineral discovery on university lands.

Also from the 1890s through the 1920s, the UT regents had to spar with Texas A&M and Prairie View over the Permanent University Fund. The Texas A&M Board of Directors had made repeated attempts to separate from UT, both administratively and financially. Its members also hoped to obtain a fair portion of the PUF. During the 1890s, A&M College only received $500 per year from the PUF. The last time it attempted to obtain a greater share of PUF money occurred in 1894 when the board of directors asked for two-fifths of the university lands. The UT regents killed the proposal because they reasoned that there was only enough money to support one "university of the first class." The A&M directors, however, were relentless in pursuing a legal separation from UT, and the matter was revisited periodically over the following years, some periods with greater frequency than others.

Although investment of the PUF was still handled by the office of the state comptroller, the University of Texas regents took an interest in how it was invested. In January 1903, the regents resolved to give support and aid for a bill submitted to the Twenty-eighth Legislature to expand the different types of investments that were permissible for the PUF. On February 12, Regent Thomas Watt Gregory reported to the board on the failure of the bill to pass the

---

[7] Chapter 102, <u>General Laws of the State of Texas Passed at the Regular Session of the Twenty-Seventh Legislature</u> (Austin: Von Boeckmann, Schultz & Co., 1901), 266-267.

legislature. He expressed his opinion that any change in the means of investing the PUF had to be made by a constitutional amendment.[8] The board of regents secretary, John J. Lane, wrote that same year that, if the university was to grow, it was in need of permanent revenues, either through a university tax or a more active endowment: the PUF.[9] There was a clear sense among them that, if the PUF was ever going to amount to anything, the regents would have to make it happen.

There was little activity regarding the PUF until 1909 when the A&M directors launched the first of many attempts to obtain a sizable share of the PUF. The directors sent an invitation to the UT regents asking to hold a joint meeting of the two boards and "if possible to reach an amicable agreement as to the disposition of the revenue arising from the permanent university fund."[10] Once again the two boards negotiated the division of the PUF. A fair settlement, according to A&M supporters, was to give the school at Bryan its independence and half of the university lands. The two boards decided to seek a constitutional amendment to provide for separation from UT, but despite the support of state gubernatorial candidate Oscar Branch Colquitt, their efforts failed in the lower house. In 1911, the two boards met again at the Driskill Hotel in Austin, both sides seeking an administrative and financial separation. Again, the two boards made no progress.[11] By

---

[8] Minutes of the Board of Regents, Meeting #103, February 12, 1903, 16.

[9] John J. Lane, "History of Education in Texas," 187-189.

[10] Henry C. Dethloff, A Centennial History of Texas A&M University, 1876-1976, vol. 2 (College Station: Texas A&M University Press, 1975), 231.

[11] Minutes of the Texas A&M Board of Directors, June 7-9, 1909, II, 161; Dethloff, History of A&M, 231.

the next year, however, it became evident that the two schools saw settlement in completely different terms.

While A&M supporters sought half of the university lands and half of the PUF, some UT supporters felt that consolidating the two institutions was the preferable solution. Proponents of consolidation, or the "one university plan," pointed out that the two schools were duplicating each others' academic efforts. The faculty at Bryan, they argued, should become part of the university faculty and move to Austin. The consolidation plan gained support from the highest levels of government. President Woodrow Wilson's recently appointed Secretary of Agriculture, David Franklin Houston, who had served as president of both UT and A&M, advocated the merging of two institutions.[12] Not all state officials agreed with Houston's assessment, but his words carried great weight for consolidation supporters and proved disheartening for the supporters of the A&M separation plan.

Governor Oscar Colquitt did not support consolidation, but he provided ample ammunition to the detractors of the A&M separation plan. Colquitt pointed out that the A&M College was much more expensive to run than the university, for its technical and scientific programs cost more than the university's liberal arts programs. He also pointed out that part of A&M's funding came from the federal government, while UT's was paid almost entirely by the state. Colquitt offered his own proposal for a constitutional amendment to create a separate Texas A&M College with its own board of regents, and 400,000 acres of the university lands, or an equal amount of stock purchased with money from university land. Similar plans offered during the 1913 legislative session included a proposal to

---

[12] Benedict, "Source Book," 479; Dethloff, History of Texas A&M, 235.

make A&M independent of UT with 600,000 acres and a property tax for the support of all colleges and universities.[13] In spite of the efforts of both institutions, no remedy from the legislature was forthcoming.

Finding such an outcome unacceptable, the A&M directors in 1915 sent the UT regents another separation proposal, one similar to the 1913 proposal. The so-called "Sackett Resolution" had the support of Governor James E. Ferguson. The resolution asked that A&M's status as a branch of the university be changed, but the effort was to no avail.[14] In January 1915, Ferguson himself called for lawmakers to consolidate the two institutions under an elaborate plan that he had devised. Texas voters in the general election on July 24, 1915, rejected the proposed amendment.

In the spring 1916, Governor Ferguson launched a barrage of accusations concerning what he saw as mismanagement of funds and unethical behavior on the part of University of Texas officials. When he vetoed the university's entire budget, his actions backfired, and on September 24, 1917, the senate voted for Ferguson's impeachment and removal from office.[15] Less than a month later, the state comptroller notified the regents that income going into the PUF was almost $200,000 per year.[16]

---

[13] Ibid, 485-487.

[14] Minutes of the Board of Regents, Meeting # 168, October 27, 1914, 22-24

[15] Benedict, "Source Book," 512, 528,539, 548-549; Kenneth E. Hendrickson, Jr., The Chief Executives of Texas: From Stephen F. Austin to John B. Connally, Jr. (College Station: Texas A&M University Press, 1995), 161-162.

[16] Minutes of the Board of Regents, Meeting #185, October 23, 1917, 26; Joe B. Franz, The Forty Acre Follies: An Opinionated

The large amount of income was welcome news to a board of regents weary from their battle with Governor Ferguson over operating expenses.

At an informal meeting in January 1919, the UT regents and the A&M directors decided to press Governor William P. Hobby for another separation amendment. Such a measure, introduced in the Thirty-sixth Legislature, proposed that the PUF be divided between UT, A&M, and Prairie View College. The bill prescribed that the University of Texas retain the right to two-thirds of the PUF and AUF while Texas A&M College got one-third. Prairie View was left in the unenviable position of getting whatever the A&M directors deemed appropriate. There was also a provision calling for the sale of the university lands and the proceeds divided as above.[17] The amendment did not pass. Land values during the period were fairly low and any gains from the sale of university lands would have been short-term.

As they looked for ways to produce income from the land, the University of Texas Board of Regents also began to look at how it might manipulate the system to put more money in the AUF. On April 27, 1920, the board members discussed the possibility of making lease money for mineral rights part of the AUF, but the royalty paid on oil and gas remained part of the PUF. The regents understood that AUF money was to be spent only for construction or permanent improvements. The idea was to put money directly in the AUF so the legislature could appropriate it to the regents for those purposes.[18] The effort to route

---

History of the University of Texas (Austin: Texas Monthly Press, Inc., 1983), 75-81.

[17] Ibid., Meeting #190, January 29, 1919, 274-275.

[18] Ibid., Meeting #197, April 27, 1920, 2.

mineral lease money into the AUF shows how the regents could manipulate a loophole.

In 1921, several important events for both the PUF and university lands took place. On January 5, the regents change the declared valuation for university lands to $10,000,000. They discussed their unwillingness to sell university lands, despite calls from some officials to do just that. They reiterated their "no sale" policy at their February meeting. In the fall, the UT regents and the A&M directors held a joint meeting at Houston once again to discuss the separation of the two institutions and the division of the PUF. This time the regents politely rebuked the directors.[19] The discovery of oil, however, only intensified the A&M directors' efforts.

The financial situation of the University of Texas changed dramatically when on May 23, 1923, the Santa Rita #1 struck oil in Reagan County. Initial production reached over one hundred barrels per day. The oil sold for $1.25 per barrel. The flurry of activity started by the Santa Rita discovery is extraordinary. Exploration permits poured in, but a sufficient administrative infrastructure did not exist. Rail-to-refinery capacity and on-site storage facilities proved insufficient. The regents were behind the curve in dealing with the extraordinary amount of production. Thus, in the following years the major oil companies quickly entered the scene and provided the badly needed infrastructure.

The regents' and Saner's inability to keep a proper accounting of oil and gas royalties led in 1924 to the hiring of Saner's first full-time assistant, Haywood Hughes. Because Saner's office was in Dallas, Hughes worked in

---

[19] Ibid., Meeting #200, January 5, 1921, 429; ibid., Meeting #208, October 21, 1921, 1-2.

the field from a little shack at Texon in West Texas. His job was to keep an accounting of oil production to ensure the proper payment of royalties to the PUF.[20] He was successful and the PUF grew rapidly. But Judge Saner and his gauger were overwhelmed by the increased workload.

In the spring of 1925, the Thirty-ninth legislature passed a bill providing for the deposit of mineral lease rentals into the AUF. Despite the objections of many state officials, Governor Miriam Ferguson signed the bill into law.[21] Admitting ambiguity regarding the constitutionality of the law, Ferguson justified her action by pointing to the deplorable conditions of campus buildings and shacks. Ferguson once proclaimed that to the average man who sees the deplorable buildings at the university, it would appear that the state is making an effort to make money and not build up higher education.[22] Ferguson, like many other state officials, believed that the UT endowment was not being used to its maximum potential.

With mineral lease money pouring into the AUF, the Texas A&M College Board of Directors decided to take legal action to secure their claim on a portion of any appropriations from it. At a meeting on September 21, 1925, board members decided to attempt an out-of-court settlement with the UT regents, but in the event that failed, they were prepared to let the courts settle the matter. The

---

[20] Ibid.

[21] Norman D. Brown, Hood, Bonnet, and Little Brown Jug, Texas Politics, 1921-1928 (College Station: Texas A&M University Press, 1984), 260.

[22] Ibid., Meeting #240, June 9, 1925; ibid., Meeting #242, September 17, 1925; ibid., Meeting #243, October 19, 1925; David F. Prindle, "Oil and the Permanent University Fund: The Early Years," Southwestern Historical Quarterly vol. 86 no. 2 (October, 1982): 287.

PUF totaled more than $5,000,000 and received a revenue of over $250,000 per month. The UT people insinuated that it might take a court to settle the matter, leaving A&M directors with little recourse. The A&M officials retained Nelson Phillips, a well-respected former judge, but he advised negotiation. The two boards held another joint meeting in Austin before a football game set for Thanksgiving Day in 1926. They established a joint committee of six people, three from each school, to find a solution for separation and to settle their respective claims for a share of the AUF. The subsequent meetings did not produce a legal split of the two institutions.[23] The UT regents, it appeared, politely rebuked the A&M College's claims to a share of the AUF, constitutional or not. The university it seemed, wanted to negotiate further about A&M's share of the AUF.

Following the discovery of oil on university lands, the UT regents embarked on a huge building program in Austin, one that reflected the ever-increasing value of the PUF. The regents spent almost $6 million from 1925 to 1936 on buildings and facilities. The same period saw enrollments at Texas institutions of higher education increase from 5,000 in 1925 to more than 14,700 in 1936.[24] Almost fifty years after the establishment of the PUF and AUF, the regents, finally, were using substantial proceeds from university lands on bricks and mortar.

---

[23] Dethloff, History of Texas A&M, 416-417; The Eagle, Bryan, Texas, November 27, 1926, December 15, 1926; Minutes of the Board of Directors, September 21, 1925, IV, 2; ibid., November 25, 1925, IV, 62; Dallas Morning News, November 25, 1926.

[24] John L. Beckham, "The Permanent University Fund: Land, Oil and Politics," unpublished manuscript on file at the Center for American History, The University of Texas at Austin, Texas, 1981.

Also because of the increased revenue from petroleum production, some state officials believed that putting mineral lease money into the AUF, rather than into the PUF, was an improper way to manage that resource. Attorney General Dan Moody thought so, too, and he filed suit against State Treasurer Gregory Hatcher to resolve the issue once and for all. Moody hoped the court would compel Hatcher to place the sum of $1,594,562 in the PUF rather than the AUF. The Texas Supreme Court issued a decision in the case, State v. Hatcher, on March 10, 1926. The state high court decided that minerals were part of the *corpus* of the estate, and they were permanent. The removal of the minerals, therefore, was the removal of a permanent part of the land. The court reversed the earlier statute, the one signed by Governor Miriam Ferguson. It had said mineral lease income be paid to the AUF.[25] From this point forward, that is after the Supreme Court decision in 1926, all petroleum-related revenue, including bonuses and rentals, went to the PUF.

Besides the legal wrangling over the proper fund for mineral lease money, there was growing concern that operators did not pay all royalties owed to the PUF. In 1926, the UT regents hired the auditing firm of Ernst and Ernst of Houston to determine if there were any royalty accounting problems. The auditors reported that the university lost money because the Reagan County Purchasing Company (RCPC), which operated a gas processing plant near Big Lake, levied a questionable gathering charge for processing gas from university land. The Texon Oil and Land Company, the gas producer, paid royalties based on the sale price of the gas, which did not include the gathering charge paid to the RCPC. A legal suit followed, and in January 1927, the regents asked Attorney

---

[25] State v. Hatcher, Texas Supreme Court, no. 4506, March 10, 1926, 1-5.

General Claude Pollard to discuss possible litigation against the RCPC. In the fall of 1927, as the case State v. Reagan County Purchasing Company got closer, the regents got word that RCPC officials wanted to try to work out a compromise. The two parties held a meeting in Dallas on November 17 and reached a settlement. The defendants agreed to reimburse the University of Texas for any and all lost revenue. The university got $1 million to add to the PUF, a one-eighth royalty on the sale price, and one-eighth of the RCPC's profit. The company was also forbidden from charging the university the bogus gathering fee that was at the root of the entire problem.[26]

Although there was a great deal of money going into the PUF, the money did not immediately translate into construction funds. To obtain some quick capital needed to pay for building expansion, the UT regents in 1928 asked the attorney general if they, as the governing body of University of Texas and the stewards of investing the PUF, had the authority to issue bonds against the fund's value.[27] Attorney General Pollard issued an opinion that the regents had such authority: that is, to issue bonds against the "income" from PUF investments, the primary revenue source for the AUF. In April the regents began looking at the cost of their building program, and in October they discussed a loan for improvement to university facilities.[28]

Petroleum production in West Texas continued to increase to the point that the existing management structure could not possibly keep up. The UT regents lobbied hard

---

[26] Haigh, Land, Oil, and Education, 148-149.

[27] Minutes of the Board of Regents, Meeting #262, February 28, 1928, 193.

[28] Ibid., Meeting #263, April 9, 1928; ibid., Meeting #266, October 1, 1928.

for the lawmakers to act. In 1929, the Forty-first Legislature passed "Chapter 282," which created the management organizations for capitalizing on university lands for the purpose of increasing revenues for the PUF. The act also created the Board for Lease of University Lands to conduct sales for mineral leases and the University Lands Survey Office to secure legal claim to the boundaries of university lands. The management agencies created under the law proved to be vitally important for the goal of increasing the value of the PUF. With the major changes going into effect, Judge R. E. L. Saner decided to retire. The regents promoted oil supervisor Elliot J. Compton to head the new University Lands Surface Office. Under his leadership, the surface department monitored grazing leases as well as petroleum-related surface activity. The regents named Hal P. Bybee, Director of the Bureau of Economic Geology, to head the University Lands Geology Office. The geology office oversaw all petroleum-related operations on university lands and assisted with information gathering for mineral sales.[29]

In August 1929, with the PUF growing by a quarter of a million dollars a month, the Texas A&M College Board of Directors asked the attorney general if he thought A&M had a legitimate claim to a share of the PUF investment income, which was in the AUF. He said he believed it did have a claim, which made more serious the board's threats to file legal action.

In early 1930, the UT and A&M boards agreed to meet in Austin. There they had an amicable exchange and a mutual commitment to work out a compromise on the issue of A&M claims to AUF appropriations. The parties agreed to form a committee of three regents and three directors to settle the issue. In March they discussed a

---

[29] Haigh, Land, Oil, and Education, 177-183.

proposal for a one-third and two-third split of the AUF appropriations. No agreement was reached, but they planned to continue trying to work out a solution. In January 1931, the UT regents gave support to a bill to cut A&M College in on a share of the AUF. The bill passed as an emergency matter effective April 8, 1931. Per the agreement the University of Texas retained all grazing lease income, sole management over investment of the PUF, and the sale of mineral leases. Texas A&M College got one-third of AUF appropriations, exclusive of grazing lease income from university lands.[30] Both UT and A&M would have to join together in the following decades to fend off attacks of other institutions for a share of AUF appropriations.

With mineral royalties flooding into the PUF, an important but misguided development took place in 1930. Texas voters amended Section 11 of Article 7 of the state constitution to allow the University of Texas Board of Regents to invest part of the PUF in bonds it issued against the PUF's own value. The measure made some lawmakers uneasy, but the voters had spoken. The regents briefly invested the PUF in PUF bonds, but the policy was short lived. Almost immediately opponents launched efforts to reverse the law. In 1932, voters passed another constitutional amendment that deleted the questionable provision. The regents could no longer invest the PUF in bonds backed by its own value.[31]

The ill effects of the great depression were not yet being felt in Texas when, in July, the UT regents expressed

---

[30] Chapter 42, General Laws of the State of Texas Passed by the Regular Session of the Forty-Second Legislature (1931), 63-65; Minutes of the Board of Directors, January 5, 1931, IV, 160-163; Dethloff, History of Texas A&M, 418-419.

[31] Beckham, "The Permanent University Fund," 18.

concern that casing head gas, a bi-product of drilling operations, was being allowed to escape into the atmosphere. J. R. Lattimer of Fort Worth told the regents that they were losing "enormous values" by not conserving the gas for a future time when its value was sure to rise. Lattimer suggested capture of the gas at the well head and piping it to a processing plant or collection facility. The regents recognized that the cost could be passed on to operators through a clause in mineral lease contracts requiring them to do as Lattimer suggested.[32]

Another important development toward conservation of resources during the down market took place on August 27, 1930, when the Texas Railroad Commission (RRC) issued its first state mandatory pro-rationing order, limiting statewide production to 750,000 barrels per day. After the Daisy Bradford discovery in October opened up vast oil fields in East Texas, oil supplies soared, and when demand did not rise commensurately, oil prices plummeted.[33] Operators ignored the RRC's production limits, prompting the UT regents to ask the legislature to conserve natural resources on university lands by passing a law to force operators to stop producing while petroleum prices were so low. Because the regents collected the royalty on the price the operator got for the oil or gas, royalties remained low. At a sealed bid sale held on July 31, 1931, the Board for Lease of University Lands only offered one 1,280-acre tract for lease, and the total bonus received for it was $640, an average price of fifty-cents per acre.

---

[32] Minutes of the Board of Regents, Meeting #281, July 16, 1930, 200.

[33] David F. Prindle, Petroleum Poltics and the Texas Railroad Commission (Austin: University of Texas Press, 1981), 21.

Because revenues from royalties continued to flow into the PUF, the University of Texas fared quite well during the depression years. On June 13, 1931, the UT regents discussed the possibility of borrowing funds for building purposes and buying municipal bonds to invest the PUF. The building program expansion resulted in the construction of nine new buildings between 1933 and 1939. Texas A&M witnessed similar growth, though far less extensive. Between 1931 and 1937, the A&M directors spent over $2.5 million on new buildings and improvements. Most of the money came from the AUF, but the directors supplemented AUF appropriations with funds from the Federal Emergency Relief Administration (FERA) and the Public Works Administration (PWA).[34] Clearly, the impact of the AUF money was important for the facilities of UT and Texas A&M.

As the price of oil began to climb, some officials looked at ways to increase revenue for the PUF by manipulating the existing system. In 1935, Major J. R. Parten, a member of the University of Texas Board of Regents, first brought up the possibility of a change to oral auction for the sale of mineral leases for university lands. The legislature amended Chapter 282, which allowed the Board for Lease of University Lands to choose between sealed and oral bidding. The Board for Lease held the first public auction of minerals on July 20, 1936. The highest bid for a single tract was $48,000 and total bonus revenue was $300,600.[35] The Board for Lease used the oral bid process successfully between 1936 and 1986. Representatives of all the major oil companies and a small number of independent operators usually attended the events, which were often exciting and interesting affairs.

---

[34] Dethloff, History of Texas A&M, 421-423.
[35] Haigh, Land, Oil, and Education, 256-258, 267, 329.

Bonus revenues reached $1,312,375 in 1942. Bonuses totaled over $3,000,000 in 1943 and topped out at $5,900,800 in 1947. Two record sales in 1953 brought in $16,238,000 in July and $10,372,500 in December in bonus revenue for the PUF.[36]

The rise in petroleum production from the late 1930s to the 1980s was largely due to new geophysical techniques, improved drilling equipment, and deeper tests. The years of World War II saw a significant rise in production on university lands, but revenues remained moderate because of wartime price controls. In 1946, fuel prices shot up after President Harry Truman ended price controls, and revenue from minerals poured into the PUF. The value of the PUF continued to rise in proportion to the increase in oil production. As drilling continued to pick up, such communities as Midland, Odessa, and Monahans saw their populations grow. An influx of oil company personnel and their families was responsible.[37]

In May 1948, the A&M board created the Texas A&M College System. A chancellor, Gibb Gilchrist, headed the new system. Over the next decade the board of directors undertook a second construction program. From 1948 to 1958, the directors spent more than $15 million dollars on new facilities.[38]

Meanwhile, in 1949, the Fifty-first Legislature passed "Chapter 186," which gave the UT regents the right to capitalize on minerals other than oil and gas on university land. Any revenue generated from minerals had to go into

---

[36] Ibid., 267-268; Patricia Anne Malin, "Oil and Gas Leasing of Texas State Lands: School Lands and University Lands" (Ph.D. diss., University of Texas, 1982), 2-4, 272.

[37] Ibid., 327-331.

[38] Dethloff, History of Texas A&M, 528, 533-534.

the PUF. There were only two such minerals known to be present: sulfur and potash. Another sub-surface resource, water, was also known to be present on university lands. In the following decades sulfur and water became important sources of revenue for the PUF. Sulfur production contributed over $8 million to the PUF. Water contracts were far less lucrative with each of the half dozen contracts bringing in a minimum royalty of $40,000 per year.[39] The sub-surface resources, such as oil and gas, were considered a part of the *corpus* of the estate and the income was deposited into the PUF.

The growth of the PUF in the post-war period prompted several important developments. The question of allowing the University of Texas Board of Regents and the Texas A&M College Board of Directors to invest the PUF in corporate stocks and bonds became an issue, and opponents defeated the proposals to make the change in 1951 and 1953. In 1956, Texas voters passed a constitutional amendment to Section 11 of Article 7 of the state constitution which expanded the bonding authority of the UT regents and the A&M directors from twenty to thirty percent of the PUF's value. The amendment, entitled "Section 11a," stipulated that no more than one percent of the PUF may be invested in any one corporation, and no more than five percent of a corporation's voting stock may be owned by the university. Stocks eligible for purchase also had to be
incorporated in the United States and have paid dividends over the last ten years. It further stated that no more than fifty percent of PUF investments shall be in corporate

---

[39] Water Exploration and Development Contract # 70, University Lands Administrative Files, January 11, 1957; Minutes of the Board of Regents, Meeting #559, January 11, 1957, 443-445.

stocks and bonds.[40] After 1956, investment returns were astronomical. At the same time, the Board for Lease of University Lands raised the royalty on oil from one-eighth to one-sixth, further increasing the principal of the PUF.

As they became more valuable monetarily, the PUF and AUF became major political issues. In 1958, the UT regents and the A&M directors issued a joint resolution to resist a proposed resolution that would allow funds from the PUF to be used for purposes other than higher education. The resolution pressured lawmakers to defeat the measure, which they did.

Later that year, at the bidding of renowned professor Walter Prescott Webb, the original walking beam and bull wheels from the Santa Rita #1 were erected on the University of Texas' main campus in Austin. The walking beam and bull wheels presence are a testament to the great wealth and opportunity that petroleum provided to the two preeminent public institutions of higher education in Texas.

With mineral royalties and investment income climbing yearly, the UT regents were well situated to continue expanding the various facilities of the University of Texas System. After many years of leasing office space, the regents began to advocate the construction of a permanent building to house the University Lands Surface Office and University Lands Geology Office in Midland. State Senator W. E. "Pete" Snelson of Midland in 1966 wrote an appropriations bill to build the Bybee Building out of AUF money.[41]

---

[40] "Section 11a Article 7," Vernon's Texas Codes Annotated, vol. 2, Sections 65.01 to 129 (West Group, 2002), 437-438.

[41] State Senator W. E. "Pete" Snelson (retired), interview with the author, March 25, 2002, tape recording.

In 1968, the Section 11a of Article 7 of the state constitution was amended to expand the number of ways the PUF could be invested. The amendment shortened the length of time from ten to five years a company was allowed to pay dividends before the regents could invest in that stock. Lawmakers also added a provision to allow for investment in "first lien real estate mortgage securities."[42] Investment returns continued to grow, topping $100,000,000 in 1970.

In 1971, the legislature passed an act to allow the UT regents and A&M directors to use the PUF for purposes other than debt retirement and permanent improvements to their respective campuses. Until that time, the AUF had to be first used to pay the interest on mature PUF bonds. The new rule stated that the governing bodies could use the money for any purpose they deemed legitimate for the function of the schools. The action provided flexibility in spending AUF money, something yet unheard of in the history of Texas higher education.[43] The law drew criticism from fiscal conservatives who feared the institutions might spend it on frivolous pursuits.

The legislature in August 1963 approved a name change for A&M from the Agricultural and Mechanical College of Texas to "Texas A&M University." Tradition loving Aggies found the name change unpalatable, but A&M officials believed the change would improve the prestige of the institution. In time, most A&M supporters came to accept the change. A similar name change took place twelve years later when the Texas A&M University Board of Directors changed its name to the Texas A&M

---

[42] "Section 11a Article 7," Vernon's Texas Codes Annotated, 437-438; Beckham, "The Permanent University Fund," 22.

[43] Beckham, "The Permanent University Fund," 22.

University System Board of Regents.[44] The changes are evidence of the growth and progress of the institution due in part to increased revenues from university lands for the PUF.

In 1973 and 1974, lawmakers in Texas set out to revise the 1876 Texas Constitution. The UT and A&M governing bodies took a particular interest in how the revisions would affect distribution and investment of the PUF. They were adamant that if it were divided among all colleges and universities in Texas, the PUF would not make any difference in a single one of those institutions. There was simply not enough money to go around. Instead, UT and A&M officials proposed opening the PUF to all institutions within their respective systems. Neither school was exactly ready to voluntarily make the PUF available to these institutions. To the relief of UT and A&M supporters, Texas voters rejected the constitutional revision, and the PUF remained inviolate. But constitutional revision revealed that the PUF was vulnerable to possible alteration.

In 1975, debate over the PUF again arose. The Texas Observer and the Dallas Morning News each ran stories about the Texas A&M University Board of Regents' supposedly lavish spending spree for a new meeting facility. The papers revealed the new building cost $1.4 million, with an extra $700,000 spent to furnish the facility. The stories increased calls for stricter accountability in spending AUF appropriations and prompted some state officials to call for the abolishment of the PUF altogether.[45]

---

[44] Dethloff, History of Texas A&M, 571, 584.
[45] Kaye Northcott, "Its on you: The biggest Aggie joke of all," Texas Observer (March 28, 1975): 1-3; Dallas Morning News, April, 13, 1975.

203

As a result of the criticism regarding PUF spending, in 1978 Attorney General John L. Hill issued an opinion stating that interest from the PUF, which went into the AUF, under sections 7, 17, and 18 of the Texas Constitution, must first retire bond obligations and then finance permanent improvements.[46] With attorney general opinions carrying the force of law, the UT and A&M regents had no choice but to comply.

Of far greater concern to the University of Texas and Texas A&M University was a proposal to repeal the state's ten-cent *ad valorem* property tax, as called for in Section 17 of Article 7 of the state constitution. The tax of $.10 cents per $100 dollar valuation benefited seventeen non-PUF colleges by providing money for construction and permanent improvements. The UT and A&M regents feared that if the *ad valorem* tax were repealed, the other state colleges would then demand a share of the PUF. Pressure from UT and A&M supporters convinced Governor Dolph Briscoe not to introduce the bill to repeal the *ad valorem* tax in the legislature.[47] Governor-elect William Clements, on the other hand, said he would call a special legislative session to settle the matter of establishing a construction fund for non-PUF schools.

In 1979 Senators A. R. Schwartz and Bob Vale made a more serious attempt to settle the problem of generating revenues for the construction costs. They introduced a resolution to divide the then $1.2 billion PUF between UT, A&M, and all the schools in their respective systems. This was essentially what the governing boards UT and A&M proposed as part of the constitutional revision of 1973. The so-called "Schwartz-Vale proposal" laid out a plan for the

---

[46] Opinion of the Texas Attorney General. John L. Hill, 1978, No. H-1167.

[47] The Eagle, Bryan, Texas, July 17, 1978.

establishment of a State Higher Education Assistance Fund, or SHEAF, to fund construction and permanent improvements at the seventeen non-PUF schools.

The *corpus* of the SHEAF would come from legislative appropriations expected to cost $40 million annually. Lawmakers projected that the SHEAF would amount to $161.4 million over the next half a decade. The Schwartz-Vale bill passed the Senate, but late in the session, supporters of Prairie View A&M asked for one-sixth of Texas A&M's one-third of the AUF. The move by Prairie View supporters caused the Texas A&M University Board of Regents to withdraw their support for the measure altogether, leaving Prairie View's request unanswered and their financial concerns unresolved.[48]

In the closing minutes of the legislative session, Rep. Wayne Peveto of Orange introduced a bill that reduced the *ad valorem* valuation to .0001 per $100 dollars and the measure passed. At this rate, the *ad valorem* tax cost more to collect than it was worth. Peveto estimated that the tax would generate just over $200 per year. The lowered tax rate left seventeen Texas colleges and universities without adequate funds to finance building projects.[49] In response, seventeen schools filed suit to force the State of Texas to collect the tax at the previous rate of $.10 cents per $100 dollar valuation, and if that was not done, they wanted to alter the distribution of the AUF.

Meanwhile, pressure to reduce state spending across the board caused lawmakers to give such duties as accounting for state agency lands to the agency to which

---

[48] The Battalion, May 30, 1979; Beckham, "The Permanent University Fund," 29.

[49] The Eagle, Bryan, Texas, May, 8, 1979; Beckham, "The Permanent University Fund," 30.

they belonged. For many years, accounting of university land income was handled in the General Land Office. The UT regents opened their own accounting office, called the Audit of Oil and Gas Production, back in the 1920s. The audit office kept a separate accounting of income from resource capitalization on university lands and was a way to keep the operators honest. In 1979, however, the Sixty-sixth Legislature transferred accounting responsibilities from the General Land Office to the University of Texas Board of Regents. The regents, in turn, established the University Lands Accounting Office to keep a record of production volume, royalty payments, rentals, and bonuses. The first director of University Lands Accounting was Ben Campbell, who left after one year to start a private CPA firm. George Clark replaced Campbell in 1982. Bob Conrad and Bryce Bales, who managed the office through 1996, followed.[50] Popular pressure to reduce spending for higher education in Texas continued, as did attempts to alter the PUF, for much of the next two decades.

In 1980, State Representative Wilhelmina Delco introduced a bill to "clarify" Texas A&M's constitutional status as a branch of the University of Texas. The bill was actually a back-door attempt to establish the validity of Prairie View's claim on a share of the PUF as a branch of A&M. Delco proposed giving the traditionally African American school, Prairie View, one-sixth of the AUF appropriations and letting UT and A&M split the other five-sixths. The Austin American Statesman reported that members of the House black caucus were prepared to introduce other bills to remedy Prairie View's financial

---

[50] Patsy Neidig, University Lands Accounting Office Land Records Supervisor, personal communication, December 2, 2003. Neidig went to work for the Audit of Oil and Gas Production from 1959, and is still employed by University Lands Accounting in 2003.

woes. For example, Representative Ron Wilson of Houston called for switching Prairie View to the UT system and with it Prairie View's share of the AUF. None of these measures made any headway during the rather contentious session and were carried over into the succeeding legislature.[51]

In 1981, the legislature again addressed the issue of construction funding for non-PUF institutions in Texas. The Senate Education Committee, known as SCR 101, put together a report offering a plan to fund construction for non-PUF schools. State Senator W. E. "Pete" Snelson, committee chairman, introduced two bills based on the SCR 101 recommendations. The bills proposed to double tuition costs from $4 per credit hour for in-state residents to $8. Tuition for non-state residents would be raised from $40 to $80 per credit hour. Even more drastic were Snelson's proposed increases at medical schools. Tuition jumped from $400 to $3,600 for Texas residents and $1,200 to $7,200 for non-residents. The bills also provided for the establishment of the Higher Education Construction Fund, which would collect half of the tuition at all state institutions as a dedicated building fund for the non-PUF schools. The tuition increase was expected to raise $52 million per year, roughly equivalent to the amount expected from a revised *ad valorem* tax.[52] Not everyone in the legislature was sold on Snelson's proposals.

---

[51] Austin American Statesman, November 18, 1980; The Eagle, Bryan, Texas, November 19, 1980 ; Houston Post, June 18, 1981; Amy Johnson, "The Haves and the Have-Nots," Texas Observer (July 10, 1981) : 4-8.

[52] Snelson, interview, March 25, 2002 ; Austin American Statesman, May 25, 1982.

Still another proposal devised in the House during the 1981 legislative session was introduced as HJR 111. Speaker Bill Clayton was responsible. HJR 111 called for revival of the *ad valorem* tax but at a reduced rate. The revived tax would be collected at a rate of $0.03 per $100 dollar valuation. Clayton proposed that seventy percent of the revenue be set aside for an endowment fund for construction at non-PUF schools. The other thirty per cent of the revenue would fund current construction and renovation projects on the campuses of the same institutions. The revived tax was expected to raise $2.13 billion between 1983 and 1992, and when the fund reached $2 billion the tax would be abolished. At that time the non-PUF schools would be allowed to issue bonds against the fund's value.[53] Neither Snelson's nor Clayton's efforts passed during the 1981 legislative session and the issue of funding for education became even more urgent over the following decade. Their efforts are important because they signal the proposal of even more drastic measures regarding control of the PUF and dispersal of the AUF.

With no remedy forthcoming in the legislature, the seventeen non-PUF institutions, as promised, filed suit over the loss of funds from the reduction of the *ad valorem* tax. In spring 1982, Governor Clements called a special session of the legislature to address the grievances of the suit. A week before the legislature convened in the special session, however, the litigant schools agreed to forego a legal solution to wait and see what the 1983 legislature would do about the problem. As the session opened, Senator Lloyd Doggett (D) of Austin bluntly asked the governor why they were there at a cost of $60,000 per day if the matter of the lawsuit was on hold until the following year. Clements

---

[53] The Battalion, April 2, 1981; Beckham, "The Permanent University Fund," 31.

stated they needed to address the question of the *ad valorem* tax. He favored a constitutional amendment to repeal the tax, and he also favored a separate dedicated construction fund for the seventeen non-PUF schools. Senator Pete Snelson of Midland offered a constitutional amendment to repeal the *ad valorem* tax. The measure sailed through the House and a Senate committee on education, but it failed to pass a final vote. The session ended with no repeal of *ad valorem*, with no building fund, but with a storm of criticism and finger pointing.[54]

Renewed threats to divide up the PUF began almost as soon as the 1982 special session ended. Senator Carl Parker (D) of Port Arthur believed a "raid" on the PUF would occur eventually. There were also threats to let the courts settle the matter if the legislature did not. In November, Governor Clements lost to Mark White in the gubernatorial race, and the new governor inherited the highly volatile issue. The Bryan Eagle reported that the chairman of the Higher Education Coordinating Board, ex-Governor Preston Smith, wrote a letter to Governor elect White. Smith urged White to consider supporting his proposal that schools within the UT and A&M systems should not get any money from general revenues until lawmakers and the voters decided whether or not to open up the PUF to other UT and A&M system schools. He explained that such a stance would be his recommendation to the legislature.[55]

By December 1982, the UT and A&M officials, apparently nervous about having to share the PUF with all Texas colleges and universities, offered a proposal to cut

---

[54] Ibid; Dallas Morning News, June 6, 1982; Snelson, interview, March 25, 2002.

[55] The Eagle, Bryan, Texas, November 20, 1982.

Prairie View in on the PUF. Many saw the move as the emergence of a preemptive strategy. Under the UT and A&M proposal, which required a constitutional amendment, Prairie View A&M would get $22 million annually in construction funds.[56] The plan was a good one and it passed, but actual appropriations for Prairie View never exceeded $10 million per year.

The year 1982 was also important regarding the history of the PUF. The sharp decline in the price of oil meant a sharp decline in revenue for the PUF. Mineral sales revenue peaked that year and declined thereafter. Declining oil prices signaled a change in the nature of the University of Texas' resource capitalization system. The UT regents came to realize that high oil and gas revenues were not a perpetual certainty. Thus, slowly over the next decade investment of the PUF became a higher source of income than mineral production.

In January 1983, State Representatives Carl Parker and Wilhelmina Delco introduced two proposals for constitutional amendments: one to spread the wealth of the PUF, the other to guarantee substantial building funds for non-PUF schools. College leaders from throughout Texas endorsed the measures, and many state officials agreed that a compromise must be reached. A combination of desperation and pressure from constituents after the repeal of the *ad valorem* tax forced compromise. The measure called for the governing boards of UT and A&M had to share AUF appropriations with sixteen other institutions within their respective systems. The legislature would appropriate $125 million a year from general revenue for a building fund for the seventeen institutions excluded from the PUF.[57] In May 1983, both houses of the legislature

---

[56] Ibid., December 21, 1982.
[57] Ft. Worth Star Telegram, January 4, 1983; Dallas Times Herald, January 4, 1983.

passed the compromise amendment, but it had to be ratified by Texas voters in the next general election, over a year away. Proponents of the amendment spent the intermediate period taking their case to the public.[58] Both the University of Texas and Texas A&M University launched publicity campaigns to educate the voters regarding the importance of the proposals.

In the November 6, 1984, election, Texas voters ratified the constitutional amendment to create the Higher Education Assistance Fund (HEAF). It provided building funds for the seventeen non-PUF universities and colleges in Texas. The *corpus* of the HEAF came from an annual $100 million legislative appropriation that began in 1985. The legislature in 1993 increased its yearly appropriation to $175 million, with an additional $50 million annually to a sinking fund for the future creation of the Higher Education Fund endowment.[59] The HEAF did not prove to be an effective measure to end assaults on the PUF.

A second constitutional amendment approved by Texas voters, popularly known as "proposition 2," amended Section 18 of the Texas Constitution to include all sixteen component schools of the UT and A&M systems in any future AUF appropriations. Prairie View got a small portion of Texas A&M's share of AUF appropriations, plus $10 million per year for ten years from UT. The amendment enlarged the UT regents' overall bonding authority from twenty to thirty percent of the PUF's value. There was also an expansion in the number of ways that bond money could be spent. Bond funds could be used for

---

[58] The Eagle, Bryan, Texas, September 23, 1984; The Houston Post, October 11, 1984.

[59] The Houston Post, October 11, 1984.

211

major repair and renovation of buildings, capital equipment like computers and furniture, and library materials.[60] The amendment went into effect in 1986, and afterward there is a discernible shift in regent focus from land management, which already had an exemplary administrative system, to investment management, which they had long managed through the finance committee of the board of regents.

In 1985 oil prices continued to decline and Land Commissioner Gary Mauro, as chairman of the Board for Lease of University Lands, pushed for a return to sealed bids for mineral lease auctions. He believed that public auctions favored the big oil companies and that the state was losing money because oil was selling for $10 a barrel rather than $40. The staff of the University Lands Mineral Interests was divided over Mauro's proposed policy change. Geologist in charge Laddie Long, as well as former geology department head Berte Haigh, thought the change to sealed bids was a bad idea. They understood that oral auctions also enabled participants to bid on tracts they might not have otherwise. For example, if one of the major oil companies showed a keen interest in a particular tract, the other bidders could drive the price up by pushing oil company representatives to bid higher. Not all UT employees and officials were opposed to the change. Wallie Gravitt, as well as regents James L. Powell and Dr. Sterling Fly, believed that in the long run sealed bids would ensure a better return for the university.[61]

The Board for Lease of University Lands held the last oral auction sale, #73, on October 23, 1985, and on

---

[60] Section 11a Article 7, in <u>Vernon's Texas Code's Annotated</u>, 437-438; Beckham, "The Permanent University Fund: Land Oil, and Politics," 22.

[61] Laddie Long and Wallie Gravitt, University Lands Geology Office geologists (retired), interview with author, March 11, 2002, tape recording.

November 10, 1986, it authorized the change to sealed bid auction. Board members held the first sealed bid sale, #74, on January 29, 1987, which was immediately noted to have been a much more mundane affair than the heyday of the oral auctions.[62]

Several developments regarding the Board for Lease of University Lands in the mid-1980s had an important impact on long-term management of the PUF. First, regents Williams and Fly, as members of the Board for Lease, raised the standard royalty on mineral leases from three-sixteenths to one-quarter, despite protestations of industry folk and some of the staff of University Lands Mineral Interests. Head geologist Laddie Long believed the royalty increase would reduce income from lease sales because the industry would find the cost of university lease too steep during the current market slump. Second, the legislature expanded the size of the Board for Lease. At the behest of Land Commissioner Gary Mauro, Texas A&M University got a seat on the board, which gave it a stake in shaping mineral leasing policies. Finally, the legislature passed a provision that made the land commissioner the permanent chairperson for the Board for Lease.[63]

In 1985, the legislature departed radically from traditional policy and discontinued appropriations from general revenues to the University of Texas and Texas A&M University for operating expenses. The schools would have to use the AUF to fund their day-to-day operations. Effectively shut off from legislative appropriations, UT and A&M supporters, opponents of the

---

[62] Mineral Lease Revenue Statistics, Minutes of the Board for Lease of University Lands, 1986-1987.

[63] Hartmann, interview, November 21, 2003: Long and Gravitt, interview, March 11, 2002.

measure, began to say quietly that the PUF might be more of a hindrance than an asset.

In 1986, the state again found itself in a funding crisis and higher education became a prime target. Moreover, there was a great deal of talk in Austin about raiding the PUF. House Speaker Gib Lewis (D) of Fort Worth, declared, "there are no sacred cows," and proposed raiding the PUF and the Public School Fund (PSF) to help solve the state's $3.5 billion budget deficit. Dallas banker and chairman of the University of Texas Board of Regents Jess Hay likened the proposal to selling the state capital.[64] Governor Mark White protested, as did much of the alumni of UT and A&M. Texas A&M officials argued that the reduced revenues would result in the loss of as many as 1,200 jobs throughout the A&M system. The decline in petroleum prices caused a significant decline in revenue going into the PUF. Investment income amounted to $84 million in 1984-1985, but was expected to drop sixteen percent to $71 million for 1985-1986. During the same period, however, investment income rose from $80 million in fiscal year 1984-1985 to $124.8 million in 1985-1986. Relentless lobbying on behalf of the University of Texas, Texas A&M University, and Prairie View A&M University thwarted Lewis' efforts to raid the PUF, but the issue of a separate construction fund for non-PUF schools remained unresolved.[65]

---

[64] The Houston Chronicle, August 17, 1986, 1, 10.

[65] Biemiller, Lawrence, "How the U. of Texas, Flexing Its Political Muscle, Foiled Budget Cutters," Chronicle of Higher Education (June 19, 1985): 12-15; The Houston Chronicle, August 12, 1986, August 17, 1986; The Eagle, August 13, 1986; It is noteworthy that in August 1986 the $3.6 billion PUF briefly surpassed Harvard's endowment of $3.5 billion.

The debate over the PUF continued after Bill Clements took office in early 1987. In fact, Governor Clements immediately raised the intensity of debate when he proposed a controversial budget plan that included a provision similar to Gib Lewis' plan to raid the PUF and PSF. Clements wanted to use capital gains from the two funds, for he thought that the funds would provide $276 million for actual operating expenses in Texas institutions of higher education. Opponents of Clements' plan, including the University of Texas Board of Regents Chairman Jess Hay, feared that withdrawals from the PUF and the PSF would not be a one-time thing. The legislative battle resulted in the PUF again remaining untouched.[66]

In October 1987, the stockmarket prices slid dramatically, thus revealing the competence of the investment system the UT regents had in place. The result for the PUF, according to Mike Patrick, the University of Texas Vice-Chancellor for Asset Management, was a loss of $300 million in stock value. Yet the PUF fared much better than the corresponding PSF, which lost thirty-three percent of the over $1 billion invested in stocks. Patrick noted that a market rally the following day regained most of the loss for both funds, but that the University of Texas would still lose "some potential capital gains that could have been used to purchase more stocks [for the PUF portfolio]." Fortunately for the PUF, a strategy to buy was about to be executed on the Friday before the crash, when the Dow dropped 108 points. Patrick stated that the buy order was not acted on, and, when the crash began, "he did some minor selling, but refrained from making major trades."[67]

---

[66] Ibid., February 8, 1987.
[67] The Eagle, Bryan, Texas, October 22, 1987.

The following month, State Auditor Lawrence F. Alwin reported that many of the non-PUF schools were misspending HEAF appropriations. The Houston Post reported that some schools misused the money to buy hand soap, drill bits, and to pay salaries. Alwin said that the University of Houston had spent so little of the money it was given that the school actually risked violating federal anti-arbitrage law. Conversely, Texas Southern University spent more on projects than it earned on interest. Texas Southern also misappropriated bond proceeds, which were earmarked for operations, to buildings. Many of the schools manipulated the fund by selling huge amounts of long-term bonds backed with fund revenue. Critics noted it was not the original intent for the HEAF to be used to retire bonds. Alwin's report estimated that as much $100 million designated for construction was diverted to other purposes.[68]

As oil revenues continued to stay low and less money went into the PUF, UT officials began to focus on investment. In 1988, an amendment to Section 11b adopted the so-called "prudent person" investment standard for the PUF. The new standard greatly expanded the ways PUF money could be invested, for it stated that the UT regents could invest in anything that any prudent person would view as a sound investment.[69] The new investment standard also caused increased criticism in the following years.

During the 1990 gubernatorial race between A&M supporter Clayton W. Williams, Jr., of Midland and State Treasurer Ann Richards, the PUF's political importance

---

[68] The Houston Post, November 11, 1987.

[69] "HJR No. 5, Sec.2," Acts of the Seventieth Legislature at the Second Called Session (1987).

grew. Williams' support for A&M ensured that he would discourage any attempts to raid the PUF to pay operating expenses for higher education. Richards' victory, however, left the future of the PUF less certain, especially with serious state budgetary battles looming.[70]

Two weeks before a 1991 special legislative session, the House Appropriations Committee planned to target the PUF as a possible source for meeting the $4.68 billion shortfall between revenues and budgeted spending. PUF investments, at the time, were generating over $200 million annually, making it a prime target. State Comptroller John Sharp's auditors, however, came up with a plan to cut the budget by over $4 billion and, thus, leave the PUF alone. House Speaker Gib Lewis, who led the 1986 attempted raid on the PUF, said he favored dividing the money among all Texas public colleges and universities. He also noted, though, that the UT and A&M lobbyists were tenacious when it came to the PUF. He called them the toughest lobbyists in the state. Nonetheless, due to the state's cash flow problem, several members of the House saw a PUF appropriation as a possible source of revenue. Sharp, whose cuts included the abolishment of over 1,000 state jobs, noted that the proponents of the PUF raid were making him look like a moderate. Governor Ann Richards supported Sharp's plan, standing firm on the idea that the PUF should be left alone.[71]

In January 1992, state district court Judge Ben Euresti, Jr., declared the entire Texas higher education system, including the PUF, unconstitutional. Judge Euresti decided the PUF was discriminatory to Tejanos, because

---

[70] The Houston Post, June 27, 1990.

[71] The Houston Chronicle, July 9, 1991; Dallas Morning News, July 12, 1991 ; ibid., July 14, 1991.

the fund was not used by any of the UT or A&M Systems' schools in South Texas. The Judge called for the institutions to correct the situation within a year, but the ruling ultimately had no effect on the PUF.[72]

In 1993, reduced income because of deep state budget cuts resulted in significant layoffs in the Texas A&M University System. Total layoffs at College Station and its component institutions would amount to ten to fifteen percent of system staff. The following year, the UT regents also scaled back the use of AUF money in its budget. The impact of diminished AUF funds in the following years led to streamlining and consolidating the various parts of the entire University of Texas System.[73]

In 1994, an oil and gas analyst employed in the accounting office, auditor Jose Luna, told his boss at University Lands Accounting Office that he believed the PUF was losing revenue. Operators piped casing head gas, a bi-product of petroleum production, from the location to a nearby gas processing plant. The plant would process the gas for transport and keep a percentage as a fee. The operator then sold his product and paid the university the royalty on that amount in cash or in kind. Luna insisted that because operators did not pay royalties on their total casing head gas production, only what they sold, the state was losing a great deal of money. Bryce Bales and Dale Sump, accounting office employees, asked for an audit of the casing head gas processing plant in Reagan County owned by J. L Davis. Following Davis' voluntary submission to an audit, for which he was not obliged to submit, no accounting problems were found and UT officials believed the matter was resolved. Luna was

---

[72] The Eagle, Bryan, Texas, January 21, 1992.

[73] Ibid., May 25, 93.

unsatisfied and a short time later walked off the job. He filed suit in Williamson County against the University of Texas Board of Regents claiming he was harassed out of his job and sought compensatory damages under a whistle blower statute. A court date was set for the summer of 1996 and both sides prepared for trial.[74]

Meanwhile, by 1995 investment of the PUF had become too complicated and too involved of a process to be conducted by the finance committee of the University of Texas Board of Regents. In response, the regents came up with a plan for a reorganized investment apparatus, for which they shared control. Lawmakers amended Section 66.08 of the Texas Education Code and created the University of Texas Investment Management Company (UTIMCO). UTIMCO was similar to investment organizations of older institutions of higher learning, and it was a completely separate corporation from the University of Texas System. The UTIMCO board was made up of three UT regents, the UT chancellor, an A&M regent, and four other individuals, ideally experts in investment management. The organization opened in 1996, and the UT regents willingly relinquished sole control.[75]

About the same time, in July 1995, Land Commissioner Gary Mauro filed suit against nine major oil companies, claiming discrepancies in oil and gas royalties, including those from university lands. The University of Texas and other state agencies joined the suit after the General Land Office revealed that state agency funds were being paid royalties on posted prices far below the market

---

[74] Austin American Statesman, July 7, 1996; Steve Hartmann, interview, November 21, 2003.

[75] Section 66.08, Texas Education Code, Vernon's Texas Code's Annotated, 33-35; Amy Strahan, "UT Investments to be Managed by New Company," The Daily Texan, July 1, 1996.

value. Land office auditors noticed the discrepancies when they began taking royalty payments in kind for the various agency lands the office managed. Luckily, because the Board for Lease of University Lands had been taking a large percentage of the production in-kind, the PUF was not affected as badly as either some other state agencies or hundreds of private landowners in West Texas. The oil companies tried to have the Third District Court of Appeals dismiss the suit, and when that failed, they appealed to the Texas Supreme Court. The high court refused the appeal, leaving the Mauro suit to resume as soon as a state district judge certified it.[76]

Also about the same time, in the summer 1996, the court date for the Jose Luna suit was fast approaching. University officials were confident they could disprove Luna's allegations of impropriety in the payment and collecting of gas royalties. At the trial, held at Georgetown in Williamson County, in July 1996, Luna claimed the University was losing "$25-50 million" from accounting irregularities on casing head gas. According to Luna, when he brought the matter to the attention of his superiors, he was harassed out of his job. Luna's attorney convinced the Georgetown jury to believe that his client was just so harassed and awarded Luna $1.2 million in damages. UT officials appealed the verdict, and Luna got about half of the original award.[77] More importantly, however, a subsequent independent audit concluded there were absolutely no accounting problems or impropriety on

---

[76] Amy Strahan, "Texas suit against oil companies nears court UT System, other state agencies claim royalties were below market values," The Daily Texan, July 1, 1996.

[77] Austin American Statesman, July 7, 1996; ibid., July 13, 1996.

behalf of university lands management agencies or the companies operating on them.[78]

Also in 1996, with UTIMCO up and running, the UT regents turned their attention to the consolidation of their capitalization system. They ordered that University Lands Oil, Gas, and Mineral Interests, University Lands Surface Office, and University Lands Accounting Office be placed under a single director, Steve Hartmann. The appointment of Hartmann to head of University Lands West Texas Operations (WTO) was a vote of confidence in his leadership in managing the university lands. The creation of University Lands WTO was the completion of the regents' efforts to streamline the operations of each aspect of resource capitalization.[79]

From 1896 to 1996, the University of Texas Board of Regents capitalized on the utilization of resources on university lands. Its continued work to expand ways the PUF could be invested, and the AUF spent, translated into bricks and mortar after the discovery of oil. From the 1923 to 1982, the PUF saw sustained growth, becoming the largest endowment fund of a public university and second only to Harvard University among all schools in the United States. The UT regents devised a system for investing the PUF during the twentieth century that evolved and became more complicated as time progressed. In the early 1990s, the regents were ready to consolidate the system. First, they created the University of Texas Investment Management Company, UTIMCO, to manage the investment of the $5.5 billion PUF. Second, they organized the land management agencies as University Lands West Texas Operations and

---

[78] The best evidence that the were no irregularities in royalty accounting is that Steve Hartmann is still in charge at University Lands West Texas Operations as of 2004.

[79] Hartmann, interview, January 21, 2002.

placed the new organization under a single director. The century witnessed significant improvement in the ways the University of Texas and Texas A&M University managed the Permanent and Available University Funds.

CHAPTER VI

CONCLUSION

The 2.1 million acres of land set aside for the University of Texas and Texas A&M University systems, commonly known as university lands, played a significant role in the financial support of both schools. President Mirabeau B. Lamar in 1838 first called for lawmakers to reserve fifty leagues of land to provide funding for the establishment and maintenance of a university. Lamar's historical legacy in more recent times has been negative due to his Indian policies, but he is largely forgotten as an visionary of Texas higher education. Building on Lamar's ideas and requests, lawmakers and the University of Texas Board of Regents devised a system of land and resource management that provided Texas' flagship institutions with an endowment unrivaled by any public institution of higher learning in the Unites States.

During the period between 1838 and 1874, Texas lawmakers passed a barrage of legislation and constitutional amendments that provided a land reserve for the establishment and maintenance of a state university, but despite their efforts no university appeared. Several factors account for delays in achieving President Lamar's goal for establishing a university supported by a fifty-league land grant. First, Sam Houston's opposition to Lamar and his policies proved to be a powerful force working against progress on the matter. Second, problems related to Indian raids along the western edge of settlement and the remote locations of selected tracts delayed the completion of land surveys, and not until December of 1856 did the first public sale of university lands take place. It occurred at the courthouse in Sherman, Texas. Third, many early purchasers of university lands had problems making their payments. And, finally, the presence of private schools, such as Baylor University, filled the immediate need for an institution of higher education. Despite such obstacles, many Texans continued to push for the establishment of a public university.

Governor Elisha M. Pease was such an early advocate. In 1858, after he urged lawmakers to establish the institution, the Seventh Legislature passed Chapter 116, an "An Act to Establish the University of Texas." The law set up a ten-member Board of Administrators to govern the institution. The law also stipulated that one in every ten sections of railroad land set aside for the state would be reserved for the university. Sectional and political divisions, however, diverted the attention of officials from establishing the school at that time.

In 1860, a university fund, built from a variety of sources, totaled more than $100,000, but developments in the following years left it virtually empty. Newly elected Governor Sam Houston opposed the university. In January 1860 he asked the legislature for a loan from the university fund for "frontier defense." The legislature passed Chapter 32, giving Houston's administration $100,000 in United States bonds from the fund. A month later Texas seceded from the Union. In January 1861, lawmakers borrowed $9,768.62 from the university fund to pay their expenses. In January 1862, the university fund totaled $1,520.97, from which lawmakers took $1,520.40, leaving it with only fifty-seven cents. Lawmakers took a total of $109,472.26 from the university fund just before and during the Civil War, money that was supposed to be paid back without interest. After the surrender and dissolution of the Confederate States of America, the state of Texas was not obliged to pay back any of the money, although it eventually did. Reconstruction in Texas resulted in the

Constitution of 1869, one that contained no provision for a state university.

Clear evidence that political divisions affected educational developments occurred in 1871 when radical Republican Governor Edmund J. Davis, who opposed repayment of the debt to the university fund, established the Agricultural & Mechanical College of Texas at Bryan. Davis applied for and received federal funding under the Morrill Land-Grant College Act (1862) and established Texas A&M in lieu of the long-anticipated state university. The money came from the sale of 180,000 acres of federal land in Colorado given the school under terms of the Morrill Act. At first, many Texas residents viewed the A&M College as a symbol of Radical Republican rule in Texas, but this idea was short lived. By the time the school opened in 1874, Democrats had taken back control of state government and the state's white agricultural elements accepted Texas A&M College as a Redeemer institution. Some officials, however, saw A&M as a symbol of Radical Republican rule in Texas. Nonetheless, Davis establishment of Texas A&M was a clear circumvention of Chapter 116, the 1858 law to establish a university. Because Davis ignored the *ante-bellum* legislation, subsequent Democratic officials were reluctant to appropriate money for A&M's operation.

After reconstruction ended, Texans were vocal about removing all vestiges of Radical leadership, most especially the Constitution of 1869. Efforts to write a new document stalled in 1874. Many officials believed that in any serious attempt at constitutional revision a constitutional convention was preferable to a legislative committee. A convention followed. When it opened in September 1875, most of the delegates were Redeemer Democrats and about half were members of the Grange, or the Patrons of Husbandry. The groups held heated debates regarding the policy of granting land for railroads and education. But they wrote a constitution, the state's current one.

The framers of the Constitution of 1876 directed the legislature to establish the University of Texas under the governance of a board of regents. In an obvious affront to Davis and Radical Republicans, they prescribed that Texas A&M College be made a branch of the university. For funding to establish the university, leaders looked to the abundant lands in the western part of the state. Lawmakers set up a system for resource capitalization that consisted of three parts: the university lands, the Permanent University Fund (PUF), and the Available University Fund (AUF). Revenue from non-renewable resources went into the PUF, which could only be invested. Revenue from PUF investments went into the AUF, along with income from the use of renewable resources, such as grass. The constitution also canceled the One-In-Ten Railroad Act of 1858; a cancellation that resulted in the loss of over 1,700,000 acres of land valued at $5 an acre. Because the railroads received a total of 17,000,000 acres of public lands, the loss of one-tenth of this land was enormous.

In exchange for the cancellation the One-In-Ten Railroad Act of 1858, the Constitution of 1876 mandated the appropriation of one million acres of the remaining public domain for the endowment of the University of Texas, the so-called "constitutional million." The constitutional million, however, proved not to be a windfall. Unlike the railroad land, which was located in parts of the state already developed and settled, the land encompassed in the constitutional million was of poor quality.

The task of choosing and surveying the constitutional million grant did not begin until 1879, when Governor O. M. Roberts spearheaded the effort. Roberts mustered funding for C. W. Holt and A. W. Thompson to survey land of and for the constitutional million acres. Likewise, Roberts was instrumental in 1881 in the passage of legislation to establish the University of Texas. The law created the board of regents as the governing body for the school. The regents served as a motivating force behind the opening of the University of Texas in the fall 1883.

The regents, along with other advocates of the university, including former Governor Roberts, pushed the legislature to make an additional appropriation to replace the estimated 1,700,000 acres denied the school after the cancellation of the railroad act. The legislature responded in 1883, the same year the University of Texas opened, with the appropriation of the so-called "legislative million." This acreage was added to the constitutional million and the remainder of the fifty leagues to form the lands that supported the University of Texas.

At the same time they appropriated the legislative million, lawmakers established the State Land Board to handle the lease and sale of all public lands, including the university lands. The regents reacted with shock, believing they should handle lease and sale of university lands. The State Land Board, whose membership included the governor, the comptroller, the treasurer, the attorney general, and the land commissioner, oversaw the sale and lease of all state lands. Because the State Land Board managed the university lands plus millions of acres of other state agency lands, sales revenue of the remnants of the original fifty leagues increased slowly.

An agent of the State Land Board, Dennis Corwin, was charged with the selection and survey of the so-called legislative million acres. Most of the land he chose was from the remaining public domain in the vast arid stretches west of the Pecos River. Corwin worked closely with the regents in the selection and survey of the legislative million and completed his work in 1885.

The regents continued to push for control over the sale and lease of the lands, believing they could increase revenue by managing the resource with an agent. The abolition of the State Land Board in 1887 and the lawmakers' decision to transfer authority over disposition of university lands to the General Land Office (GLO), rather than the University of Texas Board of Regents proved disappointing. From 1887 to 1895, the GLO staff sold a significant portion of the original fifty-league grant, but did so during a period of low market prices. As a result income was minimal. Because the PUF and AUF were not growing quickly enough to keep up with the needs of the university, the regents desperately sought additional sources of revenue. The regents could have focused more attention on the sale of the lands than either the State Land Board or the GLO and would have brought in more income.

Finally, in 1895, at the prompting of outgoing Governor James Hogg, the Twenty-fourth Legislature passed Chapter 18. It invested in the University of Texas Board of Regents the authority to sell and lease university lands. Thus, the regents entered into the land business, and over the following century they devised a system to manage the lands that had a direct impact on the eventual size of the PUF. The passage of Chapter 18 signaled a new era in the history of the university lands.

In the century from 1896 to 1996, the board of regents managed university lands for the purpose of putting money in the PUF and AUF. The development of resource management on university lands was a slow process whereby the regents devised an *ad hoc* system that did not conflict with the Constitution of 1876. Management offices developed from the use of an individual agent who worked under the land committee of the board of regents.

In January 1896, the regents hired Thomas J. "Tom" Lee to sell and lease university lands on their behalf.

From 1896 to 1996, surface leasing of university lands for grazing purposes brought in significant income. In 1896, ranchers held most of the surface leases. They ran cattle, sheep, and goats; but over the century, surface use became increasingly diversified. In late 1899, Tom Lee inexplicably left employment of the university and the regents replaced him with "Judge" R. E. L. Saner. Under Saner's leadership, from 1900 to 1929, surface leasing to ranchers continued, but easements also became a common instrument for lease of university lands. Saner used the easement to lease everything from railroads to pipelines to utility lines. To increase income for the PUF and AUF, he was also instrumental in the development of other uses for university lands during the early twentieth century.

After the Spindletop discovery in 1901, the University of Texas Board of Regents were at the vanguard of petroleum developments in the state. Its members were instrumental in the creation of a state mineral survey later that year and played an important role in the development of oil and gas law. In 1913, 1917, and 1919, their efforts resulted in the so-called "permit laws." The Santa Rita #1 discovery of May 21, 1923 was drilled under such a permit. The discovery of oil on university lands changed the financial situation for the cash strapped school, which used the money to initiate an unprecedented construction program during the 1920s and 1930s.

On yet another level altogether, the Santa Rita discovery played a significant role in the development of the petroleum industry in West Texas. Although, the Texas & Pacific Abrams No. 1 well in Mitchell County came in first, it was the Santa Rita #1 that heralded the 1920s boom in the oil fields of the Permian Basin.

After the discovery of oil, the increased revenue to the PUF led the board of regents to launch an effort to expand the ways in which the revenue could be invested. Board members hoped to expand the ways that the AUF could be spent. With proceeds from the investment of the PUF going into the AUF, getting a better return on PUF investments was of growing regent concern. With investments confined to low yield government bonds, PUF income was not likely to achieve its maximum potential.

In 1929 "watershed" events occurred in the history of university lands. In response to accounting problems caused by an unexpected volume of petroleum production in the 1920s, the legislature created management offices for university lands, including the University Lands Surface Office, the University Lands Geology Office, and the University Lands Survey Office. In addition, the legislature established the Board for Lease of University Lands to conduct mineral sales on the land. The capitalization of minerals and the potential for wealth encouraged lawmakers to grab some responsibility for controlling the lands, hence, the Board for Lease of University Lands. The board for lease originally had three members, which included the land commissioner and two UT regents. The Board for Lease conducted sealed bid sales of mineral leases on university lands from 1929 to 1936, when it switched to oral bid auction. The Board for Lease used the oral bidding method quite successfully between 1936 and 1986.

Very important for the history of higher education in Texas, the University of Texas and Texas A&M in 1931 finally reached a settlement regarding division of the PUF and AUF. Texas A&M got one-third of AUF appropriations and, of course, UT retained the other two-thirds. The regents also managed to keep exclusive control over revenues from grazing leases, investment of the PUF, and the sale of mineral leases. In the decades after Texas A&M got its share of the PUF and AUF other Texas schools sought revenue from the endowment money.

From 1929 to 1996, the University Lands Surface Office changed in a number of important ways. Elliot J. Compton, Billy Carr, and Steve Hartmann implemented conservationist policies on university lands. Such development continued into the 1990s. To reduce overgrazing, surface office policies allowed lessees to set their own animal limits. The surface office also continued to monitor petroleum-related surface activity. Other policies implemented over the century included the assessment of damages for different surface activities and the use of bonuses for leasing of surface area. The use of the bonus component discouraged speculation in university grazing leases and insured that lessees were serious about remaining for long periods of time. It also enabled lessees, who opted not renew their leases, to recoup some money spent on improvements.

In the post-war period, University Lands Surface Office personnel implemented further conservationist policies. They also undertook a number of important agricultural experiments. Under Billy Carr the surface office devised custom range management plans for each surface lease, developed the flexible grazing lease, and began collecting revenue from wildlife harvest. Carr initiated a reclamation experiment in Reagan County known as the Texon Scar. He also directed several important agricultural experiments on university lands. Over the duration of the century, however, grazing revenue only comprised a fraction of income on university lands.

Likewise, from 1929 to 1996 the University Lands Geology Office, later called University Lands Oil, Gas, and Mineral Interests, saw an evolution both in its organization and its policies. After 1929 Hal P. Bybee and a highly trained professional staff manned the geology office. As petroleum exploration and production became more technical and complicated so did the workload of the geology office. In the post-war period, additional discoveries in the Permian Basin and the periodic increase of royalty rates proved to be lucrative for UT and Texas A&M.

As oil prices dropped after 1982, revenue from university lands decreased. In response, University of Texas regents gave Texas A&M a seat on the Board for Lease of University Lands, sharing responsibility for mineral lease sale policy. During the same period, Land Commissioner Gary Mauro pushed for a switch to sealed bids for mineral leases. Although it was unpopular with the geology office staff, Mauro's decision proved to be a prudent one. It returned the bidding edge to the major oil companies, which could afford to operate through extended periods of low oil prices.

From the 1970s to the 1990s, the issue of funding for higher education increased in importance. As a result, other universities made repeated attempts to alter the management and distribution of the PUF and AUF. Relatedly, when state revenues failed to provide money, budget cutters looked to higher education appropriations, reasoning that Texans would agree to a tax increase for education, but not one for prisons or asylums. Also, some lawmakers saw the PUF as a legitimate target for badly needed funds at other schools. Other lawmakers saw the PUF as a way to get the funds they desired from the legislature. Attempts to alter the PUF and AUF to include other schools, became a means to get UT and A&M support for general revenue appropriations for those institutions.

The attempts to alter the PUF and AUF in the mid-1980s revealed a changing attitude towards public funding for higher education. It also demonstrated the political influence wielded by the University of Texas and Texas A&M University. The two large schools derived their influence not only from the wealth of money in the PUF and AUF, but in the alumni who held influential positions in state government and business. Of course, the wealth of the institutions was also due in part to the management of the university lands.

The University of Texas and Texas A&M University secured the PUF and AUF from other schools in 1986. Texas voters in that year approved a constitutional amendment that created the Higher Education Assistance Fund (HEAF). The HEAF served as a construction fund for non-PUF schools; that is, the seventeen universities and colleges that were not part of the UT and A&M Systems. Lawmakers started the HEAF with an annual appropriation of $100 million, a sum they increased in 1993 to $175 million annually. The HEAF provided badly needed construction money and dramatically decreased attempts to alter the PUF and AUF.

The decline in oil revenues in the 1980s and 1990s is also reflected in a decreasing value of the PUF. The revenue pull off from petroleum production caused the regents to look at new ways to increase the PUF and AUF. The regents shifted the focus from management and leasing of university land to intensive management of investment of the PUF's principle. In 1996, lawmakers established the University of Texas Investment Management Company (UTIMCO). UTIMCO was a non-profit investment company managed by a board of directors, which included the chancellor of the University of Texas System, three University of Texas regents, an A&M regent, and four other individuals with investment expertise. The same year they created UTIMCO, the UT regents consolidated the management offices for university lands.

The shift in focus to investment management paralleled regent efforts to reorganize the university lands management offices. University Lands Surface Office, University Lands Oil, Gas, and Mineral Interests, and University Lands Accounting Office were all placed under a single director, Steve Hartmann, and were thenceforth collectively known as University Lands West Texas Operations (WTO). The University Lands WTO personnel continued to manage the lands with environmentally conscious policies to insure their viability as an income source for the PUF and AUF for the foreseeable future.

The Board for Lease of University Lands evolved its policies from 1929 to 1996. Public auctions brought in considerable revenues from 1936 to 1986, but declining oil prices caused some officials to push for a return to sealed bids. In 1984, the legislature added a Texas A&M regent, bringing the total membership to four. During the same period lawmakers passed a measure that made the land commissioner the permanent chairman of the Board for Lease. In 1991, the Board for Lease approved a policy of taking royalties in kind. By marketing the crude oil through the University Lands Accounting Office, revenues for the PUF saw a demonstrable increase.

Some important conclusions may be drawn regarding the management of the lands between 1896 and 1996. In 1896, members of the University of Texas Board of Regents were quite active in developments on university land. By mid-century, initiative and expertise had begun to originate more from staff members of the University Lands Surface Office and University Lands Oil Gas and Mineral Interests Office. The regents became less involved in land matters as various experts in the field increasingly took more control of university lands operations. Likewise, the level of technical expertise in the management offices improved over the century. The management offices and policies developed in an *ad hoc* fashion in response to crisis and problems. As the century progressed, however, the regents and the management offices' staff began to develop policies to preempt problems, rather than simply to act in response to trouble.

Money derived from the sale and lease of university lands contributed significantly to the impressive facilities of the both the University of Texas and Texas A&M University Systems. The amount of funding for building programs at both schools in the decades after the discovery of oil is directly related to the careful management and utilization of university lands, the PUF, and the AUF.

As this study shows, the development, use, and management of university lands played an important role in the financial support of the University of Texas and Texas A&M University. Originally, the lands served as a means to establish a "university of the first class," but later they became the means to support it. Income from the lands translated into bricks and mortar for both schools and their component institutions. After the establishment of offices to manage the lands in 1929, the regents' involvement gradually diminished. The management offices were directly linked to the phenomenal growth of the PUF until the 1980s, when the regents refocused their efforts on management of PUF investments.

BIBLIOGRAPHY

Manuscript Collections and Archives

Abell-Hangar Collection, Permian Basin Petroleum Museum Archives Center and Library, Midland, Texas.

Agricultural and Mechanical College of Texas Board of Directors Minutes, Directors Office, Texas A&M University, College Station, Texas.

Albert and Ethel Herzstein Library, San Jacinto Museum of History, La Porte, Texas.

Board for Lease of University Lands, University Lands West Texas Operations, Midland, Texas.

Haigh, Berte R. Collection, Permian Basin Petroleum Museum Archives Center and Library, Midland, Texas.

Lamar, Mirabeau B. Papers, Texas State Archives, Austin Texas.

Pickrell, Frank T. Collection, Permian Basin Petroleum Museum Archives Center and Library, Midland, Texas.

University of Texas Board of Regents Minutes, Ashbell Smith Hall, University of Texas, Austin, Texas.

Legislation and Legal Sources

Acts of the Seventieth Legislature at the Called Session. Austin: 1987.

Gammel, H. P. N. The Laws of Texas, 1827-1897. 10 vols. Austin: Gammel Book Company, 1898.

General Laws of Texas Passed at the Regular Session of the Twenty-Seventh Legislature. Austin: Von Boeckmann, Schutze & Co., State Printers, 1901.

General Laws of the State of Texas Passed by the Thirty-Third Legislature at its Regular Session. Austin: Von Boeckmann-Jones, 1913.

General Laws of the State of Texas Passed by the Thirty-Fifth Legislature. Austin: A. C. Baldwin & Sons, State Printers, 1917.

General and Special Laws of the State of Texas Passed by the Regular Session of the Forty-First Legislature. 1929.

General and Special Laws of the State of Texas Passed by the Forty-Second Legislature at the First Called Session. 1931.
General and Special Laws Passed by the Fifty-First Legislature at the Regular Session. 1949.

Laws of the Republic of Texas Passed by the First Session of the Third Congress, 1839.

Report of the Commissioner of the General Land Office to the Governor of Texas, Austin, December 31, 1886. Austin: Triplett & Hutchins, State Printers, 1886.

Report of the Commissioner of the General Land Office to the Governor of Texas, for the Two Years Ending August

31, 1888. Austin: Eugene Von Boeckman, State Printer, 1888.

Rogan, Charles. Report of the Commissioner of the General Land Office, State of Texas, From August 31, 1900, to September 1, 1902. Austin: Von Boeckman, Schultz, & Co., State Printer, 1902.

State v. Hatcher, Texas Supreme Court, No. 4506, March 10, 1926, 1-5.

Vernon's Texas Codes Annotated. West Group, 2002.

Walsh, W. C. Report of the Commissioner of the General Land Office of the State of Texas for the Fiscal Year Ending August 31, 1880. Galveston: Book and Job Office of Galveston News, 1880.

_____. Biennial Report of the Commissioner of the General Land Office of the State of Texas from August 31, 1880, to August 31, 1882. Austin: E. W. Swindells, State Printer, 1883.

Newspapers

Austin American Statesman, 1973-1996

The Battalion (Texas A&M University), 1975-1996

Bryan Eagle, 1958-1996

Daily Texan (University of Texas), 1900-1996

Dallas Morning News, 1879-1996

Dallas Times Herald, 1888-1991

Fort Worth Star Telegram, 1909-1996

Galveston Daily News, 1865-1900

Houston Chronicle, 1901-1996

Houston Post, 1880-1996

Interviews and Personal Communications

Burkes, Sharon. University Lands West Texas Operations, administrative coordinator. Personal communication with author, January 14, 2002 and August 2, 2002, Midland, Texas. E-mails in possession of the author.

Hartmann, Steve. University Lands West Texas Operations, executive director, Interview by author, January 28, 2002, Midland, Texas. Tape recording.

Long, Laddie F. and Wallie Gravitt. University Lands Geology Office, geologists, retired. Interview by author, March 11, 2002, Midland, Texas. Tape recording.

Neidig, Patsy. University Lands Accounting Office, land records supervisor. Personal communication with author, January 21, 2003 and December 2, 2003, Austin, Texas. E-mails in possession of the author.

Owens, Buck. University Lands surface lessee, Interview by author, May 21, 2003, Barnhart, Texas. Tape recording.

Shivers, Lynward. University of Texas Office of General Counsel, senior attorney, retired. Personal communication with author, January 14, 2004, Austin, Texas. Telephone call.

Smith, Leslie. University Lands West Texas Operations, senior accountant. Personal communication with the author, August 4, 2003, Midland, Texas. E-mail in possession of the author.

Snelson, W. E. "Pete." Texas State Senator, retired. Interview by author, March 25, 2002, Austin, Texas. Tape recording.

Books, Articles and Other Sources

Arnesen, Edwin P. "The Early Art of Terrestrial Measurement and Its Practice in Texas." In One League to Each Wind, ed. Sue Watkins, 1-17. Austin: Texas Surveyors Association, 1964.

Arnold, J, Barto, III. "Texas Antiquities Committee." Handbook of Texas Online. (2003). <http://www.tsha.utexas.edu/handbook/online/articles/view/TT/mdt5.html> [Accessed Mon Aug 11 21:29:49 US/Central 2003].

Barkes, Eunice. Report on an archeological survey of parts of Sections 8, 9, 12, and 13 of Block 19, University Lands, Pecos County, Texas. Texas Antiquities Committee Permit No. 257. Midland, Texas: By the author, 1980.

Barr, Alwyn. Reconstruction to Reform: Texas Politics, 1876-1906. Austin: University of Texas Press, 1971.

Beckham, John L. The Permanent University Fund: Land, Oil, and Politics. Austin: Unpublished manuscript on file at the Center for American History, The University of Texas at Austin, 1981.

Benedict, Harry Y. ed. "A Sourcebook Relating to the History of the University of Texas; Legislative, Legal, Bibliographical, and Statistical," University of Texas Bulletin No. 1757. (October, 1917).

Benner, Judith Ann. Sul Ross: Soldier, Statesman, Educator. College Station: Texas A&M University Press, 1983.

Biel, Laura. "Regents Expected to Approve Rail Gun Testing in West Texas." The Daily Texan (February 9, 1988).

Biemiller, "How the U. of Texas, Flexing Its Political Muscle, Foiled Budget Cutters." Chronicle of Higher Education (June 19, 1985): 12-15.

Brown, Norman D. Hood, Bonnet, and Little Brown Jug: Texas Politics, 1921-1928. College Station: Texas A&M University Press, 1984.

Carleton, Don E. A Breed So Rare: The Life of J. R. Parten, Liberal Texas Oilman, 1896-1992. Austin: Texas State Historical Association, 1998.

Carlson, Paul H. The Plains Indians. College Station: Texas A & M University Press, 1998.

_____. Texas Woollybacks: The Range Sheep and Goat Industry. College Station: Texas A&M University Press, 1982.

Carr, Billy. "Report on Surface Leasing on University Lands in West Texas, December 1973." Midland, Texas: University Lands Surface Department, 1973. Photocopied.

Clark, James A. Three Stars for the Colonel: The Biography of Ernest O. Thompson, Father of Petroleum Conservation. New York: Random House, 1954.

_____. The Tactful Texan: A Biography of Governor W. P. Hobby. New York: Random House, 1958.

Cotner, Robert C. James Stephen Hogg: A Biography. Austin: University of Texas Press, 1959.

Dallas Newspaper Artists Association, R. E. L. Saner. Makers of Dallas. Dallas: Dallas Newspaper Artists Association, 1912.

Daniel, Forrest. "Texas Pioneer Surveyors and Indians." In One League to Each Wind, ed. Sue Watkins, 57-62. Austin: Texas Surveyors Association, 1964.

Dethloff, Henry C. A Centennial History of Texas A&M University, 1876-1976. 2 Vols. College Station: Texas A&M University Press, 1975.

Ferguson, W. Keene. Geology and Politics in Frontier Texas, 1845-1909. Austin: University of Texas Press, 1969.

Franz, Joe B. The Forty Acre Follies: An Opinionated History of the University of Texas. Austin: Texas Monthly Press, Inc., 1983.

Freeman, J. D. "The Early Surveyors of Texas." In One League to Each Wind, ed. Sue Watkins, 279-293. Austin: Texas Surveyors Association, 1964.

Gambrell, H. P. Anson Jones: The Last President of Texas. Austin: University of Texas Press, 1964.

Gould, Lewis L. Progressives and Prohibitionists: Texas Democrats in the Wilson Era. Austin: University of Texas Press, 1973.

Gracy, David B. "George Washington Littlefield: A Biography in Business." Ph. D. diss., Texas Tech University, 1991.

Green, William Elton. "Land Settlement in West Texas: Tom Green County, a case study." Ph. D. diss., Texas Tech University, 1981.

Haigh, Berte R. Land, Oil, and Education. El Paso: Texas Western Press, 1986.

_____. "Santa Rita, The Oil Well." The Permian Historical Annual 17 (December, 1977): 57-67.

_____. The Story of University Lands. Midland: Unpublished manuscript on file at the Permian Basin Petroleum Museum, Midland, Texas, 1937.

Haley J. Evetts. George W. Littlefield: Texan. Norman: University of Oklahoma Press, 1943.

Haley, James L. Sam Houston. Norman: University of Oklahoma Press, 2001.

Helms, Doug. "Great Plains Conservation Program: A Short Administrative and Legislative History." In Great Plains Conservation Program: 25 Years of Accomplishment. SCS Bulletin No. 300-2-7 (November 24, 1981) : 1-18.

Hendrickson, Kenneth B. Jr. The Chief Executives of Austin: From Stephen F. Austin to John B. Connally, Jr. College Station: Texas A&M University Press, 1995.

Holden, William Curry. Alkali Trails, or Social and Economic Movements of the Texas Frontier, 1846-1900. 2d ed. Double Mountain Books – classic reissues of the American West. Lubbock: Texas Tech University Press, 1998.

Kerr, John Leeds. Destination Topolobampo: The Kansas City, Mexico & Orient Railway. San Marino, Ca.: Golden West Books, 1968.

Kinch, Sam, and Stuart Long. Allan Shivers: The Pied Piper of Texas Politics. Austin: Shoal Creek Publishers, Inc., 1973.

Lane, John J. "History of Education in Texas." United States Bureau of Education Circular of Information No. 2 (Washington, 1903).

_____. History of Education in Texas. Austin: Henry Hutchings, 1891.

Lang, Aldon S. "Financial History of the Public Lands in Texas." The Baylor Bulletin Vol. 35 No. 3 (July, 1932).

Lee, R. Ernest. "Pioneer Surveyors." In One League to Each Wind, ed. Sue Watkins, 49-62. Austin: Texas Surveyors Association, 1964.

Linkin, Barbara. "Vineyard Workers Threaten to File Suit." The Daily Texan (July 16, 1986).

Long, Laddie F., Charlie Timberlake Jr., and James B. Zimmerman. "Tour of West Texas Lands." Midland, Texas: University Lands Geology Office, 1965. Photocopied.

Malin, Patricia Anne. "Oil and Gas Leasing of Texas State Lands: School Lands and University Lands." Ph. D. diss., University of Texas, 1982.

Mallison, Sam T. The Great Wildcatter: The Story of Mike Benedum. Charleston, West Virginia: Education Foundation of West Virginia, 1953.

Mauer, John Walker. "Constitution Proposed in 1874," Handbook of Texas Online (2002). <http://www.tsha.utexas.edu/handbook/online/articles/view/CC/mhc12.html> [Accessed Sun Jan 18 21:14:52 US/Central 2004]

McKay, Seth Shepard. Seven Decades of the Constitution of 1876. Lubbock: Texas Technological College Research Funds, 1944.

Miller, Thomas Lloyd. The Public Lands of Texas. Norman: University of Oklahoma Press, 1971.

Moneyhon, Carl H. Republicanism in Reconstruction Texas. College Station: Texas A&M University Press, 1980.

Moore, Richard R. West Texas After the Discovery of Oil: A Modern Frontier. Austin: Jenkins Publishing Co., 1971.

Myres, Samuel D. The Permian Basin: Petroleum Empire of the Southwest, Era of Discovery, From the Beginning to the Depression. Vol. 1, El Paso: Permian Press, 1973.

_____. The Permian Basin: Petroleum Empire of the Southwest, Era of Advancement, From the Depression to the Present. Vol. 2, El Paso: Permian Press, 1977.

_____. ed., Pioneer Surveyor, Frontier Lawyer: The Personal Narrative of O. W. Williams. El Paso: Texas Western Press, 1968.

Northcott, Kaye. "Its on you: The biggest Aggie joke of all." Texas Observer (March 28, 1975) : 1, 3-5.

Olien, Diana Davids, and Roger M. Oil in Texas, The Gusher Age, 1895-1945. Austin: University of Texas Press, 2002.

Parker, Edith Helen. "History of School Land Grants in Texas." Ph. D. diss., University of Texas, 1952.

Pickle, Joe, and Ross McSwain. Water in a Dry and Thirsty Land The First Fifty Years of the Colorado River Municipal Water District. Big Spring: CRMWD, 2000.

Pierson, William Whatley, Jr. "Texas *Versus* White." Southwestern Historical Quarterly 18, No. 4 (April, 1915): 341-367.

Prindle, David F. "Oil and the Permanent University Fund: The Early Years." Southwestern Historical Quarterly 86, No. 2 (October, 1982): 277-299.

_____. Petroleum Politics and the Texas Railroad Commission. Austin: University of Texas Press, 1981.

Ramsay, Jack C. Jr. Thunder Beyond the Brazos: Mirabeau B. Lamar, a Biography. Austin: Eakin Press, 1985.

Ramsdell, Charles William. Reconstruction in Texas. 2d ed. Austin: University of Texas Press, 1970.

Richardson, Rupert, Adrian Anderson, Cary D. Wintz, and Ernest Wallace. Texas: The Lone Star State. Upper Saddle River, New Jersey: Prentice Hall, 2001.

Rister, Carl Coke. Oil! Titan of the Southwest. Norman: University of Oklahoma Press, 1949.

Roberts, O. M. "A History of the Establishment of the University of the State of Texas." Southwestern Historical Quarterly 1, No. 4 (April, 1898): 233-265.

Schleebecker, John T. Cattle Ranching on the Plains, 1900-1961. Lincoln: University of Nebraska Press, 1963.

Schwettman, Martin W. Santa Rita: The University of Texas Oil Discovery. Austin: University of Texas Press, 1943.

Sellards, Elias H. "The University Deep Well in Reagan County." University of Texas Bulletin No. 2901. (October, 1929): 175-201.

Sibley, Marilyn McAdams. George W. Brackenridge: Maverick Philanthropist. Austin: University of Texas Press, 1973.

Spillman, W. J. "Adjustment of the Texas Boundary in 1850." Southwestern Historical Quarterly 7, No. 3 (January, 1904): 177-195.

Strahan, Amy. "UT Investments to be Managed by New Company." The Daily Texan. (June 1, 1996).

_____. "Texas suit against oil companies nears court UT System, other State agencies claim royalties were below market value." The Daily Texan. (July 1, 1996).

Turpin, Solvieg A. West of the Pecos: A Cultural Reconnaissance on University Lands, Terrell County, Texas. Texas Antiquities Permit No. 1414. Austin: Borderlands Archeological Research Unit, 1995.

"UTIMCO: About Us." UTIMCO Website. <http://www.utimco.org/scripts/internet/about.asp> [Accessed Sat Nov 15 20:15:32 US/Central 2003].

Warner, Charles A. Texas Oil and Gas Since 1543. Houston: Gulf Publishing Company, 1939.

Weathers, Michael "Doc," Kenneth R. Moore, Donald L. Ford, and William E. Black. "Surface Reclamation in the Big Lake Field." AAPG Division of Environmental Geosciences Journal 1, No. 1 (June, 1994): 50-56.

Webb, Walter Prescott. The Great Plains. New York: Grosset and Dunlap, 1931.

Weber, Bruce J. Will Hogg and the Business of Reform. Ph.D. diss., University of Houston, 1979.

Zimmerman, James B. "Dollars for Scholars: University Lands' Contribution to the Permanent Fund of the University." The Permian Historical Annual 7 (December, 1967): 41-45.

Index

1895 mineral law, *131*

A&M College, *34, 39, 43, 68, 114, 172, 187, 189, 191, 195, 196, 200*

ab intio, *30*

Adelsverein, *16*

Allen, W. Y., *7*

Alwin, Lawrence F., *216*

Amerada Petroleum Corporation, *159*

annexation, *14, 15, 17*

Archer, Stephenson, *91*

Atlantic Refining Company, *162*

AUF, *59*

Available University Fund (AUF), *2, 79, 145, 181, 226*

Ayers, J. P.. *See* House Committee on Education, *See* House Committee on Education

Bales, Bryce, *206, 218*

Barkes, Eunice, *125*

Battle Creek Massacre:, *12*

Baxter, George W., *82*

Baylor University, *14, 224*

Bell James H.. *See* UT Board of Regents

Bell, John G., *34*

Bell, Peter H., *18*

Benedum, Michael Late, *144*

Benson, Jim, *177*

Best, *99, 100, 102, 103, 148, 149*

Big Bend Manufacturing Company, *94*

Big Lake Oil Company, *144, 146*

Binyon, Lee, *106*

Black, Charles, *148*

Board for Lease of University Lands, *2, 104, 106, 108, 131, 151, 154, 156, 157, 162, 173, 175, 176, 195, 197, 198, 201, 212, 213, 220, 230, 232, 234, 236*

Board of Administrators. *See* Chapter 116

Brackenridge, George W., *94*

Bradley, Tinsey, *178*

Briscoe, Dolph, *204*

Bronitsky, Gordon, *125*

Brown, W. M., *61*

Bryan

    site of A&M, *34*, *35*, *42*, *68*, *155*, *175*, *186*, *187*, *192*, *204*, *205*, *207*, *209*, *211*, *215*, *218*, *225*, *238*

Bureau of Economic Geology, *105*, *137*, *141*, *152*, *195*

Burgess, William, *90*

Burkes, Sharon, *i*, *128*

Burnet, David G., *29*

Bybee, Dr. Hal P., *v*, *105*, *116*, *152*, *153*, *158*, *160*, *170*, *195*, *231*

Calhoun, John C.. *See* annexation

Camp, J. L., *40*

Campbell Ben, *206*

Campbell, Dave, *i*, *177*

Carr, Billy, *114*, *115*, *119*, *125*, *167*, *170*, 231

Chapter 116

    established UT, 23, 24, 34, 45, 64, 224, 225

Chapter 128, *48*

Chapter 144, *20*, *21*, *22*

Chapter 148, *29*

Chapter 15, *20*

    aka Railroad Grant Act, *19*

Chapter 159, *53*

Chapter 167, *29*

Chapter 173. *See* permit law of 1913

Chapter 18, *53*, *76*, *77*, *78*, *228*

Chapter 20, *72*, *73*

Chapter 23, *26*

Chapter 27, *63*

Chapter 28, *89*

Chapter 282, *106*, *151*, *152*, *154*, *195*, *198*

Chapter 32, *24*, *25*, *38*, *224*

Chapter 33, 66

Chapter 39, *52*

Chapter 43, *29, 38, 40, 41*

Chapter 44. *See* Texas A&M College

Chapter 47, *26*

Chapter 48, *41*

Chapter 49, *53*

Chapter 5, *25*

Chapter 50, *26, 27*

Chapter 51, *41*

Chapter 52, *26, 27*

Chapter 6, *27, 63*

Chapter 69, *48*

Chapter 72, *63*

Chapter 73, *57*

Chapter 75

   est. UT, *57*

Chapter 86, *26*

Chapter 88, *63*

Chapter 89, *48*

Chapter 92, *17*

Chapter 99, *71, 74, 136*

Childress, P. L., *100*

Civil War, *5, 26, 27, 32, 48, 65, 224*

Clark, Edward. *See* secession

Clark, George, *206*

Clayton, Bill, *208*

Clements, William, *204, 208, 209, 215*

Coke, Richard, *35*

Collinsworth, James, 6

Colorado River Municipal Water District (CRMWD), *117*

Colquitt, Oscar Branch, *186*

Compromise of 1850, *18, 27*

Compton, Elliot J., *103, 105, 114, 148, 152, 160, 195, 231*

Condra, Gary, *119*

Confederate States of America, *25, 26, 27, 224*

Conklin, J. A., *106*

Conklin, W. P., *106*

Conrad, Bob, *206*

Constitution of 1836, *6*

Constitution of 1845, *15, 28*

Constitution of 1866, *28, 30*

Constitution of 1869, *31, 36, 37, 40, 44, 225*

Constitution of 1876, *37, 40, 43, 44, 56, 60, 78, 155, 181, 182, 226, 228, 245*

constitutional million, *2, 47, 48, 52, 78, 226, 227*

constitutional revision, *39, 42, 203, 204, 225*

Cooper, Oscar, *76*

Corwin, Dennis, *65, 67, 69, 70, 85, 150, 227*

Cox, Don, *127*

Creath, Norris, *106, 160*

Cromwell, Carl, *143*

Cullen, Ezekial W., *7*

Daisy Bradford, *197*

Davis, E. J., *31,* 32, 33, 34, 35, *39,* 43, 168, 218, 225, 226

Davis, J. L, *218*

De Kalb College, *14*

de Zavala, Lorenzo, *7*

Delco, Wilhelmina, *206, 210*

Devine, Thomas J.. *See* UT Board of Regents

Dick Dillard, *102*

Dixie Oil Company, *105*

Doehne, Rick, *i, 177*

Doggett, Lloyd, *208*

Domaines-Cordier, 121

Drennan, Gene, *120*

Duval Corporation, *117, 172*

Edwards, A. N., *59*

Eighteenth Legislature, *62, 63, 64, 65, 66*

Texas, *66*

Eighth Legislature, *24, 25*

Eleventh Legislature, *29*

Ernst and Ernst, *148, 149, 193*

Euresti, Ben, Jr., *217*

Evans, Ira H., *32*

Evans, Jim, *i, 120, 127*

Ferguson, James E., *141, 188*

Ferguson, Miriam A., *147, 191, 193*

Fifteenth Legislature, *48*

Fifth Legislature, *18*, *19*, *237*

Texas, *143*

fifty-cent law, *53*

Fisher, Harward, *165*

Five Wells Cattle Company, *93*

Flanagan, J. W., *31*

Flanagan, Webster, *75*

flexible grazing lease program, *119*

Fly, George W. L.. *See* House Committee on Education

Fly, Sterling, *173*, *212*

Foote, C.B., *60*

Fourteenth Legislature, *38*, *39*, *40*, *41*, *42*

Fourth Congress, *8*, *10*

Fourth Legislature, *18*, *77*

Friend, Frank, *v*, *106*, *107*, *155*, *160*

Gaines, Scott, *107*, *118*, *159*, *163*

Galey, John, *132*

Gardiner, Charles W., *35*

Garland, William M., *111*

Gavnan, Henry C., *89*, *132*

General Land Office, *ii*, *12*, *13*, *21*, *37*, *38*, *55*, *62*, *71*, *79*, *81*, *82*, *92*, *93*, *97*, *98*, *100*, *103*, *107*, *109*, *113*, *122*, *132*, *134*, *137*, *138*, *140*, *150*, *155*, *173*, *181*, *206*, *219*, *228*, *237*, *238*

Gilchrist, Gibb, *199*

Goen, Guy, *119*

Grant, Ulysses S., *31*

Graves, L. G., *102*, *148*

Gravitt, Wallie, *158*, *166*, *171*, *175*, *212*

Gray, Tommy, *127*

Grayson, Peter W., *6*

Great Plains Conservation Program, *115*, *244*

Gregory, Thomas Watt, *185*

Grice, Sandy, *125*

Griffin, Charles, *30*

Grimmer, C. E., *106*

Groos, J. J., *41*

Grothaus, F. E., *34*

guayule, *94*

Haigh, Berte R., *v*, *14*, *83*, *84*, *87*, *137*, *144*, *152*, *163*, *164*

Hall, R. M., *72*

Hamilton, A.J., *27*

Hamilton, Morgan, *31*

Hartmann, Steve, *i*, *105*, *120*, *128*, *161*, *178*, *179*, *219*, *221*, *231*, *234*

Harwood, Thomas, *67*

Hatcher, Gregory, *193*

Hay, Jess, *214*, *215*

Haymon, Krupp, *143*

Henderson, James Pinckney, *15*

Henderson, Thomas S., *77*

Higher Education Assistance Fund (HEAF), *211*, *233*

Higher Education Construction Fund, *207*

Hill, Benjamin F., *134*

Hill, J. E., *109*

Hill, John L., *204*

Hill, Robert T., *89*

Hobby, William P., *189*

Hogg, James S., *74*, *75*, *78*, *182*, *228*

Hogg, Will C., *141*

Holt, C. W., *55*, *226*

House Committee on Education, *57*

Houston, David Franklin, *187*

Houston, Sam, *5*, *6*, *8*, *9*, *10*, *14*, *15*, *24*, *25*, *36*, *223*, *224*, *244*

Hubbard Richard B.. *See* UT Board of Regents

Hughes, Haywood, *101*, *146*, *190*

Hunt, Tim, *i*, *177*

Hunt, William H., *12*

Indian depredation, *48*

Ireland, John, *62*, *63*, *64*

Irion, Robert, *7*

Johnson, Andrew, *29*

Jones, Anson, *10*, *243*

Jones, Anson, *7*, *10*

Kansas City, Mexico & Orient Railroad (KCM&O), *95, 143*

Kennedy, William, *16*

Lamar, Mirabeau B., *v, 2, 4, 5, 12, 36, 223, 247*

Landreth, Ed, *102, 150*

Lane, John J., *33, 57, 81, 184, 186*

Lang, Aldon S., 20, 97

Lattimer, J. R., *197*

Lee, Thomas J. "Tom", *80, 83, 93, 132, 183, 229*

legislative million, *2, 63, 64, 65, 67, 69, 70, 78, 85, 90, 227*

Lewis, Gib, *214, 217*

Littlefield, George, *96*

Long, Laddie, *158, 165, 171, 175, 212, 213*

Lucas, Captain Anthony, *133*

Luna, Jose, *218, 220*

Mackenzie, Ranald S., *49*

Marland Oil Company, *146*

Mauro, Gary, *174, 176, 212, 213, 219, 232*

McKandles, Melba, *i, 128*

McKinney, Dr. Charles, *120*

McLeary, J. H., *61*

McMurry, Mike, *120*

Mexican War, *17, 18*

Moody, Dan, *148, 193*

Moore, M. B., *55*

Moore McInnis Bill, *133*

Moore, Kenneth R., *124, 248*

Moreno, Joachin, *85*

Morgan, George D., *160*

Morrill Land-Grant College Act, *33, 225*

Morrill, Justin,, *33*

New Mexico. See Compromise of 1850

Ninth Legislature, *26, 136*

One-In-Ten Railroad Act. See Chapter 116

original fifty leagues, *9, 14, 21, 35, 50, 51, 83, 90, 97, 227*

Ousley, Clarence N., *96, 138*

Owens, Buck, 83, 94, 123, 124, 128

Owens, Clint, *83, 93, 94*

Panhandle & Gulf Railway Company, *95*

Parker Drilling Company, *170, 171*

Parker, Carl, *209, 210*

Parten, J. R., *157, 160, 198, 241*

Patrick, Mike, *215*

Paul Davis water field, *168*

Payne, F., *87*

Peacock, John A.. *See* House Committee on Education

Pease, Elisha M., *19, 22, 29, 30, 59, 224, See* UT Board of Regents

Penn, R. L., *91*

Permanent University Fund

PUF, *2, 45, 135, 143, 147, 149, 158, 181, 185, 191, 192, 196, 202, 205, 208, 212, 226, 241, 247*

permit law of 1913. *See* Chapter 173

permit law of 1917, *141*

Peveto, Wayne, *205*

Pfeuffer, George, *68*

Phillips Petroleum Company's University EE No. 1, *169*

Phillips, Nelson, *192*

Phillips, William Battle, *89, 133, 137, 141*

Pickrell, Frank, *104, 143, 149, 150*

Plymouth Oil Company, *144, 146*

Polk, D. B., *119*

Polk, James K., *15, 17*

Pollard, Claude, *194*

Poteet, Gibbons, *106*

Powell, James L., *212*

Prairie View A&M, *53, 185, 189, 205, 206, 207, 210, 211, 214*

Prather, William L., *80*

Prince Carl of Solms-Braunfels, *16*

257

Public School Fund (PSF), *150*, *214*

PUF, 2, 3, 45, 48, 53, 61, 63, 66, 68, 76, 108, 135, 147, 148, 155, 172, 174, 175, 178, 179, 181, 182, 183, 184, 185, 186, 187, 188, 189, 190, 191, 192, 193, 194, 195, 196, 198, 199, 200, 201, 202, 203, 204, 206, 207, 208, 209, 210, 211, 213, 214, 215, 216, 217, 218, 219, 220, 221, 226, 228, 229, 230, 232, 233, 234, 235

Pyote, Texas, *103*

Quaker Peace Policy, *49*

Radical Republicans, *30*

Ragsdale, Smith. *See* UT Board of Regents

Ralph Lowe Estate No. 1 University well, *171*

Rattlesnake Bomber Base, *112*, *117*

Reagan County Purchasing Company, *146*, *149*, *193*

Reconstruction, *29*, *30*, *34*, *36*, *42*, *54*, *71*, *224*, *240*, *246*, *247*

Reconstruction Acts of 1867, *30*

Redeemer Democrats, *37*, *42*, *43*, *225*

Reese, T. S., *90*

Reynolds, J. J., *31*

Richards, Ann, *216*, *217*

Rio Grande Oil Company, *144*

Roberts, Oran M., *25*, *29*, *50*, *56*, *58*, *59*, *62*, *78*, *226*

Rogan, Charles, *83*, *87*, *88*, *133*, *135*

Ross, Lawrence Sullivan "Sul", *71*

Royalty in Kind\ program, *178*

Rutersville College, *14*

Sackett Resolution, *188*

San Elazario grant, *74*, *85*

Saner, R. E. L., *v*, *83*, *87*, *90*, *96*, *98*, *99*, *103*, *131*, *132*, *133*, *146*, *150*, *160*, *184*, *195*, *229*, *242*

Santa Rita #1, *v*, *104*, *143*, *144*, *145*, *177*, *180*, *190*, *201*, *229*

Santa Rita Townsite Company, *100*, *101*

Sayers, Joseph D., *54*

Sayers, W. B.. *See* Camp-Sayers Committee

Sayers, W. B., *40*

Scharbauer, John and Clarence, *92*

Schwartz, A. R., *204*

secession, *24, 25, 26, 27, 29, 50*

Secession Convention, *25*

Sellards, Elias H., *151*

Sharon Burkes, *128*

Sharp, John, *217*

SHEAF, *205*

Sheridan, Philip, *30*

Sims, Bill, *175*

Sixteenth legislature, *50*

Sixth Legislature, *20, 21*

Sixty-sixth Legislature, *122, 173, 206*

Slaughter, John B., *34*

Smith, Ashbel, *7, 59, 61*, *See* UT Board of Regents

Smith, Levi, *145*

Smith, Thomas S., 90

Snelson, W. E. "Pete", *ii, 116, 170, 201, 207, 209*

Snodgrass, Ruby, *106, 163*

Spindletop, *89, 133, 229*

Starr, James. *See* UT Board of Regents

State Land Board, *37, 63, 65, 67, 69, 71, 78, 79, 181, 227, 228*

State School of Mines and Metallurgy, *139, 163*

State v. Hatcher, *147, 193, 238*

State v. Reagan County Purchasing Company, *194*

Staton, William H., *94*

Ste. Genevieve, *121, 125*

Story, L. G., *57*

Sump, Dale, *218*

Taylor, Zachary, *17*

Tenth Legislature, *26, 27*

Terrell, A. W., *61*

Terrell, John J., *136*

Texas & Pacific Abrams No. 1, *143*, *229*

Texas & Pacific Railroad, *49*, *87*

Texas A&M Agricultural Experimental Station, *115*

Texas A&M College, *5*, *108*, *199*, *225*, *226*

Texas Antiquities Code, *125*

Texas Gulf Sulfur Company, *172*

Texas Railroad Commission, *75*, *156*, *157*, *162*, *167*, *197*, *247*

Texas Rubber Company, *94*

Texas Supreme Court, *147*, *193*, *220*, *238*

Texon, *99*, *101*, *103*, *105*, *114*, *123*, *124*, *125*, *143*, *144*, *145*, *146*, *148*, *149*, *170*, *191*, *193*, *231*

Texon Oil and Land Company, *143*, *149*, *193*

Third Congress, *7*, *8*, *237*

Thirteenth Legislature, *35*

Thirty-fifth Legislature, *141*

Thirty-third Legislature, *139*

Thomas William Ward, *12*

Thomason, R. Ewing, *160*

Thompson, A. W., *55*, *226*

Thompson, R. M., *56*

Throckmorton, James W., *27*, *29*, *59*

Tobin, Edgar, *160*

Transcontinental Oil Company, *144*

Treaty of Guadalupe Hidalgo, *17*

Tucker, Hugh, *143*

Turpin, Solvieg, *126*

Twelfth Legislature, *31*, *32*, *34*

Twentieth Legislature, *71*, *72*, *73*

Twenty-first Legislature, *73*, *74*

Twenty-fourth Legislature, *76*, *78*, *131*, *228*

Twenty-seventh Legislature, *89*, *184*

Tyler, John. *See* annexation

Udden, J. A., *138, 141*

University 1-B deep well test, 150

University Land Department, *81, 87*

University Lands Accounting Office, *122, 128, 174, 179, 206, 218, 221, 234, 239*

University Lands Legal, *107, 159, 163*

University Lands Legal and Surveying, *107*

University Lands Oil, Gas, and Mineral Interests, *128, 131, 165, 173, 177, 179, 221, 231, 234*

University Lands Surface Office, *2, 105, 114, 115, 118, 119, 120, 123, 125, 126, 127, 128, 151, 152, 156, 157, 170, 179, 195, 201, 221, 230, 231, 234*

University Lands Survey Office, *2, 106, 151, 154, 195, 230*

University Lands West Texas Operations, *i, 3, 79, 105, 127, 128, 161, 178, 179, 221, 234, 236, 239, 240*

University of Texas Board of Regents, *2, 37, 67, 79, 108, 139, 176, 181, 189, 196, 198, 200, 206, 214, 215, 219, 221, 223, 228, 229, 234, 236*

University of Texas Investment Management Company (UTIMCO), *3, 178, 219, 233*

Vale, Bob, *204*

Van Zandt, Isaac, *15*

Vansiclele, B.A., *12*

von Roemer, Ferdinand, *16*

Waggener Leslie, 69

Walker, J. H., *107, 150, 155*

Walsh, W. C., *55, 62*

Waple, Joseph, *10*

Ward, Thomas William, *11*

Weathers, Michael "Doc", *i, 124, 177*

Weichert, Ernest, *166*

Western Union Beef Company, *82*

Wharton, John, *7*

White, Mark, *209, 214*

Williams Kittrell, Pleasant, *22*

Williams, Clayton W, Jr., *216*

Williams, Dan C., *173*

Williams, O. W., 70, *85, 90, 91, 134, 246*

Wilson, N. T., *82*

Wilson, Robert, *6*

Wilson, Ron, *207*

Winkler, C. H., *138*

Woolward, C. A. P., *74*

Wooten, Thomas D., *64*

Yates, Andrew J., *7*

Zimmerman, James B., *116, 149, 165, 245*